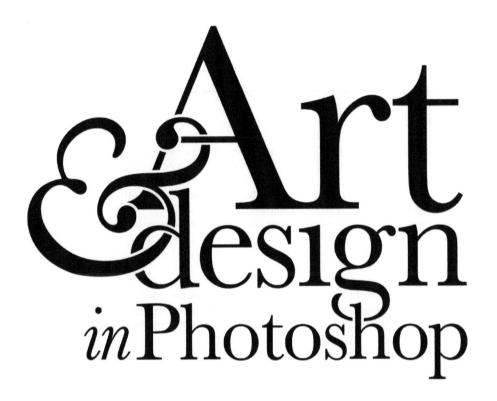

Steve Caplin

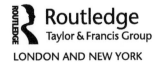 Routledge
Taylor & Francis Group

LONDON AND NEW YORK

First published 2009 by Focal Press

This edition published 2013 by Focal Press

Published 2017 by Routledge
2 Park Square, Milton Park, Abingdon, Oxon OX14 4RN
711 Third Avenue, New York, NY 10017, USA

First issued in hardback 2017

Routledge is an imprint of the Taylor & Francis Group, an informa business

Notices

Practitioners and researchers must always rely on their own experience and knowledge in evaluating and using any information, methods, compounds, or experiments described herein. In using such information or methods they should be mindful of their own safety and the safety of others, including parties for whom they have a professional responsibility.

To the fullest extent of the law, neither the Publisher nor the authors, contributors, or editors, assume any liability for any injury and/or damage to persons or property as a matter of products liability, negligence or otherwise, or from any use or operation of any methods, products, instructions, or ideas contained in the material herein.

British Library Cataloguing in Publication Data
A catalogue record for this book is available from the British Library

Library of Congress Cataloging-in-Publication Data
A catalog record for this book is available from the Library of Congress

ISBN 13: 978-1-138-40109-9 (hbk)
ISBN 13: 978-0-240-81109-3 (pbk)

Contents

Art & Design in Photoshop   Contents

Introduction

THERE ARE MANY books that will teach you how to use Photoshop. This isn't one of them.

Throughout all the editions of *How to Cheat in Photoshop* – a book which will, incidentally, teach you how to use Photoshop – I've maintained a website and reader forum to help readers with their photomontage-related problems. This has included a regular weekly contest, the Friday Challenge. And I've noticed that one of the major issues facing Photoshop artists is not how to use the Curves dialog, or the Pen tool, or how to save work for the web. One of the major stumbling blocks, it turns out, is the design process.

There are several areas of difficulty. Typography has been a particular problem: with so many dozens of fonts shipping with every new computer, and with thousands more available through the internet, how are we to select one that's appropriate for the task we're working on? Is there more to choosing the right font than merely picking one that stands out on screen, or which happens to appeal to us? Of course there is, which is why I've devoted a chapter to explaining how typography works, and how to make it work in your favor.

There are several different visual arts disciplines, and each has its own set of conventions and received wisdom. Art students will be familiar with the laws of perspective and the notion of balance; photographers will recognize the Rule of Thirds, and how movement must flow from the edge of an image towards the center; designers will understand how to lay out a page that incorporates white space and visual elements to break up the text, and how to draw the reader's eye through a layout.

At this point, I have a confession to make. I didn't go to art school. I'm not a trained photographer, or an accredited designer. (When pressed, I tend to refer to myself as an 'unqualified success'.) All the 'rules' that I suggest in this book are those I've figured out through years of trial and error, of creating montages and then wondering why they don't look as good as they should do. Only later, in some cases, have I found that there's a perfectly good rational explanation for why some compositions work and others don't, and when this is the case I've tried to phrase the explanations in a way that's meaningful to photomontage artists.

Of course, not all of this book is on a purely theoretical level. After a couple of chapters in which we explore the basic principles of typography and design, we roll up our sleeves and get down to the work of examining individual design concepts, to see how they're put together. We'll explore the fields of art and commerce, of packaging and advertising, to see what works and what fails to make the grade.

While the main theme of this book is the intrinsic design ideals that underlie each topic, we will of course show how you can achieve the effects yourself. This book isn't designed for you to reproduce the examples I've created, but rather for you to see the principles in action so you can go on to produce your own better, more original designs. It's not a cookbook, so much as a spare parts catalog.

At the back of the book you'll find a Photoshop Reference section. It's referred to several times within the tutorials; use it to brush up your Photoshop knowledge on specific points.

Of course, any Photoshop artist will occasionally struggle with some sticking point in the application itself. And so I'd like to invite all readers of this book to visit the Reader Forum at *www.howtocheatinphotoshop.com* where you can ask questions, exchange ideas and show off your work. If you have any difficulties with Photoshop techniques, or with tutorials in this book, post a message there and I (or another reader, if they get in first) will do my best to help you out the same day.

Steve Caplin
London, 2008

This book is dedicated to Carol, of course.

I'm grateful to the following:

Ben Denne and Hayley Salter of Focal Press

Keith Martin, for helping create the keyboard shortcuts font

MacUser magazine, for allowing me to repurpose some of my artwork

Adobe Systems Inc., for making Photoshop in the first place

The type designers Ray Larabie, Dieter Steffmann, Manfred Klein, Christophe Feray, Andrew Leman, Paul Lloyd, Graham Meade, Pat Snyder, Julius B. Thyssen, Walter Velez and Ben Weiner for so generously creating their outstanding fonts and making them freely available to designers.

Some of the images in this book are from Wikimedia Commons, part of Wikipedia. Some are images I've photographed myself. The remainder are taken from the best subscription site I know: **www.photos.com**. With a huge range of royalty-free photographs available for instant download, both cutout objects with clipping paths and full frame images, it's always my first stop when I'm looking for the perfect image. Many thanks to them for allowing me to include low resolution versions of some of their outstanding pictures in the tutorials in this book. On the CD you'll find a link to the photos.com home page, and a special offer for a discount membership.

How to use this book

THIS BOOK ASSUMES that you have a fair working knowledge of Photoshop. It's beyond the scope of this book to teach readers how to use the Pen tool, or the Curves adjustment, or Layer Masks. That's what *How to Cheat in Photoshop* is for. But just in case any readers come across a wholly unfamiliar concept, there's a crash course in Photoshop basics at the end of the book: the final chapter, Photoshop reference, outlines some of the most common tools and techniques.

Some Photoshop tutorials, both in print and on the internet, will specify precisely what you have to do, step by step. I tend to avoid including numerical values wherever possible: rather than telling you to apply a 6-pixel bevel with a depth of 65, for example, I'll ask you to adjust the bevel until it looks right. The purpose of this book is not to get you to recreate the examples on these pages, but to help you to understand the principles so that you can then apply them to your own work. So I make no apologies for being a little vague at times. This is deliberate, and it's in order that you can work the details out for yourself.

On each of the tutorial pages in this book, you'll see an indication of whether there's an associated image, texture or font on the CD. These are provided so you can try the tutorials out with the book propped up against your monitor (you'll never need to turn the page, as each tutorial is complete on a double page spread). The font required for each tutorial is mentioned in the text.

If you get stuck anywhere, the Reader Forum for my other book, *How to Cheat in Photoshop*, is available for your use. Post a question and it will most likely be answered the same day:

www.howtocheatinphotoshop.com/cgi-bin/simpleforum_pro.cgi

Finally, have fun with this book. It's what working in Photoshop is all about. If you aren't enjoying it, then you aren't doing it right.

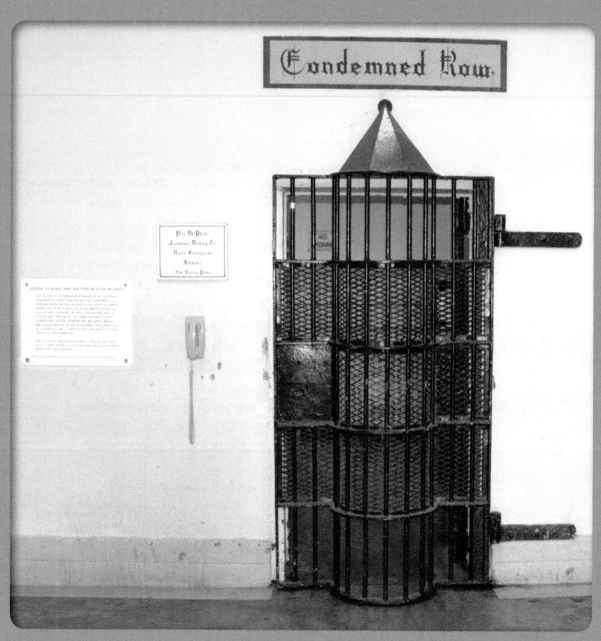

Entrance to Death Row, San Quentin prison.

Typography

The photograph on the facing page shows the entrance to the holding block for prisoners awaiting the death penalty at San Quentin prison, California. This isn't a museum exhibit, but the current entrance to the only Death Row facility in the whole of the state.

The iron cage itself looks like something from a torture gallery, but what interests us here is the choice of typeface, both in the sign above the door and in the notice regarding the use of the telephone. It's a highly stylized version of an Old German gothic lettering style, of the kind that was popular four hundred years ago.

We're not suggesting that being typographically up to date is uppermost in the mind of the prison governor, but consider the subtext of this choice. Does this typeface put us in mind of a progressive, efficient 21st century correctional facility? Or does it make us think of a medieval dungeon, complete with iron cages for the display of the executed?

Whether we're conscious of it or not, the typefaces we're presented with affect our emotional response to the subject. When we work in Photoshop, we must ensure that the fonts we choose are appropriate to the message we want to send. In this chapter, we'll look at how different typefaces can send the right or the wrong message.

Ty·pog·ra·phy

1. The art and technique of printing with movable type.
2. The composition of printed material from movable type.
3. The arrangement and appearance of printed matter.

[French *typographie*, from Medieval Latin *typographia*: Greek *tupos*, impression + Latin *-graphia*, -graphy.]

American Heritage Dictionary

Serif fonts

Serif type can be recognized by the fine lines on the end points of all the strokes, roughly at right angles to the stroke.

The form was devised by ancient Greek and Roman stonemasons, who found that if they tried to carve a thick stroke – such as the letter I – there was a strong chance that the stone would split while they were carving.

To prevent this happening, they first carved short 'stoppers' at the top and bottom of the intended stroke, to prevent the stone splitting beyond this point. These were the beginnings of serifs.

Although modern serif fonts have these serifs at most junctions, the Romans used them only where they were needed: so there were no serifs at the joins in the letters N and M, for instance, since the corner made its own natural stop point.

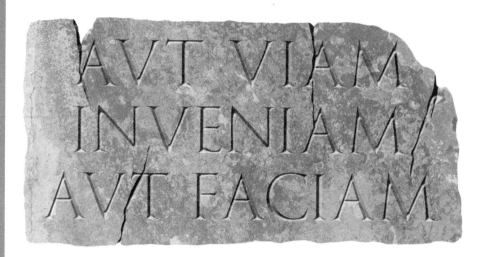

SERIF FONTS may have originated with ancient stonemasons (see left), but their appeal has lasted to the present day. The serifs themselves form a visual rule at the top and bottom of all the characters, making it easier for the eye to follow each line of type.

Because of their increased legibility, serif fonts are used for extended reading: novels, newspaper articles and most magazines use serif fonts for the main body of the text as they make it easier to read large chunks of text. There are exceptions – see the following pages on sans serif fonts for details.

All serif fonts are based, more or less, on the Roman originals. So-called 'old style' serifs originated in the 15th century with designs such as Garamond: these are

Serif type
Garamond (oldstyle)

characterized by a variation in thickness between horizontal and vertical strokes, inspired by calligraphic writing, and usually feature an oblique stress – the letter 'o', for example, will tend to have its stress at an angle, rather than directly vertical.

Serif type
Baskerville (transitional)

'Transitional' serif fonts first made their appearance in 1757, and are characterized by strong differences in weight between the thick and thin strokes. This font was designed by John Baskerville, who had to reinvent not just the printing press but paper-making techniques in order to reproduce his fine designs.

In around 1800, a new form of serif appeared, known as 'slab serif' or 'Egyptian'. These have very little variation in weight, and have thick, chunky serifs that are far bolder

Serif type
Egyptian (slab serif)

than had previously been seen. They're most commonly seen in Victorian and 'Western' posters, and are distinctively retro in appearance.

Serif type
Times (modern)

The first truly 'modern' serif font was Times Roman, designed for *The Times* newspaper in 1932 by Herbert Morrison. Intended to be the most readable font that could easily be reproduced on newsprint, Times has been a firm favorite ever since, and is the standard serif font installed on contemporary computers.

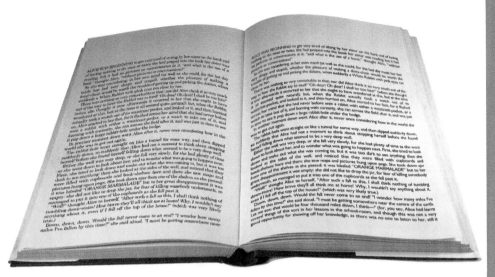

Because the serifs form horizontal lines above and below each character, serif fonts are much easier on the eye: the serifs guide the reader along each line. Text that requires sustained reading on a wide measure is almost always set in a serif font, whether it's in a book, a magazine or a newspaper. Serif fonts also have more variations in weight than sans serif, which makes the page more 'colorful' and appealing. In the example above, the left-hand page is set in a serif font; the unattractive right-hand page is in sans serif.

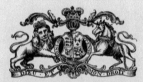

HER MAJESTY THE QUEEN

has great pleasure in inviting you to a

Buckingham Palace Garden Party

no jeans · no touching · watch your language

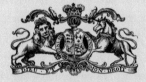

HER MAJESTY THE QUEEN

has great pleasure in inviting you to a

Buckingham Palace Garden Party

No jeans • no touching • watch your language

Serif fonts convey tradition and respectability (top), as opposed to the more modern appearance of sans serif typefaces (bottom). When this is a key requirement, only a serif font will do the job correctly.

● Serif fonts have changed considerably over the years. If you're replicating an antique document, or a Victorian book, or a contemporary newspaper, make sure you choose a font that existed at the time.

● Because of the variable line weights in serif fonts, you may find the fine strokes become hard to discern when complex effects such as chrome are applied to the type layer. Bold versions of serif fonts will always hold a chrome effect more clearly than regular weights. Pay close attention to legibility: if in doubt, use a heavier weight of the font to ensure that it will be readable.

● The variable weight in serif fonts means that we can condense or expand them to a considerable degree without them looking distorted – something we cannot do with sans serif fonts. If you need an extra-narrow font and don't have a condensed type available, consider shrinking a serif font instead.

● Times Roman is the most commonly used font on computers. This is a good reason to avoid it in your artwork: it's so bland and commonplace that it just tends to look dull. Choose a font that expresses the feeling you want the artwork to evoke in your audience.

● When setting long pieces of text, such as body matter in books or magazines, choose a serif font for its legibility, rather than its uniqueness. If a font is quirky and distinctive, it's less likely to be legible when set in large chunks. Save the fancy fonts for your headlines, where only a few words have to be read at a time.

Sans serif fonts

A BCD EFGHIJK LMNOPQRSTUVWXYZ

'Sans' is the Latin word for 'without' – and, pronounced rather differently, it's also the French word for the same thing. A sans serif font is, literally, a font without serifs.

Although sans serif fonts are much closer to handwriting, they didn't appear as typefaces until the early 19th century.

Sans serif fonts appear in a variety of forms, but are characterized by a largely even weight with minimal distinction between thick and thin strokes. They're more resolutely 'modern' than serif fonts, and are used to catch the eye in posters and newspaper headlines.

Sans serif fonts are not designed for continuous reading, but are clearer and more legible at a distance than serif fonts. Almost all road signs use sans serif fonts for their clarity and lack of ambiguity.

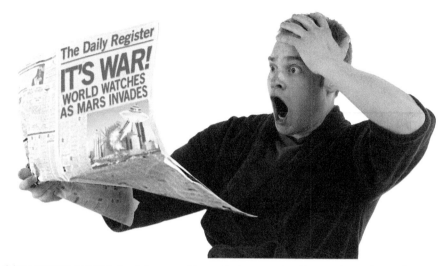

SANS SERIF FONTS don't have serifs, as their name implies, and so take up less space than their serif equivalents. For this reason, they're used in print where a large amount of information needs to be compressed into a small space: so while newspapers will use serif fonts for main articles, they'll almost always use sans serif for television and financial listings, weather reports and other detailed purposes. They're harder on the eye for long periods of continuous reading, which is why you rarely see books set in a sans font.

The earliest sans serif fonts appeared in around 1800, and were called 'Grotesque' or 'Gothic' – that's gothic in the sense of vandalistic. Very bold, and designed for posters and

Sans type
Impact (grotesque)

headlines, they were initially considered too ugly for any other purpose. Contemporary versions include Franklin Gothic and Akzidenz Grotesk.

Sans type
Johnston (humanist)

In 1913, the London Underground subway system commissioned a 'humanist' font created by Edward Johnston. Designed for increased legibility, its revolutionary design led to fonts such as Gill Sans, Frutiger and Optima: these fonts had a weight variation that made them more appealing and less austere than earlier sans serifs.

More extreme are the 'geometric' fonts such as Futura, designed in 1927, as well as Avant Garde and Century Gothic. As their name implies, these are based on pure

Sans type
Futura (geometric)

geometric forms, and tend to have a perfectly round letter O. These fonts typify the 1930s in look and feel, reminiscent of the Art Deco movement with its emphasis on geometric simplicity and lack of clutter.

Sans type
Helvetica (transitional)

The 'transitional' sans serifs are typified by Helvetica, which appeared in 1960. With a perfectly even stroke weight, it was designed to be an everyday sans font for general purpose use, and has remained the standard for sign design ever since. Other fonts similar to Helvetica are Univers and Arial. The style is sometimes called 'anonymous' sans serif, due to its plain, uncluttered appearance.

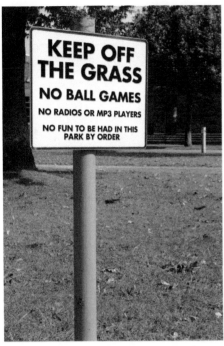

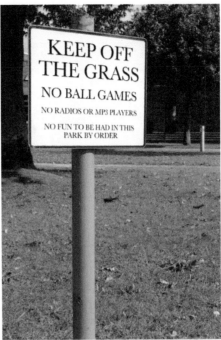

Sans serif fonts have an immediacy that's hard to ignore. Notices such as the one above have far more impact when set in sans serif (left) than they would in a serif font (right). Because the characters are less fiddly, they're also far easier to read from a distance: this is why road signs are typically set in sans serif typefaces.

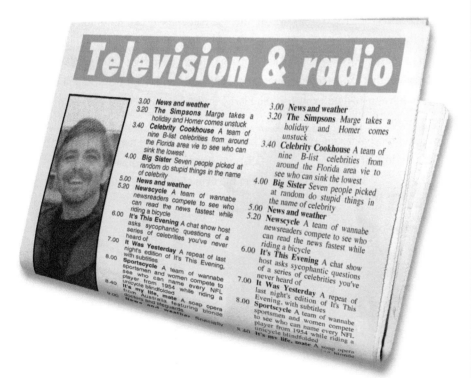

Because the letterforms are simpler, sans serif fonts are easier to take in at a glance. This means they can be used smaller with the same degree of legibility. In the example above, a sans serif font has been used for the listings on the left; a serif font, of an optically equivalent size, has been used on the right. The listings on the left are clearer and easier to scan, but take up less space on the page.

● Sans serif fonts tend to come in many more weights than serif fonts. This is partly because they have to communicate quickly in a variety of conditions, and partly because you really can't condense them artificially. Here are examples of Futura Condensed Medium (left) and Futura Medium that has been artificially condensed to the same width (right).

RR

The 'real' font is elegant in weight, and an attractive shape; the artificial version has poor balance, and introduces a weight variation that wasn't there in the original.

● For informational signs, Helvetica is still about the best choice there is. But for just about any other purpose it's just too commonplace and too bland to be of interest; any text set in Helvetica screams that it's been created on a computer, thanks to its ubiquity on every operating system.

● When recreating historical documents or signage, try to use fonts appropriate to the period. Use Grotesque fonts for Victorian posters, Gill Sans or Futura for items set in the 1930s to 1950s, and – as an alternative to Helvetica – try the Adobe font, Myriad, for a contemporary sans serif that combines legibility with a modern, clean look. The headlines in this book are set in the sans serif font Griffith Gothic.

Picking the wrong font

PETROLEUM SPIRIT

DANGER

HIGHLY INFLAMMABLE
WHEN FILLING
· NO SMOKING ·
BRAKE WHEELS
STOP ENGINE
EXTINGUISH ANY
FLAME LIGHTS

The Danger sign above is not just inappropriate, it's downright dangerous in its own right. Is this the kind of warning we'd take seriously? Or would we see this lettering as a suggestion, rather than a strict command?

Typography is an art, not a science. Our appreciation of which font to use is based as much on an emotional response as on a close examination of the correct classification of a particular typeface.

But why should this matter to the Photoshop artist? Because we're chiefly concerned with reproducing a plausible version of reality. Viewers of our work will be able to tell at a glance when something is wrong, and we'll lose their trust.

On these pages we'll look at typography that has gone wrong; on the following pages, we'll take the same examples and show how to put it right.

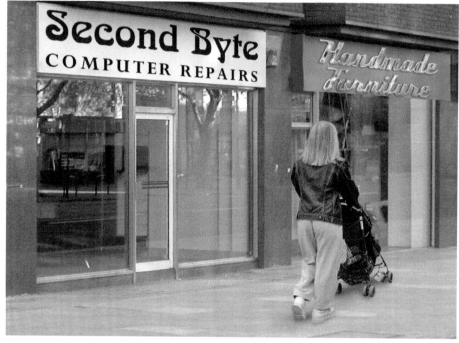

What's in a font? Two examples of design gone wrong

THE COMPUTER REPAIR STORE on the left has chosen two fonts for its signboard: Arnold Bocklin and Perpetua. They may have looked attractive in the catalog, but they don't fit the purpose. Old fashioned and nostalgic, they convey entirely the wrong message for a business that claims to be operating in a high tech industry. We wouldn't trust these people to have up-to-date expertise. Similarly, the store on the right claims to be selling handmade furniture: but the typeface is one more commonly seen on car radiator grilles. It speaks of mechanization rather than hand tooling and individual attention.

The lettering on this brass plaque (left), for instance, is designed to give prospective clients confidence in the firm of attorneys. But the casual nature of the typography has the opposite effect: this doesn't look like the sort of outfit in which you'd place your trust. Being seen as friendly is one thing; portraying your business as overly casual can backfire. And while this may be an obvious example, the opposite can be less immediate.

Fonts that are too modern, or too casual, can turn us off

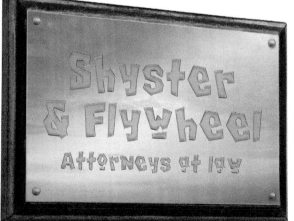

Too casual? Would you trust this firm to represent your interests?

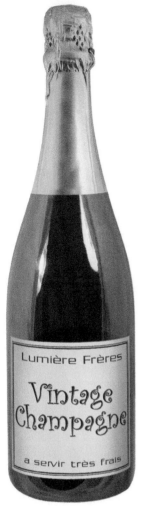

How much would you pay for a bottle of champagne that looked like this? Would you present this as a gift?

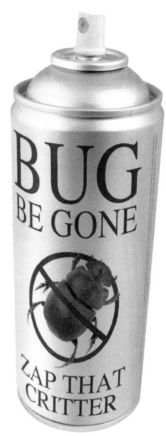

Would you be confident that this spray has the power to destroy the bugs in your home?

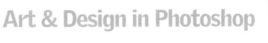

JUICY FOOD

● So far we've talked exclusively about the choice of typeface when creating logo, packaging and shop signs. But color also plays a vital role in the process. Consider the logo above: would you choose to eat at this establishment?

Sc^i
SCIENCE MUSEUM

Sc^i
SCIENCE MUSEUM

● Two logos for a science museum. The lettering style works, suggesting a mathematical formula: but the brown and red are warm colors which suggest homeliness rather than the raw spirit of scientific discovery. Does science really have a color?

when we're looking at items that should be conveying tradition and luxury, such as this champagne bottle. Photoshop artists will frequently resort to that old standby, Times Roman, for all sorts of purposes for which it's patently unfit – such as the bug-killer spray can above. The stolid, boring, traditional serif font has no place in a situation like this.

What's needed is something that shouts, that has energy to it: this sort of design requires a font with an edginess that's wholly lacking in Times Roman.

There's nothing technically wrong with the Burger Bar lettering on the left: it displays the name of the restaurant clearly. to represent their brands. But does this look like the kind of place you'd go for a satisfying meal? Or is it somehow lacking?

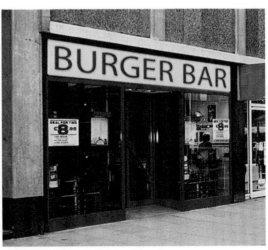

Would you expect this outlet to sell juicy burgers?

PETROLEUM SPIRIT

DANGER

HIGHLY INFLAMMABLE
When Filling
· NO SMOKING
BRAKE WHEELS
STOP ENGINE
EXTINGUISH ANY
FLAME LIGHTS

This Danger sign is clear and unambiguous. The typeface is a plain, bold sans serif that reeks of authority: ignore this at your peril. I photographed this sign in 2008, and it's likely it had stood in place for fifty years: there was no need to replace it when it was obviously doing the job perfectly.

When choosing a font, we need to think above all about the effect it will have on the reader. It's not just a question of what looks attractive on the page, but of whether it's going to do the job we demand of it.

As we've seen on this and the previous pages, fonts can be modern or old fashioned, commanding or inviting, playful or serious, strong or insipid. It's up to us to make the right choice, which means we need to be psychologists as well as Photoshop artists. Because the wrong choice can be catastrophic.

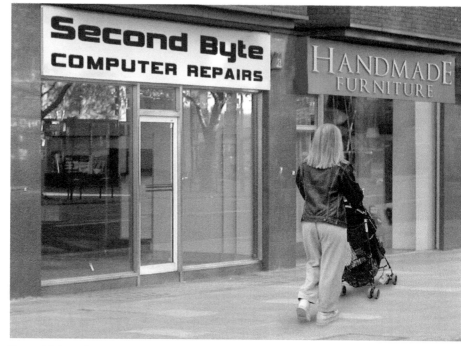

The careful choice of typeface can make all the difference to a business's public image

THE FONTS ON THESE TWO STORES are now far more appropriate to the nature of their businesses. The computer store uses a font whose clean lines and unfussy approach speaks of competence and reliability. But the font is just quirky enough to show that it's decidedly modern: the tail on the 'y' and the compressed shape of the 'S' lend this an up to date quality without being transitory.

The handmade furniture store now looks like the sort of place where care is taken, where design matters, and where quality will be more important than mere cost. Enlarging the first and last letters of the word 'Handmade' is a typographic trick that's used to express tradition and old fashioned values: it harks back to label design of the 1940s, suggesting the care and attention that would have been taken in a bygone era.

The brass plaque (left) may not show this firm of attorneys to be bright, thrusting young people with their eye on the future. They do, however, now look stolid and reliable, and rather more trustworthy than they did before, if perhaps a little unimaginative.

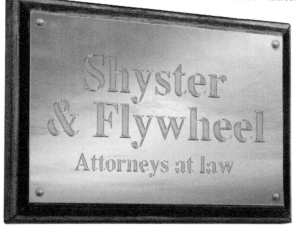

They may not be forward looking, but they'll do the job you need

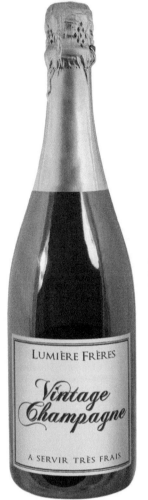

A vintage bottle, indeed, and one you'd be proud to hand over at a dinner party: this is clearly quality stuff

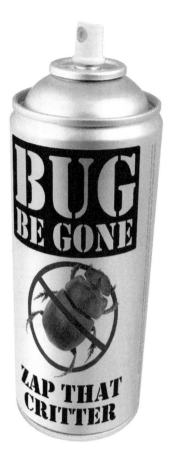

One spray from this can and your home will certainly be bug free

JUICY FOOD

● Red and yellow are the colors we associate with food, probably because they represent cooking flames. You'll see these colors used in fast food logos more than any other because they work on a subliminal level: they suggest the idea of eating.

Scⁱ

SCIENCE MUSEUM

Scⁱ

SCIENCE MUSEUM

How much difference does a wine label make? All the difference in the world. Most people buy wine based on how impressive the label looks, and that's especially true of champagne – particularly when we can't afford the more expensive brands.

The use of the stencil font for the bug spray can suggests military strength: and the choice of black and yellow for the product name is reminiscent of nuclear warnings. Both of which make us think of killing power, which is what this product needs.

The burger bar uses a plump, juicy lettering to convey the meatiness of its products. Check out the lettering used by McDonald's, or Burger King, or Wendy's, and you'll see fat, thick lettering – albeit in a variety of different typographic styles.

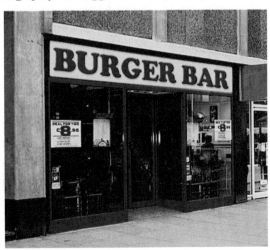

Full, fat, plump: all you can eat, and all you need

● Blue and green are both good, solid scientific colors. Perhaps it's because they're cool, dispassionate, detached. They suggest an antiseptic environment as well, which is why hospitals so often use shades of blue and green in their floor and wall coloring.

You don't need to make everything scream for attention in order to get your point across

The arrangement of type is essential for creating the mood and feel that we intend. We can take great liberties with relative sizes in order to achieve this goal.

The poster for the movie *Pirates of the Caribbean*, above, shows the two key words pulled out and centered above each other. The more insignificant 'of' and 'the' are tiny in comparison: they've been shrunk down to a size that's almost unreadable, and tucked into the space above the 'N' where there happens to be a suitable gap.

Similarly, the letter 'C' has been detached from the word which follows it, and enlarged and wrapped around the 'A' in the shape of a cutlass.

When designing posters, we need to be prepared to use several different text blocks, often splitting words themselves, to experiment with size and placement.

WHEN BEGINNERS USE WORD PROCESSORS to design posters, flyers and other information sheets, there's always a strong tendency to make everything as big as possible, filling all the space on the page. After all, the bigger the text, the more readable it's going to be, right? Well, to some extent – but balance is more important.

In the flyer above left, all the text is more or less the same size. Which means that nothing here stands out; the result is that most people would walk straight past this without noticing it. And the purpose, first and foremost, is to attract attention.

The second example, above right, changes the balance of the text dramatically. The fact that this is a public lecture isn't important; so that piece of information can go in tiny text right at the top. Similarly, the date isn't something to scream out loud, since if anyone's interested in the lecture they'll take the trouble to find out the date. By making the word 'Life' huge, we guarantee it will attract attention; the remainder of the lecture title slots neatly beneath it. Giving Professor Frink so much white space around him means his name can go far smaller. It stands out because of its location, not because of its size.

The third version, on the facing page, is another reworking of the design. Here, we recognize that the words 'the' and 'and' are minor, and don't need the same emphasis as the words which follow them; and so they're pulled out and made smaller. In addition, we've now set them in a far lighter version of the font to make them less imposing.

We've made another change in the third version, and this is to move the words 'the', 'and' and 'by Professor Frink' off-center. Although you might expect that centering everything produces a neater design, it also produces one that's dull and monotonous. Symmetry is rarely a bonus in design terms. Instead, off-setting the words gives the design a more edgy feel, which in turn draws attention to it. By making the wording less of a comfortable symmetrical device, we force people to read it.

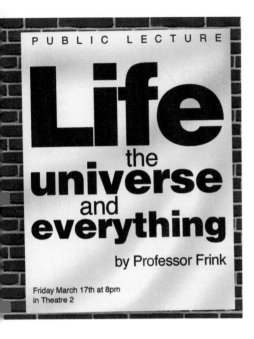

When we off-center text, though, we need to make it all line up with some element of the design to avoid it looking messy. This is where the designer's eye comes in: there are no set rules to make it look right. In our lecture example, the word 'the' lines up with the vertical stroke on the 'f' above it; the 'd' in 'and' lines up with the bottom of the 'v' above and the corresponding angle in the 'y' below, and the 'by' lines up with the left of the 'y' above it.

The typography for the poster for the movie *The Diving Bell and the Butterfly*, below, is a good case in point. Here, the text all appears to be randomly arranged; but there's a strong vertical line that runs through the left of the 'n' in 'Diving', the beginning of 'Bell', and the vertical stroke of the first 't' in 'Butterfly'. In addition, the 'g' of 'Diving' fits neatly into the space between the 'B' and the 'l' of 'Bell'.

Compare this with the second version of this lettering, in which I've moved the word 'Bell' a fraction to the right. Here, the text is awkward: the words sit uncomfortably together, the 'B' of 'Bell' presses too close to the 'g' above it. The whole effect is one of disharmony.

It's not that we consciously look for elements that line up with each other when we view these posters, any more than the casual viewer would recognize when an inappropriate font is used; but we notice when something's wrong, and we trust the design that much less.

Ultimately, the size and arrangement of type on a page comes down to what looks right. But we have to learn what looks right, since it isn't always immediately obvious. In particular, if something is wrong it can be hard to spot exactly what the offending element is – and even harder to put it right. But as with all Photoshop work, learning to use the tools is the easy bit; getting the design right is the trickiest part of the process.

MORE INFO

● In the first Public Lecture poster, on the far left, the text was all in one big block. And we kept it in a single block in the second version, even though the relative sizes changed – adding spacing and increasing leading as required. But in the third version, we separated it into individual words in order to achieve the correct placement. It would have been possible to leave it in a single block, adding spacing before the words as required; but the effort would have been huge, and the degree of control minimal.

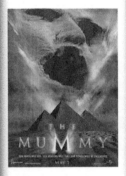

● There's nothing special about the middle 'M' of 'MUMMY' here – except that enlarging it makes a good graphic device. Feel free to be creative with type!

● When we resize text in Photoshop the type remains live – it isn't yet in the form of individual pixels, as most Photoshop layers are. This means we can make text larger or smaller at will, without worrying about pixellation or raggedness. But the moment we 'rasterize' the type by turning it into a regular layer, we lose that ability. Always get the basic arrangement of text final before rasterizing: remember, a lot of effects can be added using masks and Layer Styles.

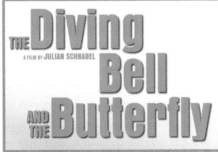

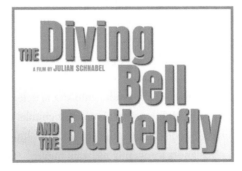

The importance of lining elements up: right and wrong

Designing with type

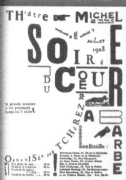

The design above was created by Ilia Zdanevich in 1923, as a poster for an event he created with Tristan Tzara. As a piece of pure typography it was years ahead of its time: even now, it has the power to shock.

Whether we're designing posters or books or magazine features, we always have to work with words. It's a constant battle between the editor – who wants as many words as possible and sees the images as an often unnecessary intrusion, and the designer – who resents the volume of wordage which means he has to reduce the size of his specially commissioned illustrations.

Often, we simply can't lay our hands on appropriate images to accompany the texts we have to lay out. But we can make the type itself do a lot of the work: here, we'll look at how to liven up a page using type alone.

Il Designato di Luciano Zuccoli

Too dull: we can make this headline look more appealing than this

Too tight: we don't need to use every square inch of space on the page

Too dense: there's no room for the text to breathe here

Parve il libro d'un uomo che avesse lunga esperienza d'anni e di casi, ed era il libro d'un giovanissimo; parve la critica implacabile d'un malcontento marito, e l'autore era scapolo. Ma era uno scapolo e un giovane che viveva a occhi aperti, in una grande città, precocemente; era l'opera d'uno scrittore nato, che a una sensibilità eccezionale accoppiava per istinto uno spirito d'osservazione fresco e sincero.

E in verità, chi volesse analizzare le qualità principali di questo libro,—di questo, e osiamo dire di quasi tutta l'opera di Luciano Zuccoli,—troverebbe ch'esse provengono dalla sincerità dell'osservazione, dalla facoltà di sentire acutamente, dalla precisione originale nell'interpretare i moti interni dell'animo e gli avvenimenti cospicui della vita vissuta. L'autore afferra movimenti psicologici non veduti da altri e li vivifica con uno spirito tra il sentimentale e lo scettico, il quale è caratteristica di lui; rende con brevi tocchi le scene, di cui mette in rilievo i particolari che sfuggono ai più e che vi lascian più duraturi l'impressione; e riflette nel giudizio delle cose e degli uomini una sua filosofia malinconica e indulgente, lepida e disperata nel tempo stesso, che se non ha stupito più nell'autore di Farfui e del L'amore di Loredana, fece la maraviglia dei critici che nell'autore di Il designato dovevano giudicare, un giovane di ventiquattr'anni.

Si è, ripetiamo, che Luciano Zuccoli, prima ancor che uno scrittore, è un uomo che ha vissuto e vive, e della vita, nonostante quella sua filosofia, è amico e ammiratore.

Indipendente come tutti coloro,—e tutti qui vuol dir pochi—i quali hanno una personalità rilevante, egli ha scelto un'opinione sua e una sua volontà; non per il piacere di contrasto, benchè un certo qual gusto per la contraddizione gli si potrebbe a quando a quando rimproverare, ma perchè non dice se non ciò che sa, che ha visto, che ha constatato; non ha gli occhi, insomma, che alla vita e alla realtà.

Parrebbe che uno spirito così formato dovesse essere arido e freddo; e sarebbe, se Luciano Zuccoli pretendesse troppo dalla realtà e dalla vita e si disgustasse facilmente d'ogni cosa dolce per quel fondo d'amaro che vi si trova quasi sempre alla fine. Ma in questo medesimo libro il lettore può aver la prova della sensibilità che l'autore ha

saputo conservare fra le delusioni, la lotta, le tempeste della sua non mai pacifica esistenza. Si leggano, ad esempio, il capitolo in cui è descritta la prima notte di matrimonio, e l'altro in cui è ritratta la protagonista tutta affaccendata nelle sue frivole compere, e quello in cui si racconta della morte e dei funerali di Laura Uglio, e si veda con qual delicatezza di tocco ha saputo lumeggiare, argomenti gravi e teneri, leggeri o tristi, scabrosi o sentimentali. E si confrontino con l'arguzia onde son delineati certi altri personaggi, con l'ironia di certe scene di famiglia, col senso di ribellione con cui sono affermate o rapidamente esposte certe verità della vita comune; e non ci si darà torto se diremo che lo studio del vero, quasi istintivo nello Zuccoli, presta alla sua opera, una varietà mirabile.

Non è certamente un autore monocorde colui che vicino a questo può allineare altri dieci volumi, in cui ciascun personaggio ha una figura sua propria; dieci volumi nei quali sfilano i tipi di tutte le classi sociali, dall'aristocrazia al popolo minuto, dal superbo patrizio del L'amore di Loredana ai ladri e ai teppisti della Compagnia della Leggera, dalla candida fanciulla di certe sue novelle alla donna ardente, volitiva, disdegnosa, che è la protagonista di Farfui, dal bambino ingenuo al libertino inquieto e curioso, dal soldato fanfarone e generoso al trionfatore freddo, taciturno e senza pietà. Mille sono i tipi che lo Zuccoli ha animato della una arte, e quelli che popolano

Il designato hanno un carattere di realtà e un rilievo indimenticabili. Il libro che vede ora la luce nella sua edizione definitiva, dopo che l'autore vi ha arrecato notevoli e pazienti ritocchi, fu pubblicato la prima volta a Milano nel 1894, presso una Casa editrice, che oggi non esiste più. Se il primo romanzo di Luciano Zuccoli era subito parso opera indipendente e originale, questo, che veniva a un anno di distanza da I Lussuriosi, diede a divedere che lo scrittore non intendeva la letteratura come un dilettantismo giovanile, ma come un'alta faticosa nobilissima arte, alla quale voleva dedicare tutto il suo ingegno. E in realtà, ingrandendo la fama dell'autore e confermando la speranza che il primo libro aveva fatto fiorire, Il designato decise dell'avvenire di Luciano Zuccoli.

Parve il libro d'un uomo che avesse lunga esperienza d'anni e di casi, ed era il libro

d'un giovanissimo; parve la critica implacabile d'un malcontento marito, e l'autore era scapolo. Ma era uno scapolo e un giovane che viveva a occhi aperti, in una grande città, precocemente; era l'opera d'uno scrittore nato, che a una sensibilità eccezionale accoppiava per istinto uno spirito d'osservazione fresco e sincero.

E in verità, chi volesse analizzare le qualità principali di questo libro,—di questo, e osiamo dire di quasi tutta l'opera di Luciano Zuccoli,—troverebbe ch'esse provengono dalla sincerità dell'osservazione, dalla facoltà di sentire acutamente, dalla precisione originale nell'interpretare i moti interni dell'animo e gli avvenimenti cospicui della vita vissuta. L'autore afferra movimenti psicologici non veduti da altri e li vivifica con uno spirito tra il sentimentale e lo scettico, il quale è caratteristica di lui; rende con brevi tocchi le scene, di cui mette in rilievo i particolari che sfuggono ai più e che vi lascian più duraturi l'impressione; e riflette nel giudizio delle cose e degli uomini una sua filosofia malinconica e indulgente, lepida e disperata nel tempo stesso, che se non ha stupito più nell'autore di Farfui e del L'amore di Loredana, fece la maraviglia dei critici che nell'autore di Il designato dovevano giudicare, un giovane di ventiquattr'anni.

Non è certamente un autore monocorde colui che vicino a questo può allineare altri dieci volumi, in cui ciascun personaggio ha una figura sua propria; dieci volumi nei quali sfilano i tipi di tutte le classi sociali, dall'aristocrazia al popolo minuto, dal superbo patrizio del L'amore di Loredana ai ladri e ai teppisti della Compagnia della Leggera, dalla candida fanciulla di certe sue novelle alla donna ardente, volitiva, disdegnosa, che è la protagonista di Farfui, dal bambino ingenuo al libertino inquieto e curioso, dal soldato fanfarone e generoso al trionfatore freddo, taciturno e senza pietà. Mille sono i tipi che lo Zuccoli ha animato della una arte, e quelli che popolano

tti qui vuol dir pochi—i quali hanno una personalità rilevante, egli ha sempre un'opinione sua e una sua volontà; non per il piacere di contrasto, benchè un certo qual gusto per la contraddizione gli si potrebbe a quando a quando rimproverare, ma perchè non dice se non ciò che sa, che ha visto, che ha constatato; non ha gli occhi, insomma, che alla vita e alla realtà.

Too wide: the three column grid gives little room for flexibility

ONE OF THE MOST DIFFICULT PROBLEMS facing a designer is what to do with a story that has no graphics, photographs or other imagery to accompany it. Simply setting column after column of long, dull text is unimaginative and turns off readers.

We can create our own design elements on a page by using purely typographical devices. Many of these seem odd when we examine them closely; but we're so used to seeing these techniques in books, magazines and newspapers that we barely even give them a second glance.

The most obvious typographic device is the 'drop cap', short for 'capital' – the enlarged first letter that spreads over three or four lines. This clearly marks the beginning of the story, drawing the reader into the article. But we can also use drop caps further down the page, simply to break up long chunks of text. They don't necessarily have to mark a change in direction in the story itself, although it helps the reader if they do.

Designers frequently use 'pull quotes' – sections of the text cut out from the main body of the work and set in a larger font, often floating within white space. These serve two

MORE INFO

Drop capitals leave the reader in no doubt as to where the story begins

Setting the first paragraph across two columns eases us into the story

Setting the author's name as a white on black byline adds a graphic element

'Pull quotes' help to add air space and interest

No need to cram everything in: white space helps the layout

Pull quotes can appear between columns, as well as within them

Additional drop caps break up large chunks of text

Il Designato

Parve il libro d'un uomo che avesse lunga esperienza d'anni e di casi, ed era il libro d'un giovanissimo; parve la critica implacabile d'un malcontento marito, e l'autore era scapolo. Ma era uno scapolo e un giovane che viveva a occhi aperti, in una grande città, precocemente; era l'opera d'uno scrittore nato, che a una sensibilità eccezionale accoppiava per istinto uno spirito d'osservazione fresco e sincero.

E in verità, chi volesse analizzare le qualità principali di questo libro,—di questo, e osiamo dire di quasi tutta l'opera di Luciano Zùccoli,—troverebbe ch'esse provengono dalla sincerità dell'osservazione, dalla facoltà di sentire acutamente, dalla precisione originale nell'interpretare i moti interni dell'animo e gli avvenimenti cospicui della vita vissuta. L'autore afferra movimenti psi-

di Luciano Zùccoli

e riflette nel giudizio delle cose e degli uomini una sua filosofia malinconica e indulgente, lepida e disperata nel tempo stesso, che se non ha stupito più nell'autore di Farfui e del *L'amore di Loredana*, fece la maraviglia dei critici che nell'autore di Il designato dovevan giudicare, un giovane di ventiquatt'anni.

Sì è, ripetiamo, che Luciano Zùccoli, prima ancor che uno scrittore, è un uomo che ha vissuto e vive, e della vita, nonostante quella sua filosofia, è amico e ammiratore.

Indipendente come tutti coloro,—e tutti qui vuol dir pochi—i quali hanno una personalità rilevante, egli ha sempre un'opinione sua e una sua volontà; non per il piacere di contrasto, benché un certo qual gusto per la contraddizione egli si potrebbe a quando a quando rimproverare, ma perché non dice se non ciò che sa, che ha visto, che ha constatato; non ha gli occhi, insomma, che alla vita e alla realtà.

Il designato hanno un carattere di realtà e un rilievo indimenticabili

cologici non veduti da altri e li vivifica con uno spirito tra il sentimentale e lo scettico, il quale è caratteristica di lui; rende con brevi tòcchi le scene, di cui mette in rilievo i particolari che sfuggono ai più e che vi lasciano più duratura l'impressione;

Parrebbe che uno spirito così formato dovesse essere arido e freddo; e sarebbe, se Luciano Zùccoli pretendesse troppo dalla realtà e dalla vita e si disgustasse facilmente d'ogni cosa dolce per quel fondo d'amaro che vi si trova quasi sempre alla fine. Ma in questo medesimo libro il lettore può aver la prova della sensibilità che l'autore ha saputo conservare fra le delusioni, la lotta, le tempeste della sua non mai pacifica esistenza. Si leggano, ad esempio, il capitolo in cui è descritta la prima notte di matrimonio, e l'altro in cui è ritratta la protagonista tutta affaccendata nelle sue frivole compere, e quello in cui si racconta della morte e dei funerali di Laura Uglio, e si veda con qual delicatezza di tocco ha saputo lumeggiare, argomenti gravi o teneri, leggeri o tristi, scabrosi o sentimentali. E non ci si darà torto se diremo che lo studio del vero, quasi istintivo nello Zùccoli, presta alla sua opera, una varietà mirabile.

uno spirito fresco e sincero

Non è certamente un autore monocorde colui che vicino a questo può allineare altri dieci volumi, in cui ciascun personaggio ha una figura sua propria; dieci volumi nei quali sfilano i tipi di tutte le classi sociali,

dall'aristocrazia al popolo minuto, dal superbo patrizio del L'amore di Loredana ai ladri e ai teppisti della Compagnia della Leggera, dalla candida fanciulla di certe sue novelle alla donna ardente, volitiva, disdegnosa, che è la protagonista di Farfui, dal bambino ingenuo al libertino inquieto e curioso, dal soldato fanfarone e generoso al trionfatore freddo, taciturno e senza pietà. Mille sono i tipi che lo Zùccoli ha animato della una arte, e quelli che popolano

Il designato hanno un carattere di realtà e un rilievo indimenticabili. Il libro che vede ora la luce nella sua edizione definitiva, dopo che l'autore vi ha arrecato notevoli e pazienti ritocchi, fu pubblicato la prima volta a Milano nel 1894, presso una Casa editrice, che oggi non esiste più. Se il primo romanzo di Luciano Zùccoli era subito parso opera indipendente e originale, questo, che veniva a un anno di distanza da *I Lussuriosi*, dové a dividere che lo scrittore non intendeva la letteratura come un dilettantismo giovanile, ma come un'alta faticosa nobilissima arte, alla quale voleva dedicare tutto il suo ingegno. E in realtà, ingrandendo la fama dell'autore e confermando le speranza che il primo libro aveva fatto fiorire,

purposes: first, to pull juicy, tempting morsels of the article out to encourage readers to look further into the piece; and second, to provide design elements, once again breaking up monotonous flows of print. Pull quotes can either appear within a column or between two columns of type.

In newspapers, you'll commonly see a typographic device whereby the first paragraph is printed large, over two columns. This makes it easier for the reader to begin reading the text. The problem is, with two regular width columns beginning just below, how do they know which one to read? The answer is to use a 'byline' – the author's name, often set as a 'wob' (white on black). These 'slugs', as they're known in the newspaper industry, aren't there to buoy up a journalist's ego: they serve a more basic design purpose.

Of course, the most significant improvement we can make is through our choice of typeface, both for headlines and for body text. But in the examples on this page, we've stuck with boring Times Roman so that we can better explore the design possibilities that type alone can offer.

MORE INFO

● Photoshop offers very little in the way of typographic tools. We can set text within a block, by dragging with the Type tool and then typing into the resulting rectangle; changing the width of the block will wrap the text, but we can't automatically create drop caps or spaces around pull quotes. Unfortunately, these need to be created laboriously, by hand, with multiple text blocks: which means we need to think about the page design carefully before we begin.

● If you're using page designs in a Photoshop document, it's always best to design them in another application – Xpress, or InDesign, or even Word – and save them as a PDF from that application, to be imported into Photoshop later. You'll generally get more control this way.

● Although the examples here show pages with no pictures, it's always possible to find photographs to accompany any text. The problem most designers face is that they're looking for relevant images; but the images are made relevant by their captions. An article on farm subsidies in a newspaper, for instance, might include a photograph of a mound of potatoes. Is this because the readers don't know what potatoes look like? Let's check the caption beneath the image: 'Farmers complained that subsidies were not at sufficient levels...' and so on. The caption may sit with the image, but it doesn't have to relate to it in any way. As long as it ties in with the main story, we're fooled into believing that the picture relates to the article. We can be easily fooled.

Customizing film logos

Reproducing a distinctive typeface, like those often associated with movies or books, is often a wonderful tool for doing a parody or satire, or making a private joke. Here, we'll make some lettering in the Harry Potter style, to go with another Harry entirely – the second in line to the throne of England.

To make this Harry Windsor lettering, we'll first make our canvas area bigger so that there's room above the original. Copying the word 'Harry' into place will help us to align the rest of the letters.

Each time we copy a chunk of lettering, we'll select it (generally with the Lasso tool) and then use `ctrl J` `⌘ J` to make a new layer from it. This way, we can manipulate each chunk independently. We'll end up with a lot of layers, but it's worth it for the convenience of increased ease of editing.

1 The original lettering is far from easy to work with. It's drawn as if lit from the center, so that the shadows are on the left on the word 'Harry', and on the right on 'Potter'. We'll have to be careful to make the new version match this lighting. We'll begin by making space above the wording, so we can copy and paste elements into it.

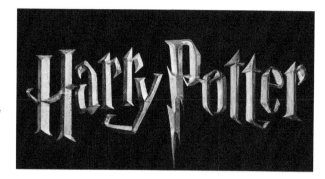

2 The 'P' of 'Potter' is marked by a strong vertical lightning bolt, so we should reproduce that with our first letter. Nothing could be easier than selecting the vertical from the 'P' and copying it to a new location. The other strokes in the 'W' are made from verticals in the 'H' and the 't'; the spike in the center comes from one of the spikes on a letter 't'. When stretched and rotated, they fit together well.

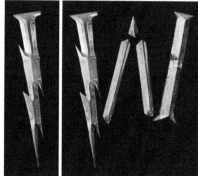
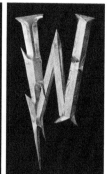

3 The letter 'i' is the vertical stroke from one of the two letter 'r' instances, flipped horizontally and with the curl cut off. There are several ways we could have made the dot on top; this one has been built from the spike on top of the 'i', duplicated and flipped vertically to make a triangle.

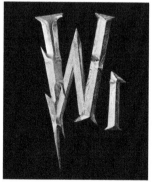
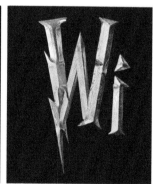

4 The 'n' seems, at first, to be a little trickier to construct. But we've already got a usable left and curved top, from the 'r'; we can repurpose it here. We need to use the 'r' from the end of 'Potter' in the original, to be certain that the lighting will be on the correct side. The other vertical stroke in the letter is the 'i' again, with the top cut off and rotated to fit into the curve on the former 'r'.

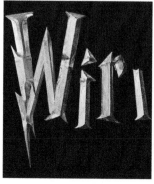
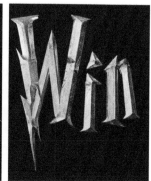

5 The only difficult part of the letter 'd' is the rounded portion – and we've already got one of those, in the letter 'o' from the word 'Potter'. We can combine this with a vertical stroke taken from the 'r' and flipped, once again; with the spiked base removed and a little distortion, it slots neatly into the side of the 'o'.

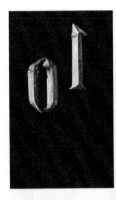

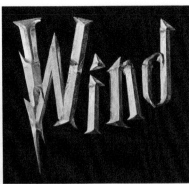

6 The only really tricky letter in this construction is the 's', which appears to have no similarity to any other letters in the words. But we do have a curved top – we can copy one from the top of the letter 'a' and flip it horizontally. It would be good to be able to rotate this to make the bottom half – but the lighting would be wrong. So we'll add a straight section and a hook at the bottom, and both of these can be taken from a letter 'r'.

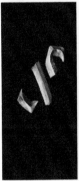

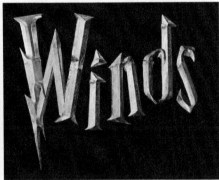

7 The final two letters of the word are easy – we already have them in the word 'Potter', and since we're not using that word at all now there's no problem about simply dragging these into place. Some tidying up is needed to blend the character elements together, and the result – when the full name is viewed as a whole – is convincing.

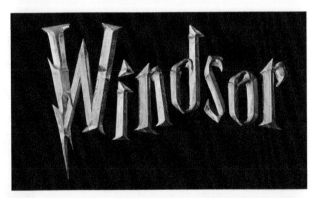

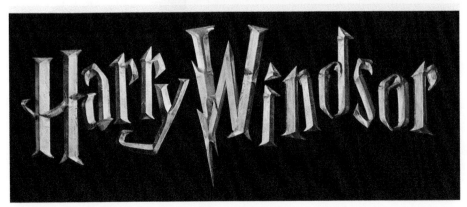

MORE INFO

● This lettering was originally part of the Harry Potter poster, which I found using Google Images. Most of the images turned up on a typical search are far too small to use: choose Large or Extra Large images from the pop-up menu on the Google Images search page to constrain your search to just those images that are big enough to work with.

● In order to work with the text, we first needed to separate it from its background. This was done by selecting the black in the poster with the Magic Wand tool. But because the lettering is so dark, a lot of it was included in the selection; QuickMask was used to paint back in the portions of lettering that had been selected by accident. See page 227 for more about using QuickMask.

● Most film lettering isn't nearly as tricky as this one: the strong side lighting and metal texture present extra problems. Even though movies and TV shows frequently use custom-designed text for their titles, you can be fairly sure that someone will have created an entire font based on it. Check out www.dafont.com for an outstanding collection of free-to-use fonts.

SHORTCUTS

 MAC WIN BOTH

Monogram letters

The picture above shows monograms carved into the rock to commemorate royal visits to the Norwegian town of Kongsberg. The most recent entry is from 1995; the earliest monogram here dates from 1623.

The rich, the powerful and the plain vain have been commemorating their initials in elaborate monograms for centuries. Monograms are routinely added to tableware, pyjamas and commemorative plaques.

The process of intertwining letters is a subtle one. We have to judge each pair of letters according to its individual characteristics in order to find the best fit. Not all pairs can be intertwined easily, which is why we often see letters at different heights in monograms.

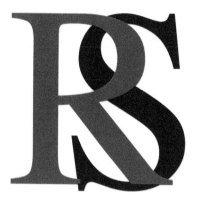

1 We'll use the letters R and S for this example, as they can be intertwined in a complex and multi-overlapping manner. First, create the two letters as separate text objects: we need to be able to manipulate them individually. I've set these in two different colors so we can see what's going on more clearly.

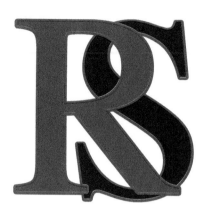

2 Use Layer Styles to add a stroke to the letters. Make sure the stroke style is set to 'outside', so it doesn't interfere with the characters themselves. Here, I've applied an 8pt stroke to both characters; the color doesn't matter at this stage.

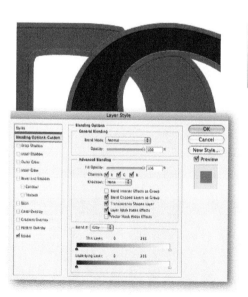

5 There's a problem. When we zoom in on the masked portion of the R, we can see that the stroke curls in unnaturally because the stroke is following the character. We want the stroke hidden along with the character: so open the Layer Effects dialog, and set the options to Layer Mask Hides Effects as shown here.

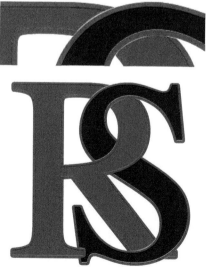

6 This presents us with a second problem. With the stroke and the mask both set to exactly 8 pixels around the letter S, we end up with a slight fringe that we can see when we zoom in. The solution is to delete the mask, and reapply it with the Expand setting set to 7, rather than 8: this hides any gaps.

MORE INFO

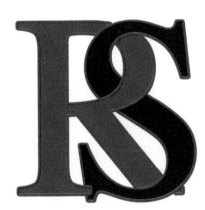

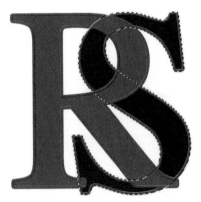

3 We need to hide the R selectively where the S lies in front of it. Load up the letter S as a selection by holding *ctrl* ⌘ and clicking on its thumbnail in the Layers palette; then use Select > Modify > Expand to make the selection 8 pixels larger (the same width as the stroke).

4 Create a layer mask for the letter R (see page 233), then use a hard-edged brush to paint out those areas where the S wants to lie in front. We could intertwine the letters two different ways; here, the tail of the R and the bottom of the bowl are painted out so they lie behind the S.

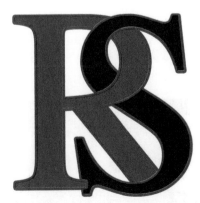

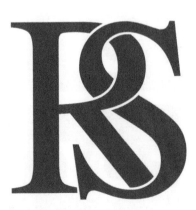

7 With the new Expand setting one pixel smaller than the stroke, we get a tighter effect. Once the letters are wound together, deselect and then paint out extraneous areas – the end of the tail on the R, for example, looked ugly; so remove it. Appearance is always more important than sticking to the rules.

8 With the characters interwined as we want them. we can look at the fill and stroke colors. Setting the stroke to white, so making it invisible against our white background, is the standard procedure for monogrammed letters; I've also hidden a little of the lower serif of the R on the mask to fit better.

● The tradition when winding character pairs together is for the elements to pass alternately above and below each other. There are, naturally, two ways of beginning this process – they're both shown above. It's up to you which method you choose, but it's worth trying both; generally, one will work significantly better than the other.

● Of course, you don't need to stick rigidly to the 'over/under' rule. When designing the lettering for the cover of this book, the way it looks was far more important than any theoretical mode of procedure.

● When intertwining three or more characters together, as is often the case, it can take time to find the perfect fit. Always put the extra time in at this stage, before you begin the masking procedures set out here: it's much more difficult to adjust the masks later, and is straightforward once the characters have been arranged in their final position. On the other hand, you should always be prepared to delete your masks and start again if the arrangement proves not to be working further down the line.

MAG NETS

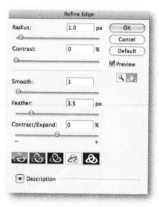

Font smoothing

MAGNETS

There are many reasons why we might want to smooth type. We might need to create rounded lettering for refrigerator magnets, as in the above example: here, plain old Times Bold has been turned into the rounded plastic form in just a few seconds.

If we're using type as the basis for a stone carving, or want it to look as if it's cast in metal, then rounding the corners can make the end result far more convincing. We also need to round the edges of type for making neon signs, embossing effects, and so on.

This technique uses the Refine Edge dialog found in Photoshop CS3 and later (and there's also a version of it in Photoshop Elements 6). You'll need this version in order to use the technique – although there is an alternative approach. See the More Info panel on the right for details.

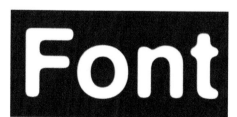

1 Begin by setting the text you want, in the font of your choice. Add extra letter spacing to give the characters room to expand – they can always be tightened up by hand later. Hold `ctrl` `⌘` and click on the layer's icon in the Layers palette to load the selection.

2 Open the Refine Edges dialog, either from the button on the Options bar or by pressing `ctrl` `alt` `R` `⌘` `⌥` `R`. With the default settings, we'll just get a slightly fuzzy version of our wording; but we're going to change the settings next.

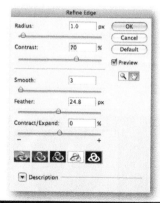

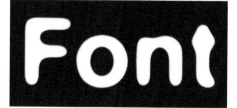

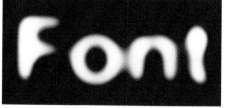

5 The higher we increase the Feather amount, the more rounded the text becomes. We can even increase it so far that the lettering begins to lose its shape, producing the highly stylized version seen here. This would be a great choice for sci-fi movie posters due to its organic, alien feel.

6 We're not constrained by the need to keep the edges crisp, of course. Here, lowering the Contrast setting to just 70% produces a blurry version of the type that's still entirely legible. Again, this would be a good choice for a sci-fi context.

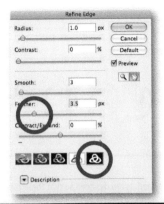

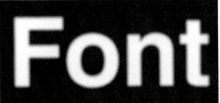

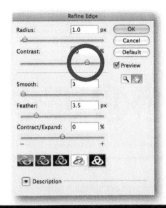

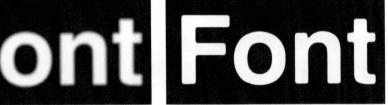

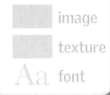
3 Click the final icon, bottom right, to view the selection as a mask. This shows the selected area in white against a black background. To begin the process of rounding off the text, increase the Feather amount. This produces the blurry, out-of-focus look we see here.

4 To get rid of that blurring, increase the Contrast by dragging the slider to the right. Dragging it all the way to 100% will tend to produce a rather ugly, stepped bitmap edge to the lettering; start at around 80% and adjust upwards if necessary.

MORE INFO

● In step 1 here, we began by spacing our text more widely than usual. To do this, select the words with the Type tool, and use `alt` ➡️ ⬅️➡️ to add letterspacing. The reason for this is that font outlines can enlarge (as seen in step 7), or merge together (as seen in step 6). By greatly increasing the spacing, we prevent this happening accidentally.

● If you don't have Photoshop CS3, you can still produce similar results – but you have to do it manually. First, merge the type into the background layer. Use Gaussian Blur to soften the edges of the text: you should end up with a result similar to that seen in step 3 (except your type will be black on white, rather than as shown here). Next, open the Levels dialog. You'll see three small triangles beneath the histogram. Drag the black and white triangles towards the center, so they almost touch the gray triangle. This simulates the Contrast step, tightening up the feathering. Move all three triangles to the left or right to expand or contract the outlines. This method is a little hit and miss – expect a fair amount of Undoing, changing the Blur amount, then trying again.

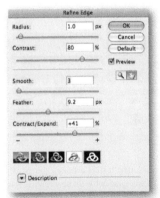

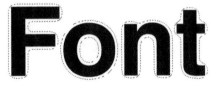

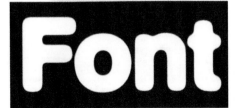

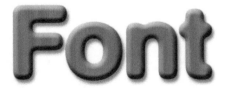

7 With the contrast back up to 80% to achieve a smooth outline, we can change the apparent weight of the font. Here, raising the Contract/Expand slider allows us to offset the outline, producing a much bolder, chunkier version of the type. The possibilities here are practically endless.

8 Finally, when you're happy with the appearance, click OK to dismiss the dialog. You'll be left with the original lettering, showing the new form as a selection outline. Make a new layer, and fill the selection with color. Here, I've used Layer Styles to add a simple emboss and shadow effect.

Don't try this at home

I was baffled each time I drove past this sign – until it was pointed out to me that Fresh Pond is the region of Massachusets where this gas station is located. But you can see why a tourist might be confused by the idea.

The sign above is an example of how a bit of typographical thought – such as setting the word 'gas' in a larger, or a different font or color – would have avoided any confusion.

But there are many worse typographic mistakes than this in common use, and we'll see examples of them each time we open a newspaper or click on a website.

Shown here are some of the most common mistakes designers make with type. They're all easily avoidable; you just need the confidence to ditch an idea once it's become clear that it really isn't going anywhere.

GOTHIC CAPS

1 Fonts such as Old English (above) and those with fancy, swash capitals are designed so that these capitals are used at the beginnings of words only. When an entire word is set in these capitals the result is an ugly, unbalanced mismatch of styles. Whatever it is, it certainly isn't Old English.

COLORDAZZLE

2 Placing opposite colors together creates an instant 'wow' effect. Unfortunately, that's all the effect is – instant. It has no lasting merit, and it's both painful and difficult to read. The effect is bad enough in one or two words; a whole paragraph set in this way is simply infuriating for the reader.

Patterns

3 Photoshop allows us to apply all kinds of Layer Styles to text – including texture overlays. You may think for a fraction of a second that this is a cool and classy way to liven up dull type, but you'd be wrong. It simply makes the text illegible. Avoid at all costs!

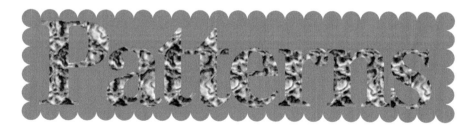

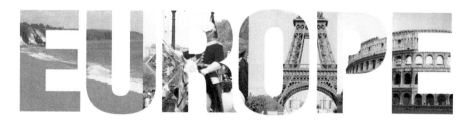

4 The idea of filling bold words with a series of images that illustrate the concept isn't a new one, and it's one that can work very well – in the right hands. But you do need to be especially careful about the placement of images: don't cut off an image half way through a letter, for instance, and don't chop people's heads off.

MORE INFO

● Try not to be tempted to 'make do' with a font from your collection if it isn't the right one for a job. It will only take a few minutes to find a shareware or freeware font that's a better fit for the design in hand, and can make all the difference to the end result.

● Typographic designs can easily take on a life of their own. We start working on a concept, and keep tinkering and toying with it in the hope that it will suddenly gel. What we really need, however, is the ability to step back and look at our work afresh. Go out of the room, make a coffee, then look at your monitor from across the room as you return: this should give you a fresh perspective on your design. Be prepared to start again if you think it isn't working.

● During every design session that includes type, take a fresh look and ask yourself: is it legible? If you're in any doubt, then fix it immediately – before you get too used to it.

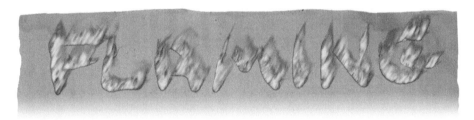

5 This sort of design is something we used to see a lot in the early days of the internet. The mentality is this: 'I've got 16 million colors available to me, and dammit, I'm going to use them all.' If you try to make every word scream for attention then none of them will be legible – it's the equivalent of shouting at an audience.

FLAMING

6 Occasionally you may be tempted – or be asked – to make words out of flame, or clouds, or water droplets, or pools of oil. It's possible, of course, but the sad fact is that however well you achieve it, it will always look irredeemably ghastly. Try to avoid the temptation.

Dear John,

I'm writing to you to ask for your help with a rather delicate matter. I think that only

7 Comic Sans is the 'handwriting' font that's bundled with every computer. Business people use it because they think it looks more casual than Times Roman. It has no place in any Photoshop work: it isn't handwriting, and it doesn't look like it. There are plenty of great handwriting fonts out there, so go and find something more original.

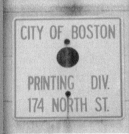

● You'd think that the City of Boston's Printing Division could have found a more typographically elegant solution to their own sign – one which would have included their name without abbreviation. This is stupidly bad typography: don't settle for it!

Joined Up

8 Some fonts, such as Deftone Stylus (above) or formal handwriting fonts like Snell Roundhand, are designed so that each letter runs into the one which follows. When they're spaced out like this the result is just plain ugly, as each character seems unnecessarily extended to the right. Respect the typographer's intentions!

All the fonts included with this book are in TrueType format, which means they can be used on both Windows and Mac computer systems.

TrueType started life with a bad reputation. Because there was no licence fee to pay to Adobe, as there was with PostScript, it was the format of choice for knock-off merchants producing copies of well-known fonts. These were often rushed out without proper care, which caused printing problems – so leading printers to ban TrueType fonts. It's always worth checking with your printer before using these fonts in commercial work. (This doesn't apply to using the fonts within Photoshop documents, of course.)

The freeware fonts tend not to have a full character set. While they will all include upper and lower case alphabets (if appropriate) as well as numbers, you may be hard pressed to find euro and pound symbols, ampersands and so on. It's also unlikely that they will have a full set of punctuation marks.

Most of these fonts are designed for special-effect use, and that's how we treat them in this book.

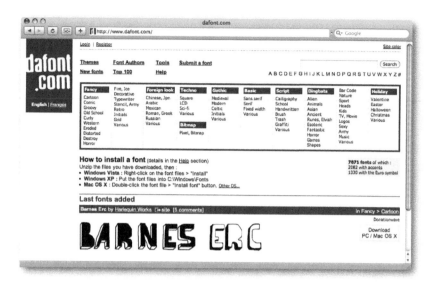

There are many sources of fonts on the internet, many of them offering fonts that are free for both personal and commercial use. My personal favorite is **www.dafont.com** which groups fonts into categories – Fancy, Gothic, Techno, Basic, Script, and so on – and then into subcategories (so Script includes Calligraphy, Handwritten, School, Brush, Graffiti, and so on). It's a fantastic resource that makes it easy to find the font you need in a hurry. You can also search by font name or by the name of the author.

The site also includes a preview feature whereby you can type your sample text to see it displayed in the font of your choice.

At the last count dafont.com listed nearly 8,000 fonts on the site. They're all provided in formats for both PC and Mac in TrueType format, and are all available for free and instant download directly from the site.

For a wider selection of fonts, both commercial (paid-for) and free, the best site I've found is **www.myfonts.com**. The site treats visitors like adults, and assumes you have a basic knowledge of the sort of font you're looking for (but see its subsite, WhatTheFont, opposite).

Most of the fonts on the myfonts.com site are available both as commercial PostScript fonts and as home-use TrueType fonts; in some instances, the TrueType versions are available for free, while the PostScript versions are paid for.

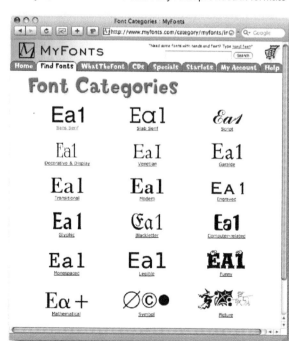

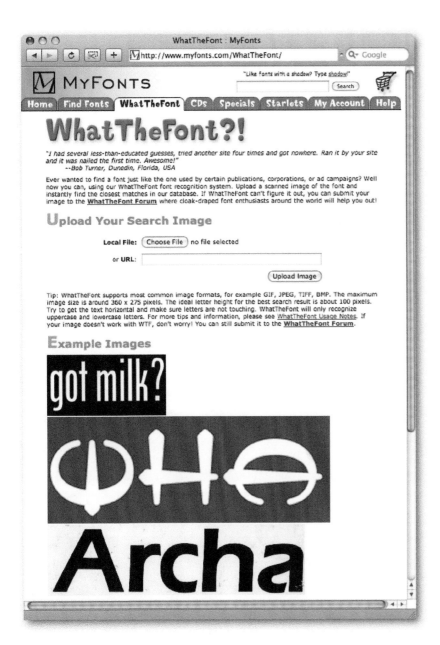

MORE INFO

The internet holds a huge variety of font resources. Here are a few of my favorites:

www.comicbookfonts.com
A collection of commercial (but affordable) fonts specifically designed for comic book artists.

www.webfxmall.com/fonts
A collection of special effect fonts.

www.identifont.com
If WhatTheFont fails you, or if you can't get enough characters, try identifont. This takes you through font design step by step, asking about specific character shapes until you arrive at the one solution.

www.fontfreak.com
Collection of mainly display fonts. Users are able to download the entire collection in a single archive.

http://moorstation.org/typoasis
The virtual home to a wide range of font authors. An attractive, well-designed site that makes finding fonts more of a pleasure.

www.planet-typography.com
News and information about new fonts and font designers. With articles on how and why certain fonts were designed – of great interest to those into typography.

www.fontlab.com
Developers of typographic software for the creation of fonts, for both Mac and Windows.

One of the most extraordinary typographic resources on the internet is **WhatTheFont**, the revolutionary font identification website located at **www.myfonts.com/WhatTheFont**. It allows you to load any image containing text on your computer, and will make a range of suggestions as to what the font used might be.

The more characters you give it to work with, the more precisely targeted the results. But even with half a dozen characters, WhatTheFont manages to pin a font down to three or four possibilities. So if you've spotted a font on a website, do a screen capture; if it's in the street, capture it with the camera in your cell phone; if it's in a newspaper, scan it into your computer. WhatTheFont will almost always be able to tell you what it is, and where you can lay your hands on it.

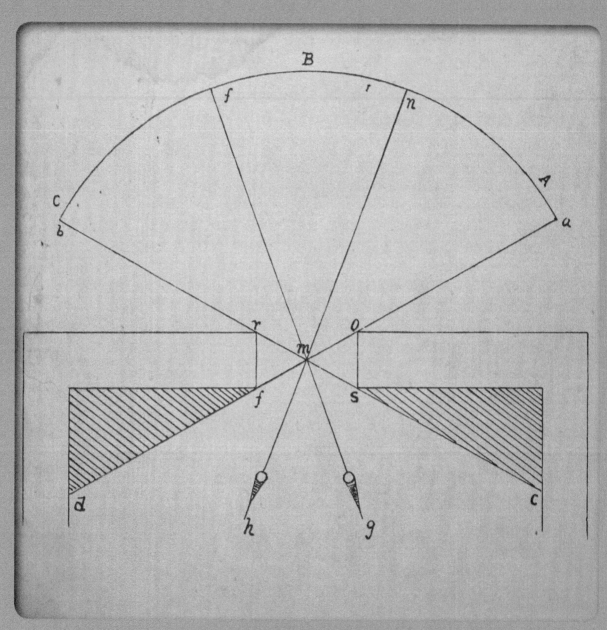

Experiments on the relation of light and shadow within a room, from *The Notebooks of Leonardo da Vinci*, edited by Jean Paul Richter, 1880

Principles of design

When we create a montage in Photoshop we're not just laying the bare facts before our viewers – we're telling a story. And we have to do all we can to make that story entertaining, informative and compelling. Otherwise, as with all poor storytellers, we'll simply lose our audience.

The rules of composition have been delineated over the centuries, evolving from first principles into a solid, robust set of guidelines. The rules that originally applied to painting were later applied to photography; and we can implement that same set of values when we're creating photomontages as well. The medium may have changed, but the art of storytelling remains constant.

In this chapter we'll look at some of the key concepts that determine how a good picture differs from one that's poorly composed. We'll look at how to lead the viewer's eye through an image, and how to make them look at just what we want them to look at.

Although all these ideas are presented as 'rules', it's important to remember that rules are, of course, just as important when they're broken. And so, along the way, we'll also examine instances of when to ignore the rules for dramatic effect, for the sake of difference or just for pure cussedness.

composition

The act or art of composing, or forming a whole or integral, by placing together and uniting different things, parts, or ingredients. In specific uses:

(a) The invention or combination of the parts of any literary work or discourse, or of a work of art; as the composition of a poem or a piece of music. 'The constant habit of elaborate composition.' – Macaulay.

(b) (Fine Arts) The art or practice of so combining the different parts of a work of art as to produce a harmonious whole; also, a work of art considered as such.

Webster's Revised Unabridged Dictionary

Facing in and out

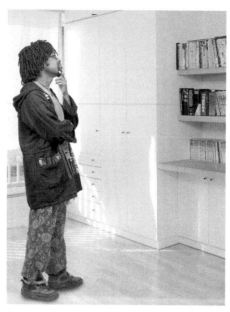 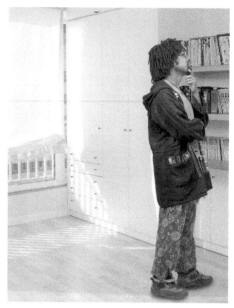

Facing in or facing out: one creates a good composition, the other unbalances the image

Michelangelo's sculpture of David is almost always depicted from this angle – and this is how the original is approached from the hallway at the Galleria dell'Accademia in Florence, Italy.

Although the statue was placed in this position, we are in fact viewing it from the side: a true front view would show David staring straight into our eyes, body turned away. Sadly, the location means it's impossible to get this view as there's a column in the way.

The direction in which a figure is facing crucially alters our impression of the scene. Here, David seems distant, almost distracted; and that wasn't Michelangelo's intention.

THE POSITION OF A CHARACTER in a scene changes the way we appraise the scene, and also affects the overall balance of the image. Here, our figure in the left version is examining his bookshelves from a distance. It's a well-balanced image: he stands on the left of the scene, the books are on the right, and the eye leads naturally from one to the other. In the second version, we've moved him closer to the books. He may be able to see them more clearly here, but the image falls apart. With all the visual interest cramped on the right of the picture, the whole left half is just dead space.

It's a good rule of thumb always to place your characters facing into the image rather than out of it. The impression given in the second image above is that he's more interested in something out of shot – in which case, if it's so interesting, why aren't we looking at it as well?

There are cases when we need to break this rule, of course. The girl in the photograph on the right isn't just turning her back on the array of fresh vegetables, she's turning away from us, the viewer, as well: displeasure and refusal are written all over her pose. By rejecting the scene, she's rejecting the contents.

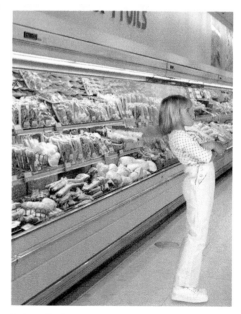

Perhaps she doesn't want to eat her greens...

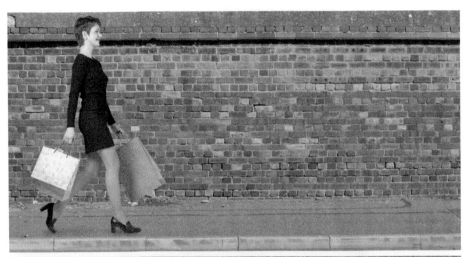

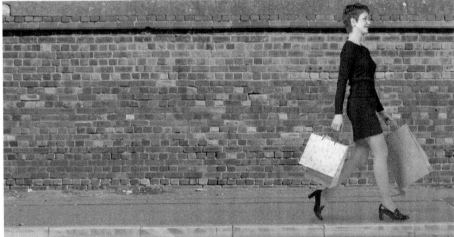

Characters, animals or objects in motion have far more power when they're walking into the scene, rather than out of it. It could be the simple human value of expectation: where we're going is of more interest than where we've been. Again, there are exceptions to this rule. In the example on the right, the focus of the image is the pseudo philosophical graffiti: the woman is there merely to add human interest. In this instance, she must face out of the scene to avoid conflicting with the focus.

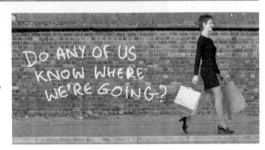

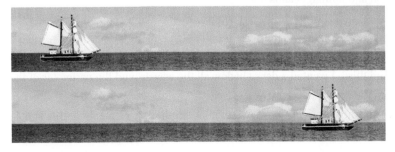

Even inanimate objects need to conform to the 'facing in' rule. Consider the balance of these two images: the first works, the second is just uncomfortable.

● In the west, we read from left to right. It may be because of this that we expect motion in this direction as well: when we 'read' an image, we tend to begin at the left and move our gaze towards the right. In the cinema, the left side of the screen is well known to be the more powerful – and many arguments have arisen between actors and directors as to who gets to stand on the left.

● Even the way a character is looking, rather than facing, can indvertently draw the viewer's attention out of the scene. Check those eyelines!

● The designer's need for photographic subjects to face into the page rather than out of it frequently leads to images being 'flipped' to make people face in the opposite direction. Sometimes, this can have drastic consequences. One well-known software firm used to publish a library of 800 CD-ROMs, containing a total of 80,000 royalty-free photographic images. Many of these images were supplied by freelance photographers, who were paid a fee for their use. One image, showing a young boy conducting an orchestra, was flipped by a designer to make him face into the page. But here's the problem: the boy had sadly died since the photograph was taken. The resulting image showed him conducting while holding the baton in his left hand – which, his parents insisted, ridiculed his memory. The photograph had been taken at a public event, and no model release had been sought. The parents sued for defamation of character, and won; the entire 800 CD library was withdrawn from circulation.

The focus of attention

When medieval artists wanted to depict saints, they painted a halo around their head. In fact, the halo concept is far older than this: haloes have been found on statues of Buddha from the 1st century AD, and on carvings of the god Ra in ancient Egypt, millennia before that.

So why did this convention take hold? Are we to believe that sacred figures in ancient times really sported a ring of gold around their heads?

Haloes are used to draw attention to the central figures in religious compositions. They've become so commonplace that we see them without noticing them. But we couldn't use this technique today without attracting adverse comments. And so, as Photoshop users, we need to find a different way to focus our images.

A man, a calculator, a room setting. But our eye wanders all over the place

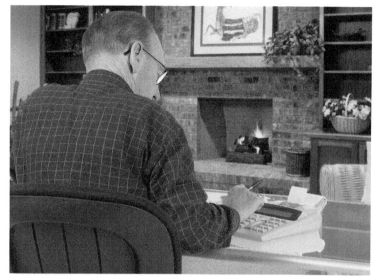

The judicious addition of shadows helps to focus the viewer's attention

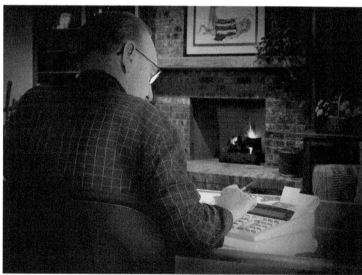

THE FIGURE OF A MAN working at his accounts, top, has all the elements: the calculator, the homely setting, the flickering flames suggesting domestic harmony. But there's no sense of drama here; with all the parts of the picture in plain view, everything cries for attention and nothing stands out.

In the second version, I've made three changes. First, I darkened and increased the contrast on the background image, to make the fire stand out more. Second, I painted a shadow onto the back of the man, to accentuate the sense of the light as emanating from the fireplace. And third, I painted a dark shadow all the way around the perimeter of the room, away from the fire.

The result is to concentrate the viewer's attention on the key elements in this simple montage – the solitary man at the desk and his calculator. Our eye is now immediately

This doctor has been photographed in his operating theater. But the mess and confusion behind him detracts from the image: it's hard to focus on him directly, with so much going on in the background.

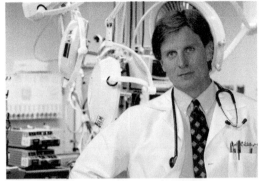

● To create the shadow on the man we first make a Hard Light layer, using a technique we'll employ many times in this book. See page 232 for more on layer modes.

Blurring the background is one solution. The use of Gaussian Blur gives a controlled out-of-focus effect that echoes the shallow depth of field preferred by portrait photographers. In Photoshop, of course, we have the luxury of being able to apply our blurring afterwards.

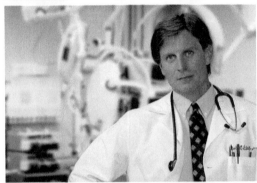

● In the doctor example on this page, we have the luxury of working with a layered image in which the doctor and his background are two separate layers. If this were a single photograph, we'd have to trace around the doctor (the Pen tool or QuickMask are best for this – see page 233) and make a new layer from him. We're then free to treat the background independently. One problem with blurring the background, though, would be that we'd be able to see a fringe of the original doctor included here: the solution would be to enlarge the doctor layer slightly, so as to cover the edges beneath.

Another approach is to add a blue tint behind the figure. This is simply achieved: create a new layer and fill it with your chosen color, then lower the opacity of that layer until the background shows through. This is a more graphic approach, but achieves its purpose – to make the foreground figure stand out.

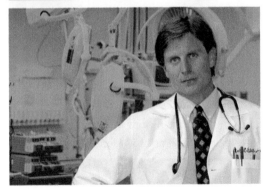

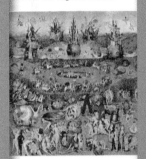

● As with every rule, there are times when this one needs to be broken. The painting above is *The Garden of Earthly Delights* painted in 1504 by Hieronymous Bosch. In order to accentuate the sense of chaos and disorder, he deliberately filled the canvas with tiny elements, each of which tell their own story in graphic detail. But there's still defining symmetry here that prevents total anarchy.

drawn to the central figure, as the less relevant perimeter of the room fades into blackness. The shadows bring a different mood to the piece: whereas before he was just working at his desk, now he's working late into the night to put his accounts in order.

There are many ways to draw attention to the focal ploint of an image. In Da Vinci's

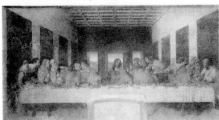

The diagonals lead us back to the center

famous painting of the Last Supper, all the diagonals point directly towards the head of the figure of Christ: wherever our gaze might wander within the picture, it's always pulled back to the middle. Photographers and photomontage artists can use similar techniques to draw the eye.

The strong diagonal

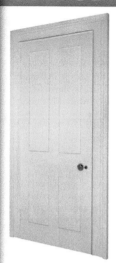

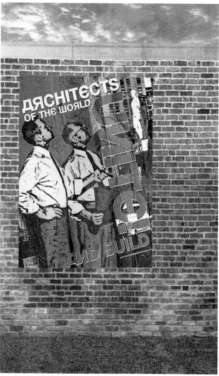 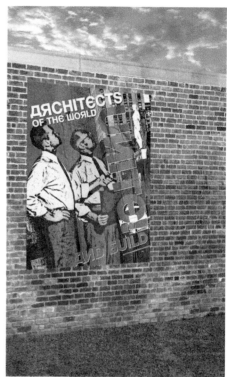

Two views of the same scene: but which looks more like real life?

Ask someone to draw a door, and you'll be presented with a squared-up rectangle. The more artistically inclined may add panels, and perhaps even a doorknob. Which, you'd think, is exactly as it should be.

The problem is that we rarely, if ever, see a door as a perfect rectangle in real life. Glance around the room you're in now, at the door, windows and ceiling: if you were to draw them exactly as you see them, they'd be irregular polygons. Only when we're flat on to a door do we see it as a rectangle, and even then parallax would mean we'd truly see it with curved edges.

Real life has no squared-up views; and so when we create scenes in Photoshop, we need to avoid them too. They look too artificial to be convincing.

LATER ON IN THIS BOOK we'll spend a chapter looking at creating posters, such as the Russian revolutionary style shown above. Of course, these posters will always look better pasted on a wall, than flat on a printed page. So why is it that the left image, above, looks more unrealistic than the angled right one?

Throughout the history of art, painters have been at pains to bring diagonal elements into their work. Partly it's for the sake of realism, showing scenes as we apprehend them in real life. Partly it's to prevent an image being divided into regular chunks by horizontal lines: in the image above left, the ground and sky form strong horizontal bands that break the unity of the scene, turning it instead into a loosely assembled pattern of close-fitting chunks.

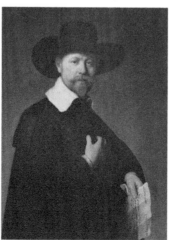

The diagonal imperative is clear in this portrait by Rembrandt

A strong diagonal element in a picture will always bring dynamism and life into the image. It helps to lead the eye through the scene, providing a clear path for us to follow as we gaze upon it. The arrangement of the head, collar, hands and sheet of paper in this painting by Rembrandt, left, is far from coincidence; they form waypoints on the diagonal that runs from top left to bottom right.

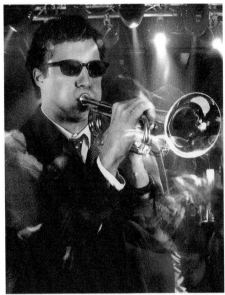 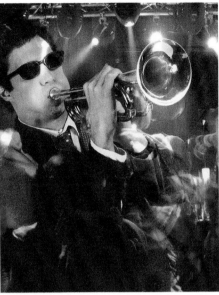

The same jazz man, the same background. But while one is static, the other has dynamism and movement

● There are many techniques we can use to integrate all the elements of a scene. The jazz trumpeter, left, has been placed in front of the colorful background. Here's how the rotated version looked in its original form:

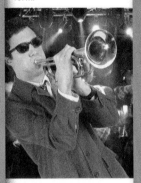

With both picture elements clearly visible, even the strong diagonal can't tie them together. But by changing the mode of the trumpeter's layer from Normal to Hard Light, we allow the background to show through and so blend the two together. You can read more about layer modes on page 232.

We can use diagonals to brighten up our montages, giving them an extra kick when they need it. The simple montage above contains just two elements, the trumpet player and the stage background. In the first, he's standing right in front of the background – but there's really no sense here that he's playing his instrument. He might just be posed for the picture; he might even be a waxwork for all the animation he shows. It only takes a rotation of his figure to produce a picture that's exciting and inviting.

Where painters created diagonals deliberately, photographers will always look for diagonals in the real world in order to photograph them. This may involve photographing a tall building from an oblique position, or rotating the camera to capture an angled view, or positioning a figure so the limbs make a diagonal shape. However it's done, photographers have long known that diagonals bring interest, shape and form to an image.

As ever, we sometimes need to break the rules. In the image on the right, the diagonals at the corners lead to a squared-up window. This gives the image a sense of calm and stillness: there's deliberately no movement in this picture. Would it work if the woman were off center?

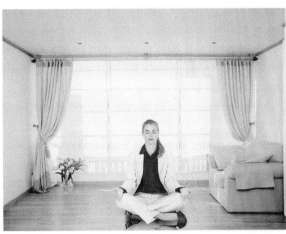

Deliberate stillness: the calm at the center

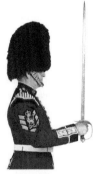

● It's worth thinking about how diagonals affect us in real life. Imagine a soldier with his sword raised. When it's leaning forward, it's an aggressive pose suggesting immediate action; when the sword is held dead vertical, the impression is of a soldier at rest.

The Rule of Thirds

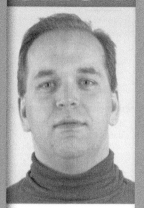

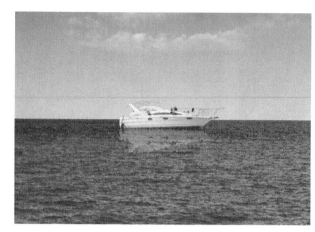

What's wrong with this picture? Why does it seem so static?

There's only one reason we'd position the subject of a composition right in the middle of the scene, and that's to take a passport photograph. In all other cases, there are better positions.

The 'Rule of Thirds' is a handy guide to positioning elements within a picture to their best advantage. It's a guiding principle that was first used by artists, who used it when creating images from scratch. The concept was taken up with enthusiasm with the birth of photography: aligning picture elements with the proportions set out by the rule enabled photographers to create compelling, powerful images.

Those who have been creating photographs or photomontages for some time will instinctively place their elements in these positions, without ever knowing that there's a guiding rule at work.

The Rule of Thirds shows how the composition misses on every count

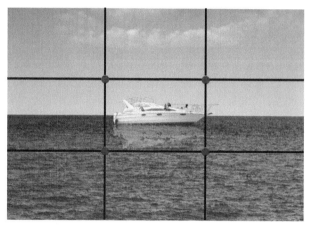

CONSIDER THE IMAGE of the boat on a clear blue sea, at the top of this page. It's got everything – a flashy yacht, a beautiful Mediterranean sea, a blue sky with one or two wispy clouds drifting by. So why does it seem so unappealing?

The answer becomes clear when we look at the so-called 'Rule of Thirds'. This is a composition technique that divides the image up into three equal horizontal regions, and three equal vertical regions – rather like imposing a tic-tac-toe board on our photograph. The horizontal and vertical lines give us the positions where our image elements have the most power and impact; the intersections, shown here as red dots, are the strongest positions in the whole composition.

As we can see when we overlay the grid on our picture, it completely fails to hit any of the sweet spots. The horizon is dead center, which divides the image in half. The boat, bang in the center of the shot, has no power whatever.

On the facing page, we try two different approaches. In the top one, we've moved the horizon line down so that it lines up with the bottom third, and the boat has been moved to line up with the 'power point' bottom left (the smaller inset image shows the grid overlay). This approach accentuates the sky, and is a pleasing composition: there's a sense of balance here that was lacking in the original. As with most rules of composition,

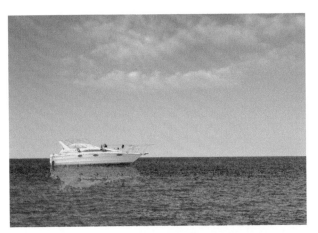

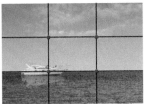

Bringing the horizon down accentuates the sky

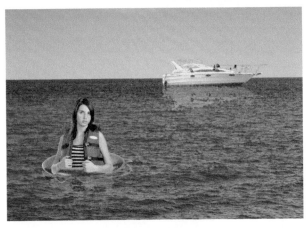

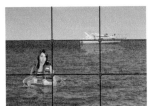

Raising the horizon gives more emphasis to the sea

● The Rule of Thirds was first written down in 1797, describing how a landscape should be proportioned for the most aesthetically pleasing effect, in J. T. Smith's book *Remarks on Rural Scenery*.

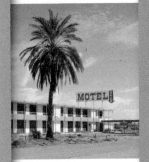

● Elements of a photograph will often fall into place without us consciously thinking about their precise position. The image above is a pleasing shot of a Californian motel; but it's not until we overlay the Rule of Thirds grid, below, that we see exactly why. The palm tree lines up with the left vertical, the roof of the motel with the lower horizontal, dividing this image up into neat, compelling proportions.

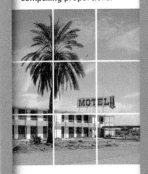

● You don't need to have the Rule of Thirds in mind when you create compositions; but if you're stuck for a reason why a montage isn't working, try applying it and readjust your scene.

it's hard to say exactly why one approach works when another fails. As viewers we have an emotional response to the arrangement that's difficult to quantify.

In the second approach, we've moved the horizon to align with the upper third, so giving emphasis to the sea. To liven this image up, we need to add an element in that wide expanse of blue, which is why the girl in the lifebelt is there. Note that she doesn't have to align precisely with the power point: these are general principles, not overriding rigid delineations. The lines and points are merely guides.

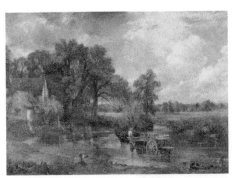

Constable's *Hay Wain*: spot the rule in action

One of the first artists to take the Rule of Thirds to heart was the famous English landscape painter John Constable. In his most celebrated work, *The Haywain*, he was careful to balance his picture elements according to the rule – although he didn't of course, opt for a slavish adherence to the precise positioning. But note how the haywain itself, bottom right, is balanced by the tree, top left.

Perspective: the horizon

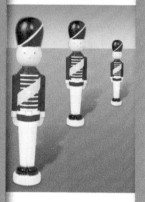

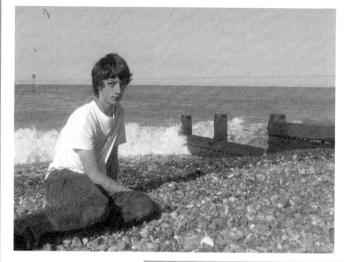

It doesn't matter whether you're sitting on the beach...

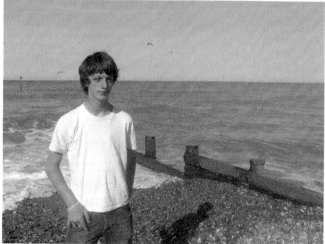

...or standing at ground level...

Two views of a simple scene. The top one shows three identical soldiers receding into the distance; in the bottom one the soldiers all appear to be different sizes. Why?

Even though we're looking at an obviously artificial background, populated by model soldiers, we still expect the rules of perspective to work. When they don't, the result is a scene that makes us feel uncomfortable and awkward: we may not be able to put our finger on exactly what's wrong, but we know that something is out of place.

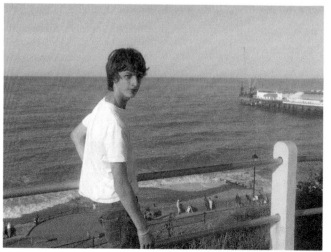

...or standing on a cliff top...

...the horizon is always at eye level.

MORE INFO

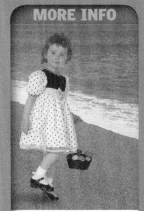

THE THREE PHOTOGRAPHS on the facing page could have been fitted into a much smaller space. But I make no apology for taking up a full page with them, because the message they convey is of supreme importance to the Photoshop artist:

The horizon is always at eye level.

You may be standing, sitting on the ground, or at the top of the Empire State Building: when you look directly forward, you'll see the horizon straight in front of you. It's by no means an obvious rule of nature, and many people don't believe it when they first hear it. But try it for yourself and you'll see it's true.

So why is this rule so important? Because it's so often broken by Photoshop artists who aren't aware of it when they attempt to make photorealistic montages. Their montages will always look false and inconsistent, and without appreciating this rule they'll never understand why.

When we create our montages, we need to position ourselves as viewers of the scene. If we add figures to this scene, then we're making assumptions about our position relative to them: we may be shorter than them, or taller, or sitting down. In general, we'd assume ourselves to be of average height, and so on an eyeline with most of the people in the scene.

In the four images shown here, the first is a view of a London street. The horizon is indicated by the converging lines of the building on the left (see following pages for more on how to read perspective out of a scene). This shows the man in blue jeans to be slightly shorter than we are, as he's just below the horizon line.

● This little girl is, naturally, shorter than we are. So when we position her on a beach, we place her eyeline well below the horizon: so far, in fact, that it's out of sight above the top of the image.

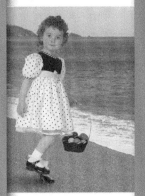

When we place a figure in the scene, we need to position him relative to the horizon. Too high, or too low, and he'll look out of place. The correct position is shown bottom left, in which his eyeline is precisely on the horizon, showing that he's exactly the same height as we are.

We could imagine that we'd crouched down to take a picture from her eye level. This brings the horizon down, and into shot. Even though we should stick to the eyeline-horizon rule, it's important to recognize that people are of different heights. In the top image, the girl is looking up at us, while in the bottom one she's looking directly forward at us. Her eyes don't move; it's all in our perception of the scene.

● When we include a number of figures that recede into the distance, placing their heads on the same level creates an immediate consistency.

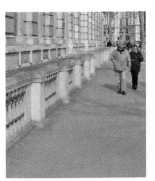

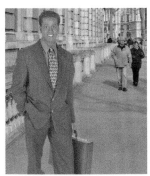

The original photograph, above left. But which scene shows the correct placement of the man in the suit?

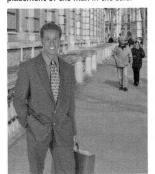

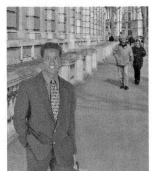

Reading perspective

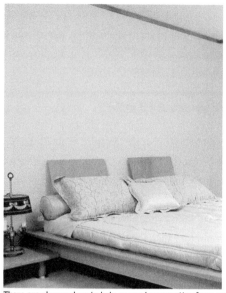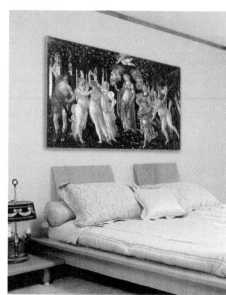

There are always clues to help us read perspective from a scene

It's easy enough to read the perspective in this scene: the railway lines clearly tend towards the vanishing point, located firmly on the horizon.

This is called 'one point' perspective, for the clear reason that all the lines in the image that are leading away from us tend to a single point. This kind of perspective is easy to see in exterior shots, where the horizon itself is on view in the picture.

Few background images are as obliging as this one, though. When we move the action from the outside to the inside, in particular, we face a different problem; with the horizon no longer visible, we need to work out its position. In so doing, we can find the location of the vanishing point, which will give us the key to the perspective of the whole image.

ON THE PREVIOUS PAGES we looked at the importance of our eye level being on the horizon in a montage – and the horizon plays a vital role in perspective illustration. We used an image of a boy at the seaside to illustrate our point. But most of our compositions are not set at the seaside, so the horizon is not conveniently visible in the image. How, then, are we to gauge its position?

We can interpret just about any scene in terms of the perspective that underlies it, and deduce the position of the horizon from the horizontal lines within it. It's all done using the concept of the vanishing point – the imaginary dot on the horizon (it's *always* on the horizon, by definition) towards which perspective lines will tend.

In the image above left, we're given clues to the perspective of the scene within the picture: the angles of the headboard pieces behind the pillows and of the cornice that divides the wall from the ceiling all suggest the perspective that's in play here. Using these clues, we can place a picture on the wall (Botticelli's *La Primavera*, in this case) in such a way that it looks as if it belongs in the scene.

Photoshop now includes a Vanishing Point filter, which can help us to create perspective views within existing images. But it's essential to know how to construct vanishing lines by hand, and so divulge the position of the horizon: it helps us not just with positioning people correctly, but with the placement of three-dimensional objects in such a way as to make them look convincing.

In the example on the facing page, the vanishing point falls rather neatly within the image. Frequently, we won't have this luxury; it may be necessary to use the Canvas Size dialog in Photoshop to extend the image greatly to either left or right, so that we can see the position towards which our vanishing lines are tending, and so correctly establish the horizon within the scene.

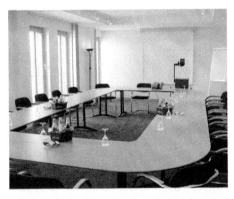

1 There's no horizon visible in this interior shot. But because it's a real photograph, we know it must have an internal consistency; there's a vanishing point in here, and we only have to find it.

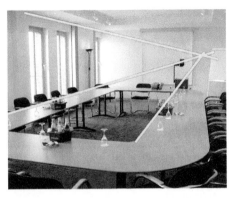

2 We can start by drawing straight lines that coincide with those lines in the image that are tending away from us: the edges of the table, the edge of the wall. Those lines will all meet at the vanishing point.

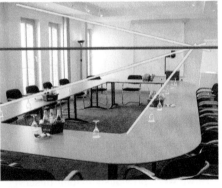

3 When we draw a horizontal line through this vanishing point, we set the horizon of our image. That's where the word comes from: horizontal lines are those which are parallel to the horizon.

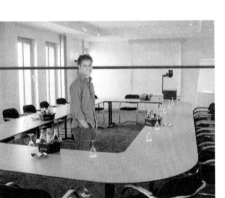

4 With the horizon now established, we can place a figure within the scene. By aligning his eyes with the horizon line, we place him at the same height as the viewer (see previous pages for details).

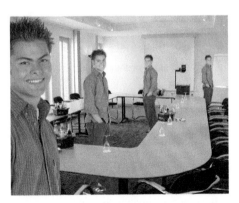

5 To illustrate the point further, we can move our figure forwards and backwards in the scene, scaling him up and down to move him closer and further away. As long as his eyes are on the horizon line, he'll be consistent with the background image.

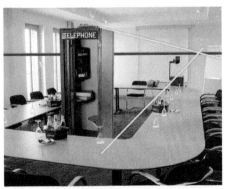

6 If we want to place a three-dimensional object into this scene, we need to first work out the perspective of the object itself – by drawing vanishing lines from it. Lining up this object's vanishing point with our existing horizon gives it its correct location.

MORE INFO

● In step 2 here we draw vanishing lines over the top of our image. We need to do this on a new layer, of course, so we can hide them later. The easiest way to draw straight lines is to use the Shapes tool, set to Fill Pixels (the third icon):

Choose a foreground color, and draw lines following the existing lines in the image. We can draw the horizon in a different color, for the sake of clarity.

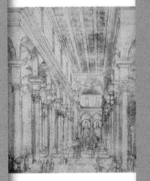

● The details of how perspective works were first expounded by the Persian mathematician Ibn al-Haytham in his *Book of Optics*, written in 1021. But the idea wasn't taken up in the West until the early 15th century, when the architect Brunelleschi found he was having trouble creating sketches that would accurately show his clients views of the proposed buildings. He went deeply into the subject, and the result of his labors was to expound a complete theory of the implementation of perspective – an example of his architectural illustration is shown above. It was Brunelleschi, as much as anyone, who gave rise to the explosion of art that was the Renaissance.

Foreground elements

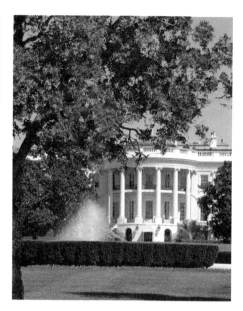

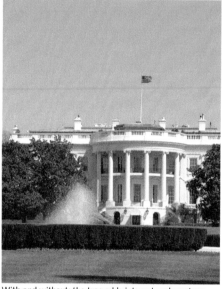

With and without: the tree adds interest and mystery

When Henri Matisse painted his series of views through open windows, it wasn't just that he couldn't be bothered to walk a couple of paces forward to get a clean view. The window is as much a key part of the painting as the scene beyond.

In a way, it's counter-intuitive; why should we deliberately choose to obscure a portion of the image? Surely it would be better for everyone if we were given a clear shot of the scenery?

In the case of Matisse's paintings, the window frames put the view into context. What might have been merely an attractive arrangement of boats, sea and sand takes on a human element: this is now the view from someone's bedroom, the scene that greets them every day when they awake. The life of the person who inhabits this room, even though it's only barely suggested, is of as much interest as the boats outside.

ABOVE: A CLEAN, CRISP VIEW of the White House. It's a beautiful sunny day, the flag's flying, the fountain is in full flow. So why is the end result so dull? It's not until we add a tree, obscuring part of the scene, that we achieve a balanced, intriguing image.

There are several reasons why the tree helps the image to work. For one thing, it adds a much-needed foreground element: without it, everything in the scene is in the mid-range, which creates a flattening effect. The tree, however, is close enough to be almost tangible, so bringing us as viewers into the action. Where we were previously distant observers, we're now more active participants. The tree is nearer to us than to the building, and belongs in our space.

There's another reason why the tree helps the composition, and that's because it brings a sense of mystery to the scene. It's almost as if we're chancing upon the building, rather than being presented with it in its entirety in one go: there's a feeling of discovery here that wasn't present before.

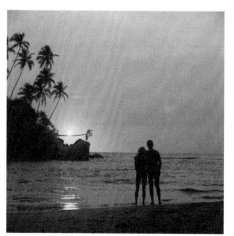

A sunset scene – but with a human scale

Photographers will frequently try to include a human element in their images, which makes them more immediate. The sunset on the left, for instance, would be a pretty enough sight on its own; but with the silhouetted couple there to enjoy the view, it becomes a romantic location.

As Photoshop artists, we can add figures to our images long after the photographs have been taken. And we can take

MORE INFO

The Coliseum, in Rome: massive, imposing and of great historical importance

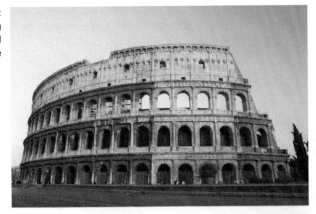

● The tree placed in front of the White House wasn't photographed in the White House grounds. It wasn't even photographed in Washington, but three and a half thousand miles away in Derbyshire, England. Does it matter? There are those who will query the accuracy of placing a tree right in the middle of the White House lawn; but if the end result is well enough achieved, who's going to suspect it wasn't real?

Adding people brings back the human element that was lacking: but is too much of the building obscured?

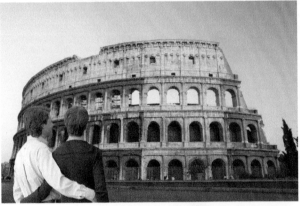

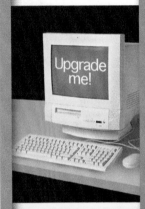

Reducing the size of the people helps to accentuate the scale of the building

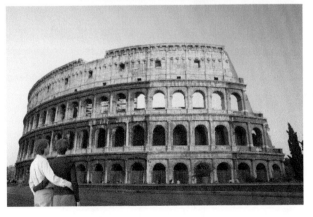

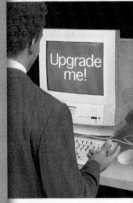

● The figure in the second image, above, adds nothing to the 'story' in this scene. But he balances the image: by looking over his shoulder, we're taking his part in viewing the message on the monitor. In this montage, the figure represents us looking at the image.

advantage of this fact to enhance and improve upon the originals: the human element in a photograph adds life – literally. The image of the Coliseum in Rome, top, is an impressive enough view of the building; but it's sterile, and lacks interest. Adding a rear view of a couple of tourists (center) draws our attention into the scene, as well as providing a 'Rule of Thirds' focus (see earlier in this chapter). But we don't need our interlopers to be anything like as intrusive as this: reducing them greatly in scale (bottom) still adds their worth, but accentuates the massive scale of the Coliseum as well.

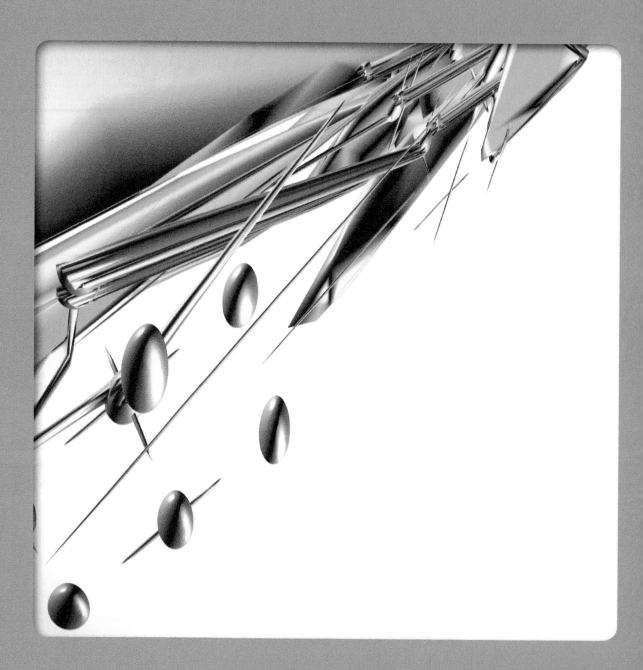

Contemporary design

It's easy to assess design from the past. We can glance at a book cover and tell if it was designed in the 1930s, the 1960s, or the 1990s. We can recognize a poster from the Jazz Age, and spot an 18th century portrait. But when it comes to the design of today, it's much harder to pin down.

It's partly that what has survived from the past, in recognizable form, is the very best – or the most typical of the period. There was probably as much variety in art and design a hundred years ago as there is today; but much of it was so ephemeral that it hasn't lasted the course. Only with the benefit of hindsight can we tell what's going to remain with us.

This chapter draws on design styles that are currently seen in advertising, in magazines, in newspapers and on the street. Not all will still be around in fifty years' time; the fickle nature of history will weed out the examples that don't quite make the grade.

contemporary

1. characteristic of the present; 'contemporary trends in design'; 'the role of computers in modern-day medicine'

2. belonging to the present time; 'contemporary leaders'

3. occurring in the same period of time; 'a rise in interest rates is often contemporaneous with an increase in inflation'; 'the composer Salieri was contemporary with Mozart' [syn: contemporaneous]

Wordnet Dictionary

Digital grids

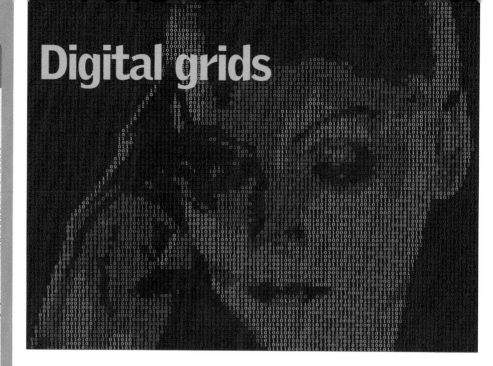

Long before computers were capable of displaying colors – or even shades of gray – programmers were printing images made of strings of letters and numbers.

Known as ASCII Art, the technique was laborious to program: but the results were often spectacular.

Here's a modern take on that technique, which is possible using a careful correspondence of values in grids and filters. Rather than relying on the weight of the letterforms to create the image, we'll use different brightnesses of an array of binary ones and zeros to create our effect.

Although the process takes a while to set up, once created it's easy to replace the original image with a different one for instant results.

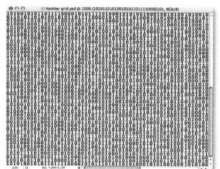

3 Turn that text box into pixels using Layer > Rasterize > Type, then duplicate the block of text so it fills the entire canvas area. Merge all the raster type layers together to create a single layer.

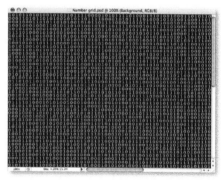

4 Inverse the type layer to make white on black text, then open the Hue/Saturation dialog. Check the Colorize button, and lower the Brightness value; drag the Hue slider to get the color you want.

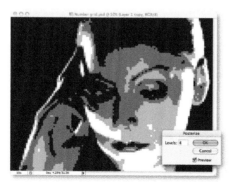

7 For a more graphic effect, use Image > Adjustments > Posterize. This process reduces the number of gray shades in the image: a value of 4 produces good results.

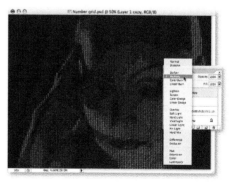

8 Now to make the numbers show through. From the pop-up menu in the Layers palette, change the mode of the layer from Normal to Multiply: now we can see through the image to the numbers below.

Art & Design in Photoshop

MORE INFO

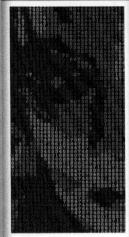

● In this tutorial we've used ones and zeros to create the text texture – but we can use any numbers we like, as in the above example. They work because numbers are set to be the same width in just about every font, to enable columns of figures to line up. If you want to use text letters instead of numbers, you'll find that most fonts won't fit neatly to the grid, because the characters are all different widths. To make the technique work with letters, be sure to choose a monospaced font such as Courier. That way, each character will fit neatly within the grid space. You can find a wide sleection of monospaced fonts available for free on many websites.

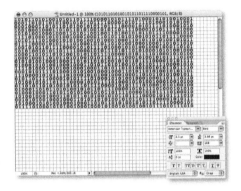

1 Begin by opening the Preferences dialog: go to the Guides, Grid & Slices section. Set up gridlines with the spacing you need for the size of the job. Here, we're using a 12 pixel grid.

2 Make sure the grid is visible (use View > Show > Grid) and create a new text box; type in a random string of ones and zeros. Adjust the size and leading until the numbers fit exactly within the grid spaces.

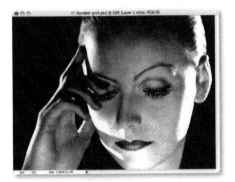

5 Now for the photograph. It helps to choose an image with strong light and shade; increase the contrast if you need to. Erase any fiddly elements in the background so that the foreground image stands out.

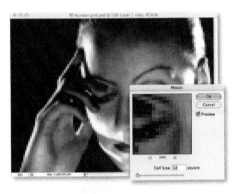

6 To treat the image to match the grid, choose Filter > Pixelate > Mosaic. This turns the image into an array of large, square pixels. A cell size of 12 will make the squares match the grid exactly.

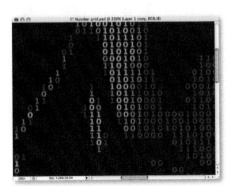

9 Zooming in on the image shows us how the Mosaic effect and the grid coincide perfectly. Each number is an entire unit – there are no cutoff portions of numbers in the whole image.

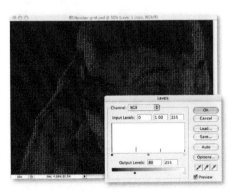

10 If you want some of the numbers to be visible in the background, open the Levels adjustment (⌘ L ctrl L) and drag the bottom left slider to the right to brighten the darker areas.

Stencil graffiti

Love it or loathe it, graffiti is as much a part of the urban landscape as streetlamps, phone boxes and discarded burger wrappers.

Where the 'tagging' that adorns so many public buildings – the scrawling of a stylized name with a felt tip pen – may be seen by many as mere vandalism, there's another side to graffiti that's far more creative. I'm not talking about the glorious, multicolored extravaganzas that are an art form in their own right, but the stencilled images that are easily repeated on just about every available surface.

Although most stencil graffiti is carefully hand drawn – such as the demonic George W. Bush, complete with horns, above – we're going to look at how you can create your own version of this street art using just about any photograph as your starting point.

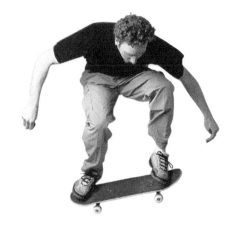

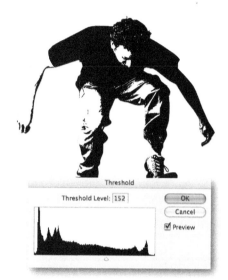

1 We could use just about any image as the basis for our stencil – a politician, a pair of lovers, any household object. I thought this figure of a boy on a skateboard suited the subject matter well; it's taken from the photos.com collection.

2 To turn the photograph into a graphic element, we first need to turn it into pure black and white. We can do this using the Threshold adjustment. Rather than applying it directly, though, we'll add it as an Adjustment Layer.

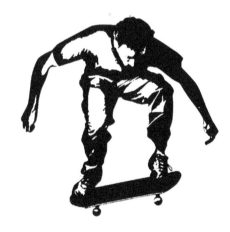

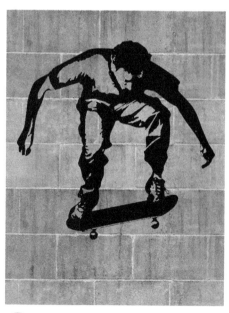

5 The Threshold adjustment made pure black and white, but followed the variations in the image too precisely. To make it look like a stencil, we need to get rid of the jagged edges: the Median filter (Filters > Noise) is the best way to smoothe out those contours.

6 Move to the Threshold Adjustment Layer, and press ⌘ E ctrl E to merge it down into the skateboarder, then make the wall layer visible (it's in the psd file on the CD). Change the layer mode of the skateboarder to Multiply so we only see the black – in this mode, all the white will disappear.

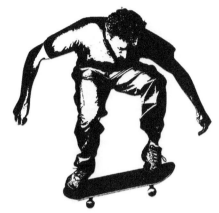

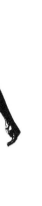

MORE INFO

● The big advantage of applying Threshold as an Adjustment Layer, rather than as a standard adjustment, is that we can see through it to the layer or layers beneath as we work on them. Using the Dodge and Burn tools in steps 4 and 5 would have the wrong effect if we'd simply applied the adjustment directly; similarly, the Median filter would have produced quite a different result on a regular Thresholded layer.

● When using the Dodge and Burn tools, you don't need to reach for the toolbar to switch between them. Holding the ⌥ `alt` key while either one of them is the active tool will give you temporary access to the other one – a real time saver.

● In step 7, we use the Polygonal Lasso tool to trace the outline. We can also use the regular Lasso, holding ⌥ `alt` as we click the corners; release the key to close the selection.

● Although we stopped at step 8 here, you could go on to add as many extra touches as you like to increase the realism. Maybe the paint should drip down the wall a little way: use the Smudge tool with a hard-edged brush, set to around 90% pressure.

③ Because this is an Adjustment Layer, it means we're looking through it to the layer beneath. Using the Burn tool, we can now darken up the arm and the trousers where the image was too faint. As before, we still get pure black and white.

④ The Dodge tool – the flip side of the Burn tool – lets us brighten the image. We can use it to good effect here, to bring out some highlights in that otherwise solid mass of black shirt. But the image is too ragged to make a convincing stencil just yet.

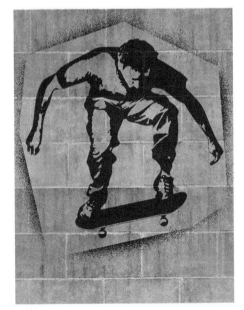

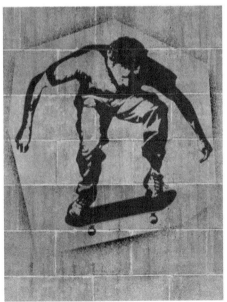

⑦ To make the spattering around the edges, draw a rough bounding shape with the Polygonal Lasso tool. Inverse the selection using ⌘ `Shift` `I` `ctrl` `Shift` `I`, and use a soft-edged brush set to Dissolve to paint some spill over the edge: this creates a spattering effect which adds a lot of realism.

⑧ To color the graffiti, open the Hue/Saturation dialog and check Colorize. Move the Lightness slider to the right to make the black brighter, and experiment with the Hue and Saturation sliders to change the color. Finally, apply some Gaussian Blur to soften all the edges, including the spattering.

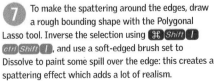

Line art: simplified

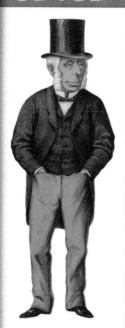

Artists have been drawing stylized images of people for as long as there have been artists. This Victorian caricature depicts a man with a head far too large for his body: but we're familiar with the genre, so we let it pass without further comment.

Where the traditional artist has to draw figures from scratch, we're able to use Photoshop to make the process rather simpler. Here, we'll start with a photograph and trace over it to define the basic outlines and features, then use a filter to generate the fine detail. The result should be an image that's immediately recognizable to anyone who's acquainted with the subject.

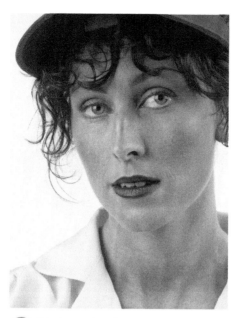

1 This close-up view of a woman seems to present some problems at first sight. The hat is an unnatural element, which doesn't blend well into the head; and that wispy hair, surely, must be almost impossible to draw.

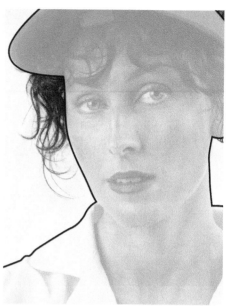

2 Begin by tracing the outline. Make a new Shapes layer, set to Shape layers mode (see More Info), and use the Pen tool to draw around the perimeter. Set a black stroke with a white fill, and lower the opacity of the layer so we can see through it.

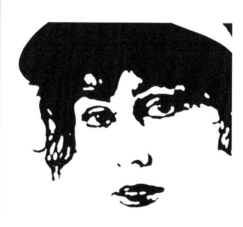

5 Make a copy of the original photograph, and drag it to the top of the layer stack. Use `ctrl` `Shift` `U` `⌘` `Shift` `U` to desaturate it (knocking all the color out), and use Filters > Artistic > Poster Edges to turn it into this stark, monochromatic view. You'll need to experiment with the sliders to get the right effect.

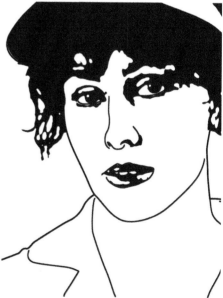

6 When we now set the mode of this layer to Multiply – having hidden the original photograph – we can see through it to the layers beneath. The black and white Poster Edges layer fits well with the drawn outlines; the first stage of the process is now complete, ready for us to add color.

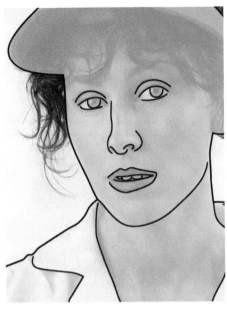

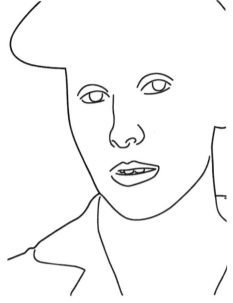

3 Make a new, empty layer. Make sure the Pen tool is now set to Paths (rather than Shapes, as before) and draw individual paths tracing the main features – around the nose and eyes, the lips, beneath the chin, and so on.

4 Choose the Brush tool, and set a small, hard-edged brush – around 3 pixels in diameter. Set the foreground color to black, and, with the Pen paths still selected, press *Enter*; the paths will be stroked with the brush size and color on the new layer.

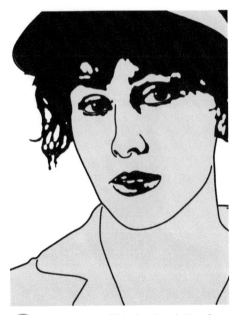

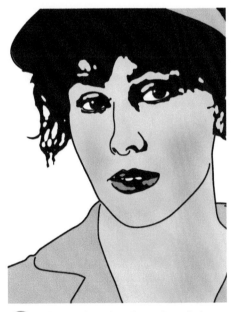

7 For the base color fill, load up the selection of the Shapes layer by *ctrl* *⌘* clicking on its thumbnail in the Layers palette, and set its mode to Multiply. Make a new layer beneath it, and fill with a flesh color: we'll be able to see through the Shapes layer to this color beneath.

8 Make a new layer above the previous color layer, using it as a clipping mask (press *ctrl* *alt* *G* *⌘* *⌥* *G*). Paint the shirt and hat with a hard edged brush, then switch to a smaller brush to add red to the lips and white in the eyes. Add shading with the Burn tool, set to midtones, on the lower color layer.

MORE INFO

● Shapes layers, used in step 2, have three modes: they can draw Shapes layers, Pen paths, or pixels on the current layer:

It's important to choose the right variant. Here, we want to choose Shapes layers: these are vector layers with editable paths, which can have both a stroke and a fill. The Fill is set by a swatch attached to the layer's thumbnail in the Layers palette; the Stroke is set using the Stroke section of the Layer Styles dialog. It's important to remember when the Pen tool has been set to Shapes mode, since you'll need to change it back to Paths mode after you've used it.

● When drawing the paths in step 3, we need to draw several individual paths that are not linked. Hold *ctrl* *⌘* and click anywhere while using the Pen tool to stop one path, in order to then draw a new one.

● In step 7 we could have changed the color of the Shapes layer swatch. But that would have made coloring difficult in step 8; this solution presents us with far fewer problems later.

SHORTCUTS

 MAC   WIN   BOTH

Line art: crosshatching

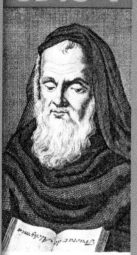

One of the earliest methods of printing pictures was using engravings. The image would be scratched into a metal surface, which was then inked, rubbed clean and pressed onto paper; the ink which remained in the scratched lines would appear in reverse on the paper's surface.

To create the sense of light and shade, a crosshatching effect was used – regular arrays of fine lines, duplicated in opposing directions for a darker result.

The technique is still used on banknotes and other hard-to-reproduce documents, and has acquired a fine art cachet for its clean lines and clarity. We'll mark our contemporary take on the style with this portrait of General James Garfield, 20th president of the United States.

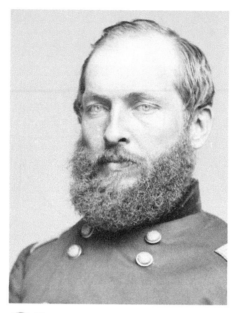

1 This crisp portrait of James Garfield will provide a good basis for our crosshatch illustration. If you're using a photograph of your own, first turn it to grayscale then, if necessary, boost the contrast to make it crisper.

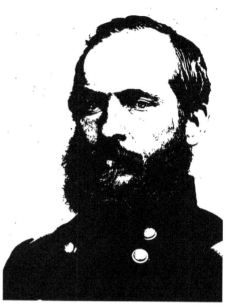

2 Take a copy of the photograph, and this time run Image > Adjustments > Threshold. Drag the slider until you get a very dark version of the portrait. There should be some clear area of skin remaining, but not very much. Choose Edit > Select All, then Copy.

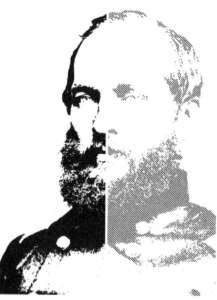

5 Take another copy of the original photograph, and run the Threshold adjustment again – but this time, drag the slider to get a much brighter image (left). Flip the diagonal line layer so it faces the other way, then repeat the Select All/Copy/QuickMask/Paste procedure to make a second set of lines.

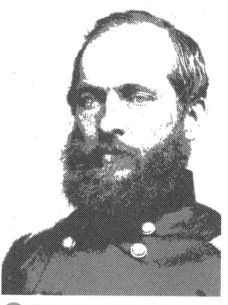

6 When we set the mode of the new diagonals to Multiply, we can see through this layer to the original diagonal line layer beneath. The opposing direction of the crosshatch produces a darker, more highly shaded area where we want it. All we need to do now is to bring back some extra detail.

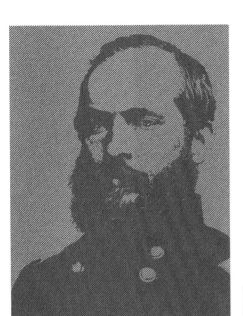

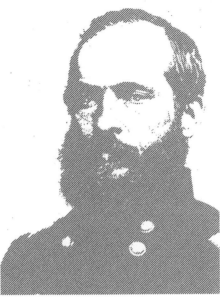

3 It's easy enough to draw a layer made of diagonal lines but it does take time, so I've provided one for you. Turn this layer on and press **Q** to enter QuickMask mode, then choose Paste (*ctrl* *V* ⌘ *V*) to paste the copied Threshold image in here.

4 Press **Q** to leave QuickMask, and the threshold image will have been turned into a selection (but see More Info). Use *ctrl* *J* ⌘ *J* to turn the selection into a new layer made of diagonal lines, and hide the original diagonal lines layer.

MORE INFO

● In step 4 we paste the threshold version of the image into QuickMask. The default setting is for unselected (masked) areas to be highlighted in red; but we want the opposite. In fact, when working in Photoshop we almost always want QuickMask to behave in the opposite way. To change the way it works, double click the QuickMask icon at the bottom of the toolbar to see this dialog:

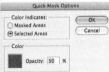

Check the Selected Areas button. Now when you paint in black in QuickMask, the area you paint will be the selected area. If you don't want to change the default, then simply inverse the selection before making a new layer. See more about QuickMask on page 227.

● If you're attempting this with one of your own photographs, be sure to erase the background first. Any complications behind the figure will produce ugly and confusing results.

● In step 5, we can flip the diagonal lines layer using Edit > Transform > Flip Horizontal.

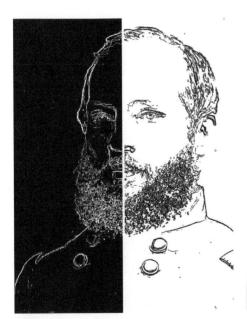

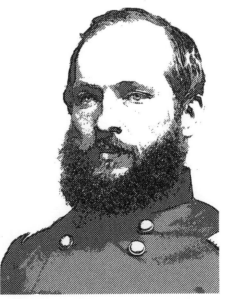

7 Run Filter > Blur > Smart Blur on another copy of the original photo. From the pop-up Mode menu at the bottom of the dialog choose Edge Only to produce this white on black effect (left). Invert the image using *ctrl* *Shift* *I* ⌘ *Shift* *I* for a black on white version (right). This gives us our fine detail.

8 Change the mode of the new detail layer to Multiply as well, and place it above the two crosshatch layers. All three combine to make a convincing crosshatching effect. There may well be some stray black pixels around the place: paint these out in white on a new layer.

SHORTCUTS

 MAC WIN BOTH

Cut paper montages

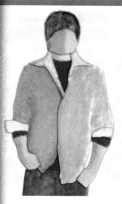

Artists have been creating collages from cut or torn paper almost since the invention of paper itself. Henri Matisse was a devotee of the form, producing many collages from torn paper.

The image above uses pieces of paper that have then been inked over. We're going to take a more conventional approach, producing striking artwork from a photograph by creating our own cutouts directly in Photoshop.

This technique is easy to achieve and is capable of producing intriguing artwork. It helps greatly if you have an original photograph to work from, as we do here. Don't feel you have to stick too closely to that original, though: while changing a person's features too much may make them unrecognizable, changing the color of their clothing can add a useful enhancement.

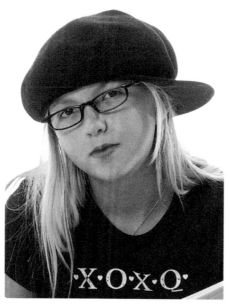

1 In our original photograph, the girl is wearing a black hat and a black T-shirt with a rather confusing logo. We'll replace this with a more conventional shirt, which won't detract so much from the focus of the piece.

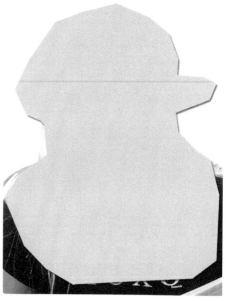

2 Begin by making a new layer. Use the Lasso tool to trace around the outline of the figure with straight lines (see More Info panel for help). Then fill the selection with a fleshtone color, and use Layer Styles to add a simple drop shadow effect.

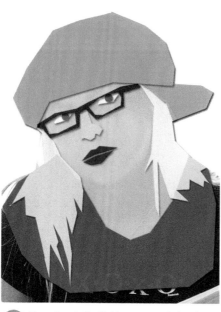

5 Now return to the first layer we created, make a new selection for, say, the hair, and make a new layer from it and recolor as before. As long as we keep making new layers from the original, they'll all be created with the same opacity and with the drop shadow, so we don't have to add it afresh each time.

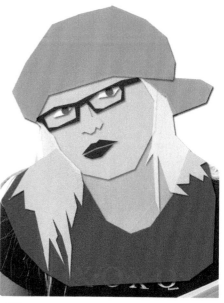

6 Finally, make a new layer for the face, going beneath the chin. Although 'logically' we should have created this layer straight after the initial layer, the combined opacity of the two means that we wouldn't be able to see the original photograph through it; this way we can see the features as long as we need to.

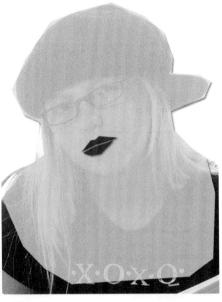

3 With the first piece of 'paper' in place, we can't see the photo beneath – so reduce the opacity of this layer to 80% so we can see through it. This procedure also gives the 'paper' a slightly translucent quality, which adds to the overall effect.

4 Make a selection within the layer we've just created – in this case, the lips. Use *ctrl J* ⌘ *J* to make a new layer from the selection, and it will appear at the same opacity, with the drop shadow intact. Fill with a suitable lip color.

MORE INFO

● In step 2, we need to trace the outline roughly, as a series of straight lines. We could switch to the Polygonal Lasso tool, but we might forget we've done so next time we want to use the Lasso tool. A better method is to hold the *alt* ⎇ key while tracing, which will give us the Polygonal Lasso temporarily – forcing the Lasso to draw straight lines between each point we click. When you release the key, the start and end points will join up to complete the selection.

● By making each new layer directly from the base layer, we copy that layer's attributes – the shadow and the opacity. Remember to return to the base layer to turn each new selection into a layer of its own.

● We've here added the texture as a final step, above the artwork. We could have added texture to our original layer, of course, and then each new layer made from it would have that texture as well; but if we found the overall effect too strong, or too weak, we'd be unable to do anything about it at that stage. By creating the texture as a separate layer above all the others, we can lower the opacity or increase the contrast to get exactly the effect we want.

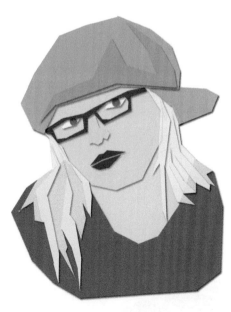

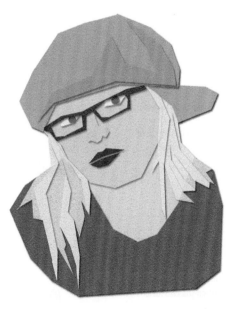

7 We could stop there – but we can add interest to the flat areas of the image by creating a simulation of shading and texture. Make new selections within both the hair and the hat regions, and use *ctrl J* ⌘ *J* once more to turn them into new layers; darken as appropriate to create the best effect.

8 As a last step, we can add the texture. Hold *ctrl* ⌘ and click on the thumbnail of the first layer we created, then make a new layer: fill the selection with 50% gray, and change the layer's mode to Hard Light. The gray will disappear. We can now add texture using the Texturizer filter –the Sandstone texture works well.

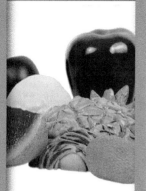

Outline and fill

1 We're starting with a photograph of an arrangement of fruit. Reduce the opacity of the fruit layer to around 30%, so it doesn't swamp us; then start drawing the fruit outlines with the Pen tool. We don't need to follow every nook and cranny in each piece of fruit.

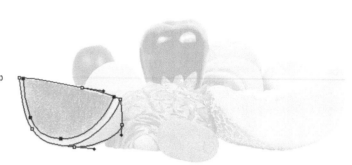

Drawings have used the outline and fill technique for hundreds, if not thousands, of years: the artist first draws the outlines, then fills in the drawing with solid colors.

The aim in the past was always to be as realistic as possible, with the fills carefully shaded and fitting neatly to the outline.

Recently, however, a variation on the theme has appeared. In this new take on the old style, the fills clearly miss the outlines: they follow the same rough shape, but fail to conform exactly to the original design.

It's a style that gives a fresh, relaxed feeling to the artwork. Where a neat fit using flat colors might have produced a sterile, almost technical style of illustration, this looser approach enables us to create drawings that look more contemporary, more stylized, and less buttoned-up.

3 Although we're using a starting photograph, we don't need to stick precisely to it: some embellishment is often required. Here, for instance, I've added a stalk on the plum, a stalk and a couple of leaves on the apple, and the signs of a stalk on the Kiwi.

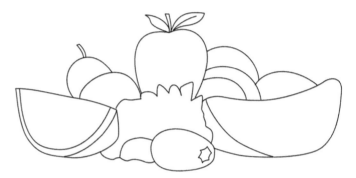

5 Choose strong, flat colors that best represent the fruit you're painting. You don't have to be faithful to the original, and in fact sampling colors from the original photograph would produce dull, lifeless work.

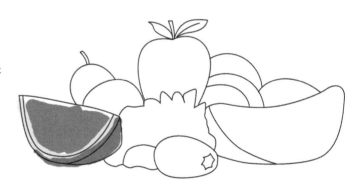

7 You have to make a judgment as to what detail is necessary. We definitely need the pips on the two melons to make them read correctly as melons, and a fair amount of detail is needed to make that pineapple clear. Add highlights to the rear fruit as well.

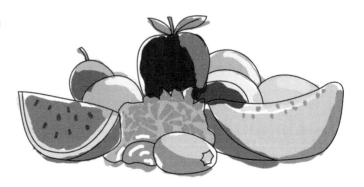

2 When you've finished, hide the original photograph. Then make a new layer, set the foreground color to black and choose a small (around 3 pixel) hard brush. With the Pen paths all active (but none selected), press *Enter* to stroke the paths with the brush on the new layer.

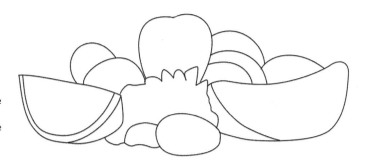

4 Make another layer, and move it behind the outlines layer. Use a hard-edged brush to start painting in some of the fills. There's no need for accuracy of any kind at this stage!

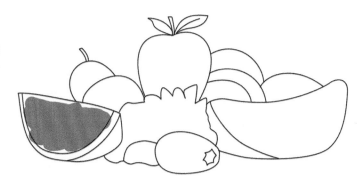

6 Paint in all the fruit roughly, making sure that every element has a fill associated with it. This is the basic fill; next, we'll add the details that will make those blobs look more like fruit.

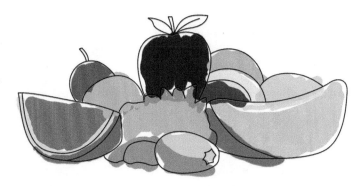

8 Finally, reduce the opacity of the fill layer – here, I've taken it down to 70% of its original strength. This gives the outlines more of a pastel feel. I've also nudged the whole fill layer down by 10 pixels, which makes a looser fit and looks better.

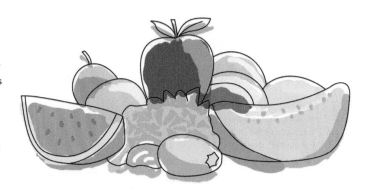

MORE INFO

● When drawing with the Pen tool, the tendency is for the tool to keep drawing a single path until it's closed off by clicking on the starting point. But we need to draw multiple open paths. To do this, after a path has been drawn, hold *ctrl* ⌘ and click anywhere away from the path. This will end the current path, so you can start drawing a new one.

● The pastel color feel we achieve in the fiinal step is typical of this sort of work: the aim is for it to look rather like a washed-out watercolor. But finding suitable pastel colors to paint with would be tricky and very time consuming. It's far better to fill with strong colors sampled from the Swatches palette; when we then reduce the opacity of the fill layer, we're adding the same amount of the pastel quality to all the colors together, so maintaining the consistency off the image.

● This style would look good with a slightly textured background, to simulate the sort of paper watercolor artists use. To reproduce this technique, use the Texturizer filter (Filter > Texture), but don't overdo it – too much texture can simply overwhelm the image.

SHORTCUTS

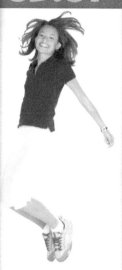

Although many manufacturers would have publicized their new MP3 players through a hard examination of their features, Apple took the lifestyle approach instead. The decision to make the iPods and the headphones in white was a break from the gray and black of everything else; and so they used the fact in their print and TV advertising, with a white iPod standing out against a black silhouetted figure.

The key to making this technique work lies in the initial choice of figure. The jumping girl, above, seems to have all the energy we need for this technique: but while it's clear from the photograph that one arm is behind her, by the time it's a silhouette she'll just have an arm missing. Choose your image with care!

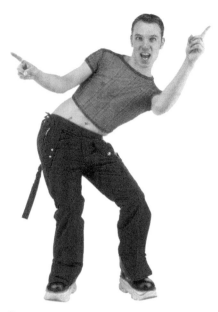

1 This figure has everything we need: a dynamic pose, a good sharp outline, and a sense of fun. Sure, his dress sense might leave much to be desired – but since we're going to turn him into a silhouette, this is not an issue.

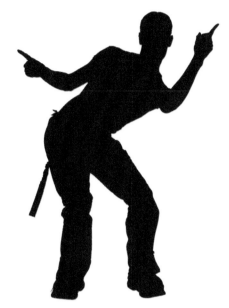

2 To fill this layer with black, first make black the foreground color (the **D** key will do this). Then press **alt** **Shift** **Backspace** **⌥** **Shift** **Backspace** to fill the layer with the foreground color, while preserving transparency (see More Info panel).

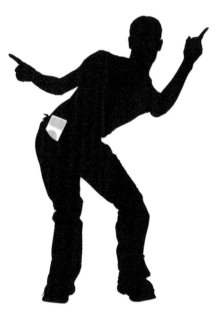

5 The iPod we've just drawn can now be reduced, if necessary, and distorted with Free Transform to make it fit into the pocket. To create the pocket effect itself, simply erase the bottom portion of the iPod (or use a layer mask): the eye will interpolate the pocket for us from the missing portion.

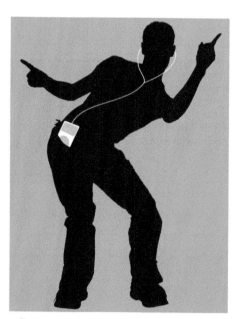

6 To make the cable, draw it with the Pen tool. Make a new layer and, with the path still visible, switch to the Brush tool. Choose a very small, hard-edged brush, and make white the foreground color; press **ctrl** **Enter** **⌘** **Enter** to stroke the path with this color. You'll need a colored background to see it, of course.

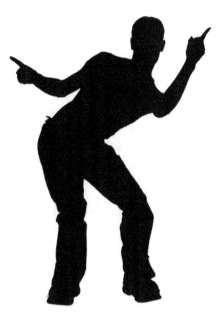

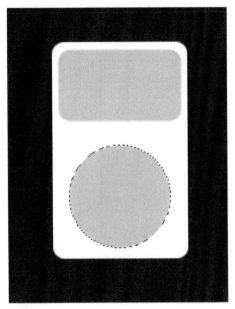

3 Simply converting the image to a silhouette isn't enough: we need to make sure that everything in this silhouette makes good sense. Here, the strap hanging from the back of his waist is a confusing item, so use the Eraser tool to remove it.

4 To draw the iPod, zoom in to an area of black and make a new layer. Use the Round Cornered Rectangle tool in the Shapes tool (**U**) to draw the basic iPod shape (see More Info panel), then select a screen and clickwheel area and fill with gray.

MORE INFO

● In step 2 we fill the layer with a different color without using any menus. Pressing *alt* *Backspace* ⌥ *Backspace* will fill any layer with the foreground color, but unless there's an active selection or the layer's transparency has been locked, the whole image area will be filled with this color. By adding the *Shift* key we prevent the color from 'leaking out' beyond the bounds of the existing image, so temporarily preserving the transparency of the layer.

● In step 4 we use the Shapes tool to create a round-cornered rectangle. The Shapes tool has three modes of operation, and it's important to choose the right one:

The first button creates a new Shapes layer, which is filled and colored using Layer Styles. The second makes a Pen path conforming to the shape. The third simply creates a pixel-fill based on the current shape, and this is the variation we want here. Set the radius of the rounded corners using the numerical Radius field that appears when this tool is chosen.

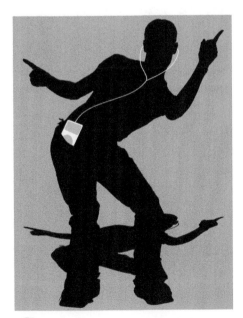

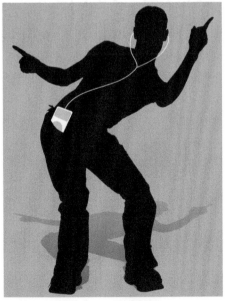

7 Making the shadow involves a couple of steps. First, duplicate the silhouette layer, and use Free Transform to compress it. You may need to paint in some extra shadow around the feet, or even erase some unwanted portions, to make the compressed version fit the body well.

8 Lower the opacity of this shadow layer using the number keys – around **5** for 50% opacity works well. Make a layer mask for this layer, and use the Gradient tool, set on black to white, to draw a vertical gradient on this mask. It will hide the shadow progressively as it recedes into the background.

Pixel art

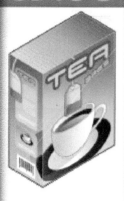

Technical artists have been drawing in isometric perspective for decades. With angles constrained to just 30° increments, and no real perspective, components of, say, an electric drill can be combined in one illustration and rearranged as necessary.

The idea was copied by the computer game Sim City, so that parks, streets and whole housing complexes could be rendered in fake perspective. The appearance caught the popular imagination, and pixel art was born. Soon, designers were taking the form to new levels.

Pixel art uses receding angles of 60° in both directions – that is, along the X and Z axes – with the vertical Y axis remaining truly vertical.

Pixel art is a fiddly, time consuming process, so we're only looking at a tiny portion here. I've included the final image for you to use as a template if you wish.

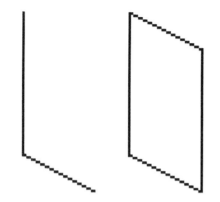

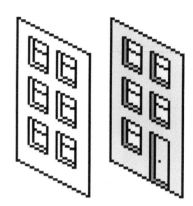

1 To draw pixel art we need to zoom right in – 500% or more is a common view. We'll begin by drawing the base of this building, going two pixels along and one up: this is the standard formula for drawing at 60°. Duplicate this for the building top.

2 We can draw a single window in the same way. Rather than drawing pixel by pixel, it's often easier to select a group of two pixels and 'steer' them with the cursor keys – see the More Info panel for details. Duplicate the windows, then fill with color.

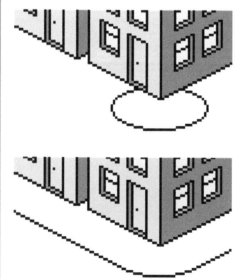

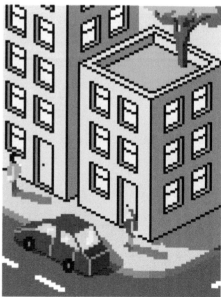

5 Drawing curves is always tricky in this isometric perspective. To make the corner of our road, start with an ellipse (with anti-aliasing turned off – see More Info panel) and add a stroke using the Stroke menu. Then erase all but the bottom corner, and continue the kerb with straight lines drawn at the usual 60° angle.

6 We can duplicate this road edge to make a thick kerb: Select All, then hold *alt* ⌥ as you nudge it downwards to make the vertical edge. Recolor it (remembering to make it darker around the turn), then fill above and below it. The dark color of the road surface helps to ground the image, giving it more depth.

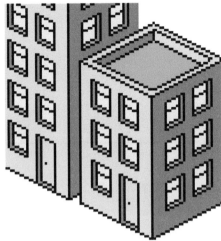

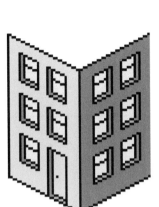

MORE INFO

● When drawing pixel art, we need to adjust our drawing and selection tools. First, the Brush tool needs to be changed to the Pencil tool – this is chosen from the pop-up list in the Brush tool icon. All the selection tools, including the Marquees and the Lasso, must have anti-aliasing turned off: otherwise, when you make a selection you'll get fuzzy edges. The same goes for the Paint Bucket tool, which you'll use to fill bounded areas with color.

● Drawing at a 60° angle can be tricky. One solution is to show a background grid, set to 1-pixel increments; when we hold *Shift* and click, the Pencil tool will draw a straight line between click points.

● Another solution to drawing at 60° is to use the Cursor keys instead. Draw a small block two pixels wide, and select it; then hold *alt* ⌥ as you use the cursor keys to nudge it one pixel up. Release the key, then nudge two pixels to the side, and you'll have made a copy in the right position. Continue this process, holding and releasing the *alt* ⌥ keys to make a copy each time, and you'll find it a relatively quick way to step your 60° path.

3 We can make the turn wall for this building by flipping a copy of the original (and replacing that door with another window). Remember to darken up this side: having a single strong lighting direction is what helps pixel art look convincing.

4 We've drawn a thick wall around the top of this building, with a patch of grass in the center. Duplicate it for the building next door, and move the layer behind; here, I've selected the top half and copied it up to make this building taller.

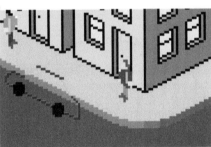

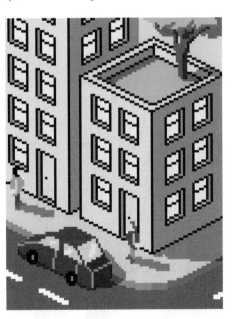

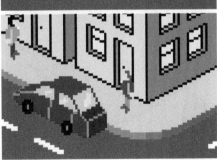

7 Drawing people at this size is always tricky; there are so few pixels to play with that it's hard to be accurate. To create a complex object like a car, begin with an outline drawn in perspective; then duplicate this outline, and fill in the spaces between – being willing to adjust the shape as you draw.

8 As always, it's the addition of shadows that makes all the difference. These are painted in black on a new layer, with that layer set to 50% opacity. The tree on the roof is drawn freehand, but with a nod towards the isometric perspective of the scene.

SHORTCUTS

 MAC   WIN   BOTH

Simpsons cartoon

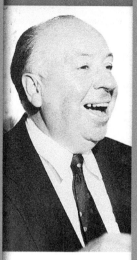

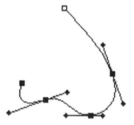

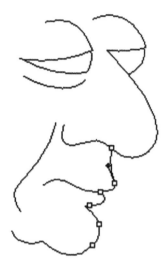

It's rather odd, when you think about it, that we should accept a world full of people with yellow skin and an overbite without thinking twice about it. But that's the power of television – in particular, the power of *The Simpsons*: the realism of the emotions is so strong that we're prepared to overlook the obvious strangeness of the appearance.

Caricatures of real people in *The Simpsons* never really look that much like the person they're supposed to represent. They use as few lines as they can get away with, which means a lot of detail gets left out; and, in common with so many cartoons, features are routinely exaggerated for comic effect, often at the expense of a more recognizable approach. We'll try the treatment on Alfred Hitchcock.

1 The nose is always a recognizable feature, so it's good to start with this. Use the Pen tool to draw the shape. When drawing with the Pen tool, you can hold `ctrl` `⌘` at any time to get the Direct Selection tool, if you need to modify the shape of the path. With this key held down, you can drag both handles and anchor points.

2 Hold `ctrl` `⌘` and click away from the path to stop drawing it; then, when you click again, you'll start a new path. Draw separate paths in this way for each of the features in turn. There's no need to make them all join up to form a closed perimeter. Try not to click right on an existing point, or you'll join the path.

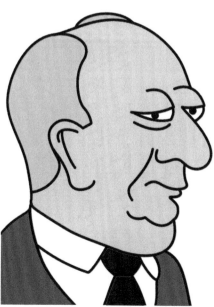

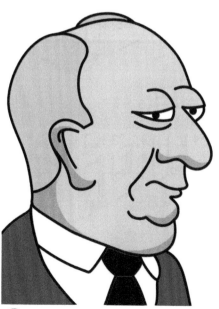

5 Continue the same process to fill the rest of the colors. Select them on the outlines layer, then expand the selection, then switch to the fill layer to place the color in. If you like, you could make separate layers for each of the fill colors.

6 You may not have noticed, but characters in *The Simpsons* frequently have shadows. Make a new layer, using the fill layer as a clipping mask; then paint in here with the darker color. Use the brush in combination with the Eraser tool to shape the shadows.

Contemporary design

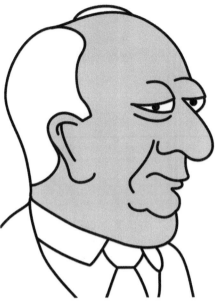

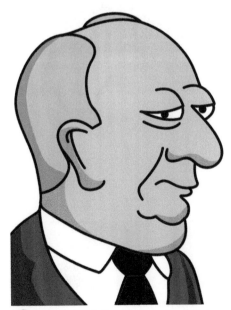

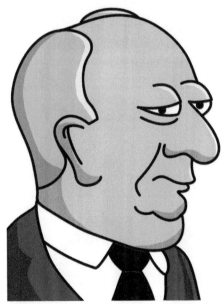

3 Draw the basic shape for the head, then add in the additional features as new paths. When you've finished, make a new layer and choose a hard-edged brush of around 5 pixels in size; with the path all visible (but none of it selected), press *Enter* to stroke the path with the brush, creating these solid outlines.

4 Click within the face area with the Magic Wand tool to select it, then make a new layer and move it behind the outlines. Use Select > Modify > Expand to expand the selection by two pixels, then choose a bright yellow as the foreground color, and press *alt Backspace* *⌥ Backspace* to fill with that color.

7 Add shadows to the other elements – the hair, the suit, and so on. We can use the shadows to produce the shape of the suit collar on the left, and to give a suggestion of an arm on the right. The shadow also helps give the hair shape.

8 As well as shadows, characters have highlights – especially when they're drawn for stills or publicity material. Set the Brush tool to 50%, and draw the highlights around the eyelids, the hair, and over the nose.

MORE INFO

● Drawing with the Pen tool is one of the hardest techniques to master in Photoshop. It's beyond the scope of this book to teach you how to use the tool: all I can do is urge you strongly to take the time to learn it, as it's one of the most useful tools of them all.

● In step 3, we use the Brush tool to 'stroke' the path, drawing along it with the current brush size and color. Make sure the foreground color is black, and that the tool is set to 100% opacity. I've also painted in the eyes in this step, using a larger brush size to paint single black dots in each eye.

● In step 5, we keep going back and forth between the outline layer (to select the regions for coloring in) and the fill layer (to add the color). We could, of course, fill with color directly onto the outline layer. But we lose editability this way; keeping the two separate makes it much easier for us to control the artwork. It also means that when we add the shadows in step 6 and the highlights in step 8, we can do so behind the outlines, without worrying about overpainting them by accident.

SHORTCUTS

 MAC   WIN   BOTH

61

Caricature

You might imagine that caricature drawings of politicians and celebrities is a fairly modern phenomenon, but you'd be far from the truth. The image above is a caricature of a Roman politician, complete with a laurel wreath around his bald pate. It's scrawled on a wall in Pompeii, and was drawn two thousand years ago.

When creating caricature drawings, we exaggerate the subject's features. The smallest anomaly, the slightest feature that's out of the ordinary in any way is blown out of all proportion, to create an image that represents the character we're satirizing.

Caricatures are often cruel, as they play on those features about which the subject tends to be most sensitive. These are, after all, their defining characteristics. But the format can also be playful, as we'll see in the example used here.

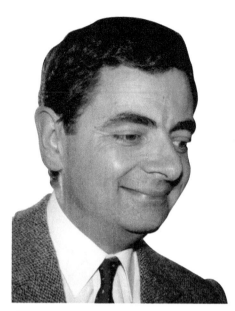

1 The comic actor Rowan Atkinson is the perfect candidate for caricature. He's known for his rubbery features, but there's nothing that really stands out on his face as being unusual. This photograph is by Gerhard Heeke, and comes from Wikipedia.

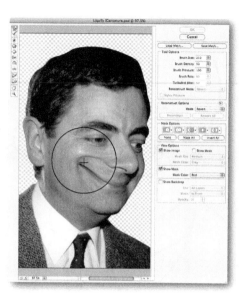

2 Open the Liquify filter (ctrl Shift X ⌘ Shift X). The default tool is the Forward Warp tool (W), and that's the one we'll use in the main. Choose a large brush size – around 250 pixels – and push the corner of the mouth up to exaggerate the smile.

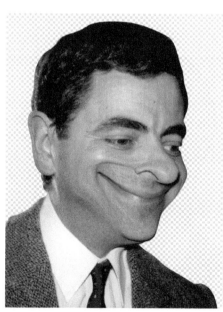

5 Rowan Atkinson has a small chin, so let's take that fact and work it into our caricature. By pushing up the jaw on either side of the chin we make the chin itself appear pointed and much smaller. Use a large brush size once again, to move larger quantities of pixels around the screen.

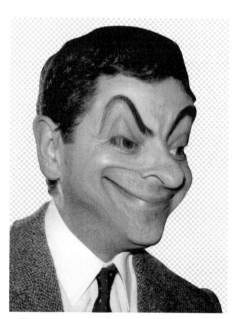

6 Those eyebrows are ripe for exploitation. With a large brush size, drag them up to make huge, larger-than-life curves. This also has the effect of making Atkinson look surprised, and brings a strong comic element to the image.

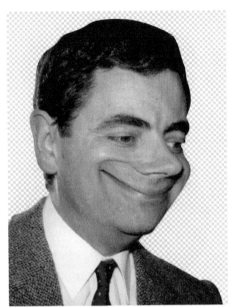

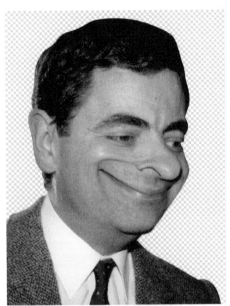

3 Still using the Forward Warp tool, push the other cheek up to match the first. You'll notice it takes the nose with it – we can fix that in the next step. We're still in Liquify, but I've cropped it to hide the interface so we can see the image more clearly.

4 Lower the brush size to around 100 pixels, and move the tip of the nose back. We can reshape the nose however we like with the Forward Warp tool; let's exaggerate the original by giving it a slightly bulbous tip, and a raised nostril.

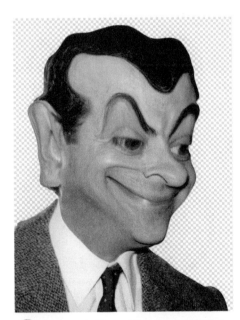

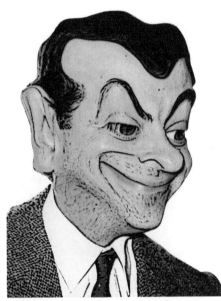

7 We can make the eyes bigger by using the Bloat tool (**B**). Click and hold within each eye: the longer you hold, the larger the eye will get. If you go too far, hold *alt* ⌥ as well to reduce the eye. Use the Forward Warp tool once more (**W**) to exaggerate the ear and the shape of the hair.

8 We could simply stop at the end of step 7, and we'd have a photographic caricature. But we can improve on the result by adding two filters. Here, the unlikely choice of Film Grain removes some of the fine detail from the face, while Poster Edges both posterizes it and adds contours that look hand drawn.

MORE INFO

● When using the Liquify filter, we need to use a surprisingly large brush size in order to create smooth warps: too small, and we'll simply end up with a wrinkly effect. The keyboard shortcut for changing the brush size is **]** and **[**, which makes the brush larger and smaller in 2-pixel increments. This can take a long time when we want big changes, so hold *Shift* as well when using these keys to increase and decrease the brush size by 20-pixel increments instead.

● In the final step, it takes two filters to achieve this effect. Rather than applying them one at a time, use the Filter Gallery to add both filters together: you can use the New Document icon at the bottom right of the dialog to add a new filter. Only by tweaking the settings of both filters can you produce exactly the right results.

● It's very easy to get carried away when using the Liquify filter, ending up with an image that looks nothing like the person you're attempting to satirize. It's better to stop earlier than you think, rather than after it's too late: you can always add more distortion later, but it's hard to take out once it's there.

SHORTCUTS

MAC WIN BOTH

Steampunk

Steampunk is a design approach that takes contemporary or futuristic technology and dresses it in the style of early 20th century scientific equipment. The glorious steampunk device above is a computer in which the flat screen has been built into an ornate mirror stand, with typewriter keys on the keyboard and many other decorative touches.

Inspired by the science fiction work of H. G. Wells and Jules Verne, steampunk first appeared in 1960, with the movie *The Time Machine*. The machine of the title was beautifully created with brass and leather fittings, making the machine itself into a work of art. The revolutionary computer game *Myst* used a very similar approach in all its styling.

We'll look at how to adapt a steampunk style to make a dull guitar into something approaching a work of art.

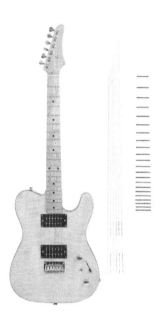

1 This is our starting point: a remarkably plain wooden guitar. We first need to copy the strings and frets to new layers, so we can place our own elements behind them. Selecting the strings can be tricky – see More Info for some suggestions.

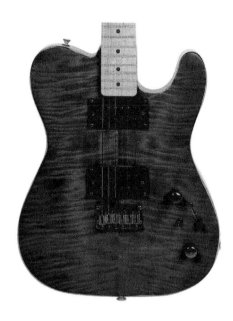

2 Select the face of the guitar body, by selecting it with the either the Pen tool or using QuickMask. Make this into a new layer, and use Curves or Levels to darken the wood, adding some red to it to get this strong mahogany look.

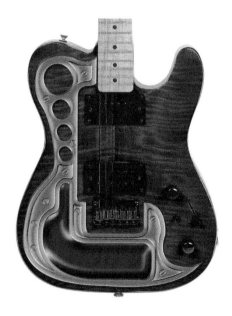

4 Hold *ctrl* ⌘ and click on the brass panel's thumbnail in the Layers palette to load it as a selection, then use Select > Modify > Contract to reduce this by, say, 16 pxels. When we now make a new layer using *ctrl* *J* ⌘ *J*, the Layer Style will come with it. The red panel is the same Layer Style, slightly modified.

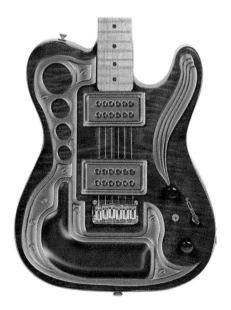

5 The two pickup elements are drawn in the same way as the brass plate, as flat objects; when the layer style from the plate is copied to this layer, it turns into polished brass. A single curved swoosh is duplicated and scaled down to make the decoration top right. This is where the saved Strings layer shows itself useful!

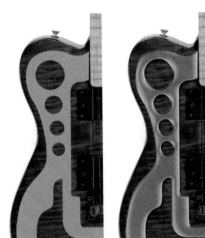

MORE INFO

● Selecting the strings in step 1 can be fiddly – but here's a fairly simple method. Use the Lasso tool, holding *alt* ⌥ to trace straight lines between click points. Zoom in to 200% and click once on each corner of the left-most string, to select it. It's easier than you'd think. Then press **Q** to enter QuickMask mode, and the selection will be shown highlighted. Make a rectangular selection with the Marquee tool that just encloses this string, then hold *alt* ⌥ as you drag it to make a copy; use Free Transform to skew and stretch it to fit the next string. Repeat for all the other strings.

● To draw the screw heads in step 4, first make a small circular selection and, on a new layer, fill with any color. Copy the layer style from the base plate to this layer, to add the brass effect to it. You'll need to reduce the Emboss amount for such a tiny object. Using the Rectangular Marquee tool, make a vertical selection one pixel wide down the middle of the screw, and delete: this will make the screw head. When this screw is now copied around the artwork, you can rotate it to a few different angles to give the impression of several separate screws.

3 The brass panel is made by drawing the design on a new layer, complete with gasket-like holes (left). The metal look is created entirely using Layer Styles: the style itself is on the CD, so take a look to see how the combination of embossing and satin works here.

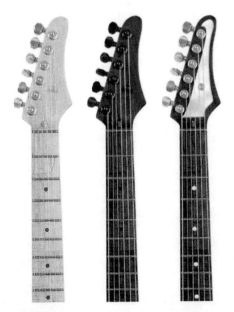

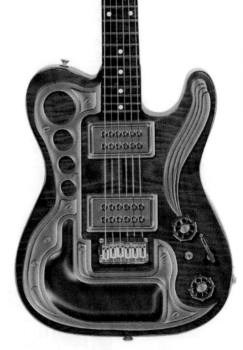

6 To treat the neck (left), first copy it all to a new layer and use Curves or Levels to darken it, to get the deep wood effect (middle). Paint out the machine heads on a layer mask for this layer. The mother of pearl plate and fret markers is simply created by applying the Clouds filter to a selection.

7 Additional elements here include the water tap knobs, replacing the original volume and tone knobs. I drew these in Photoshop, but it would have been just as easy to find photographs of them using Google. This is the kind of job where you never quite finish adding decoration – much like the real thing, in fact.

SHORTCUTS

MAC **WIN** **BOTH**

Line action and texture

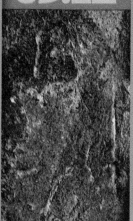

1 For our homage to Lewis Carrol's *Alice Through the Looking Glass* – his sequel to *Alice in Wonderland* – we'll need a picture of Alice. This is taken from the excellent photos.com library of royalty-free images, and has the right sense of boredom for our purpose.

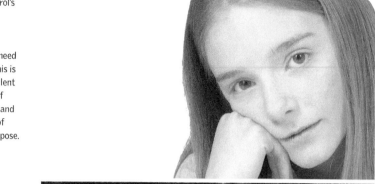

Photographers love taking pictures of textures. Rusty metal, worm-eaten wood, decaying brick, all are sought out by those keen to capture the feel of the surfaces for posterity.

In the 1990s, a need arose for all those dozens of textures that had filled shoeboxes and transparency folders. A number of Photoshop artists began to incorporate textures into their work, overlaying it on top of images to create rich, dense imagery that brought a new tactile quality to photomontage illustration.

More often than not, these textures are accompanied by 'line action', as it's sometimes called: orthogonal lines and circles that delineate areas of the composition, marking edges and creating an almost mathematical sense of purpose and proportion.

3 To make the image darker and more mysterious, create a new Curves adjustment layer from the pop-up menu at the bottom of the Layers palette. Drag the center of the line down to make a curve; as it's an adjustment layer, it will darken all the layers beneath it.

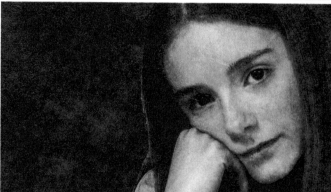

5 We need to change the mode of the brick layer to make it blend in with the underlying layers. We could use Hard Light, or even Multiply; after some experimentation, I found that Overlay mode produced the most pleasing results.

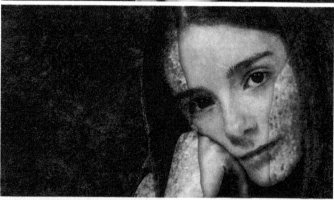

7 The horizontal rules are drawn by making a selection 2 pixels thick with the Marquee tool, filling this with white and then duplicating it around the artwork. The circles are made by taking circular selections and using Edit > Stroke to apply a 2 point white stroke to them.

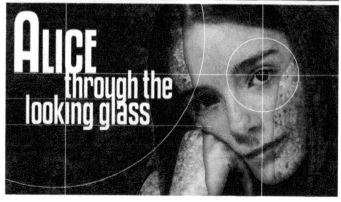

ALICE through the looking glass

2 The first texture is a scan of a piece of leather, placed behind the Alice character. To make her interact with it, change the mode of her layer from Normal to Hard Light: this lets the leather show through, creating a more unified image.

4 Our second texture is a photograph of a piece of brickwork. Make a layer mask for it, and use the Lasso tool to select and hide a portion above Alice. Then add a drop shadow to the layer using Layer Styles, so it appears to stand above the Alice layer.

6 The text here is set in Ray Larabie's font Kenyan Coffee. It's a modern but plain font, which will work well with the outline style we'll apply later. Place all the font layers into a single group, then duplicate the group and flatten it to make a single layer (see More Info).

8 Reducing the opacity of the lines to 50% and placing them below the brick allows the texture to show through, which integrates them into the image. The Alice lettering is filled with orange, and the layer mode changed to Screen; the outline is an Outer Glow, added using Layer Styles.

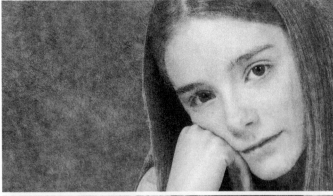

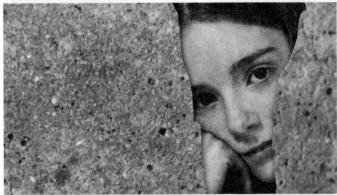

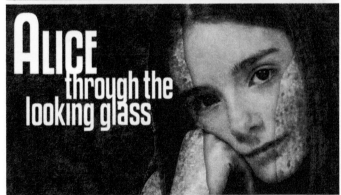

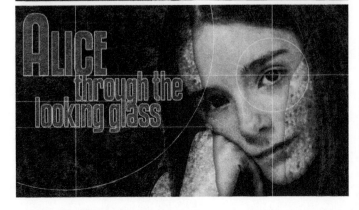

MORE INFO

● In step 6, we put all the text layers into a single group. The easiest way to do this is to select them all in the Layers palette, then choose New Group from Layers from the pop-up menu at the top of the palette. This allows us to move them as a unit, to lower the transparency of the whole group, and to hide and show them. But when we want to add a layer style, it's a lot easier to do to a single layer. Duplicate the group (so we don't lose the original contents), and hide the original; then select the new group, and use *ctrl E* / *⌘ E* to merge the group into a single layer.

● When changing the opacity of all the lines, it helps to place all the layers we used to create them into a group as well. We can now lower the opacity of the group as a whole. In this way we make a uniform opacity throughout: if we simply lowered the opacity of each line layer in turn, we'd get extra bright spots at the intersections where the pixels doubled up. This would be both unsightly and distracting.

● In step 4, we could simply erase a chunk from the layer. But the layer mask means we can edit it later.

SHORTCUTS

 MAC WIN BOTH

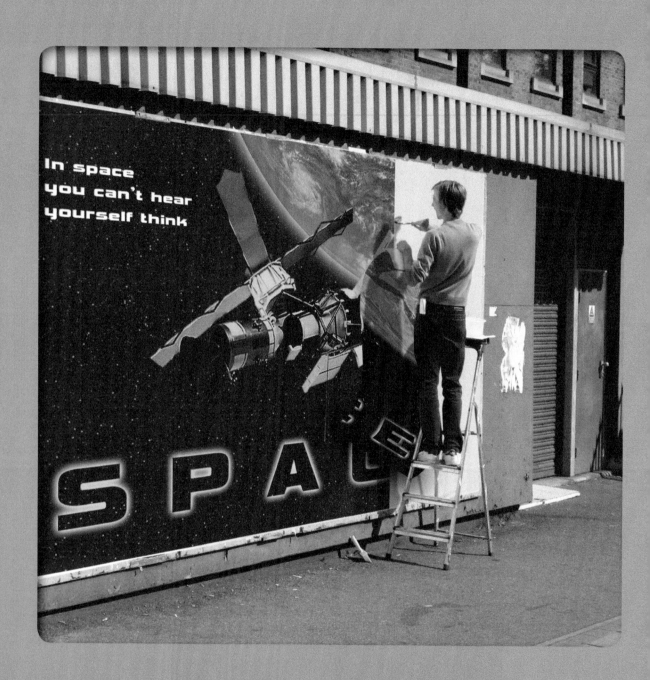

Poster design

We're advertised at in magazines and in newspapers. We're assailed by commercials on TV, in the cinema, even on the DVDs we buy. Is the only way to get away from them to go for a long walk?

Not if you live in the city, it isn't. Posters shriek at us from all sides: from billboards, from hoardings, from bus stops. In subways, in shop windows, and on placards on the street.

With so many signs all fighting for our attention, the advertising agency that designs them has to work hard to grab our interest. In some European countries, a grinning face holding the product is enough to send housewives scurrying for that brand of washing powder; but for most of us, advertising is a subtle and sophisticated art that tries to win our hearts through emotional and intellectual content.

In this chapter we'll look at how different kinds of posters are put together, from Victorian times to the present day.

poster

1. A large, usually printed placard, bill, or announcement, often illustrated, that is posted to advertise or publicize something.

2. An artistic work, often a reproduction of an original painting or photograph, printed on a large sheet of paper.

American Heritage Dictionary

1838, from post in the verbal sense of 'fasten to a post' (1633).

Online Etymology Dictionary

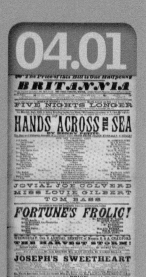

Victorian playbill

The huge explosion of typographic design in the 19th century gave poster designers a vast new range of fonts to work with. Some were bold some delicate, some playful; the choice was immense.

Printers would buy in sets of typefaces at set display sizes, and frequently they wouldn't own more than one or two sizes of a particular font. This, in part, explains the way the reader is overwhelmed with such a huge variety of type styles: it's almost as if a different font were used for each size.

Liberties were often taken with the design, to fit in with the available space. In the example above, the word 'the' in the main headline has been rotated 90° to fit. Today, we'd reduce the point size of the headline slightly to make it occupy the space, but the Victorian printers had no such luxury.

1 We need to load a lot of fonts to make this poster work. Here I've used the fonts Headline One, Fette Egyptienne, and Plastische Plakat-Antiqua for the main headline. Set each line so that it takes up the full width of the page.

2 The cast of characters is set in the font Slab Serif HPLHS, a very condensed serif. We can't set tab stops in Photoshop – the program's word processing capabilities are very limited – so we'll have to make the text up by hand.

5 Photoshop doesn't support 'leader dots' as there are no tabs to be placed, so we have to type them in by hand. A string of full stops would be too tight, so type 'dot space dot space' in the gaps. Leaving a couple of extra spaces helps the text to look more hand set, as if the type were slightly damaged.

6 The rest of the poster is set in the same fonts we used earlier, with the addition of Cairo for the 'To be, or not to be' line. Victorian posters tended to be very wordy: you can't get away with minimal information here. Take the time to write extra lines to make the effect more convincing.

ANNOUNCING AN EXTRAVAGANT PRODUCTION
IN FULL COSTUME, OF
HAMLET
Prince of Denmark
FEATURING THE TALENTS OF SUNDRY MEMBERS OF THE ACTING PROFESSION

ANNOUNCING AN EXTRAVAGANT PRODUCTION
IN FULL COSTUME, OF
HAMLET
Prince of Denmark
FEATURING THE TALENTS OF SUNDRY MEMBERS OF THE ACTING PROFESSION

Hamlet, the troubled prince
Claudius, the king and usurper of the throne
Gertrude, his queen, and mother to Hamlet
Polonius, a courtier
Ophelia
Laertes

ANNOUNCING AN EXTRAVAGANT PRODUCTION
IN FULL COSTUME, OF
HAMLET
Prince of Denmark
FEATURING THE TALENTS OF SUNDRY MEMBERS OF THE ACTING PROFESSION

Hamlet, the troubled prince .... Mr. Geoffrey Beaverwax
Claudius, the king and usurper of the throne .... Mr. Arbuthnot de Vere
Gertrude, his queen, and mother to Hamlet .... Miss Fanny Giggleswick
Polonius, a courtier .... Mr. Jeremiah Foole
Ophelia } children of above .... { Miss Fatima Wimsie
Laertes } .... { Mr. Freddy McGinger

ANNOUNCING AN EXTRAVAGANT PRODUCTION
IN FULL COSTUME, OF
HAMLET
Prince of Denmark
FEATURING THE TALENTS OF SUNDRY MEMBERS OF THE ACTING PROFESSION

Hamlet, the troubled prince .... Mr. Geoffrey Beaverwax
Claudius, the king and usurper of the throne .... Mr. Arbuthnot de Vere
Gertrude, his queen, and mother to Hamlet .... Miss Fanny Giggleswick
Polonius, a courtier .... Mr. Jeremiah Foole
Ophelia } children of above .... { Miss Fatima Wimsie
Laertes } .... { Mr. Freddy McGinger

TO BE PERFORMED WITH NUMEROUS SCENIC PAINTED BACKDROPS, WITH MANY FANTASTICAL ITEMS NEVER SEEN UPON THE STAGE.
TO INCLUDE THE FAMOUS MONOLOGUE
To Be, or not To Be
AS CONCEIVED BY MR. BEAVERWAX TO THE DELIGHT OF AUDIENCES THROUGHOUT THE CIVILIZED WORLD.
TO BE PERFORMED THREE TIMES DAILY

ANNOUNCING AN EXTRAVAGANT PRODUCTION
IN FULL COSTUME, OF
HAMLET
Prince of Denmark
FEATURING THE TALENTS OF SUNDRY MEMBERS OF THE ACTING PROFESSION

Hamlet, the troubled prince   Mr. Geoffrey Beaverwax
Claudius, the king and usurper of the throne   Mr. Arbuthnot de Vere
Gertrude, his queen, and mother to Hamlet   Miss Fanny Giggleswick
Polonius, a courtier   Mr. Jeremiah Foole
Ophelia   Miss Fatima Wimsie
Laertes   Mr. Freddy McGinger

ANNOUNCING AN EXTRAVAGANT PRODUCTION
IN FULL COSTUME, OF
HAMLET
Prince of Denmark
FEATURING THE TALENTS OF SUNDRY MEMBERS OF THE ACTING PROFESSION

Hamlet, the troubled prince   Mr. Geoffrey Beaverwax
Claudius, the king and usurper of the throne   Mr. Arbuthnot de Vere
Gertrude, his queen, and mother to Hamlet   Miss Fanny Giggleswick
Polonius, a courtier   Mr. Jeremiah Foole
Ophelia ⎱   ⎰ Miss Fatima Wimsie
Laertes ⎰ children of above   ⎱ Mr. Freddy McGinger

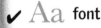
(3) To create the names of the actors playing the parts, we need to duplicate the character list. With the Move tool, hold *alt* ⌥ as you drag it to make a copy, then add *Shift* to move it horizontally. Right align the text using the button on the options bar.

(4) The last two entries, Ophelia and Laertes, will share a string of leader dots. The words 'children of above' can be set on the 'Laertes' line, shifting the baseline of the words up slightly. The curly brackets are set in condensed Times Regular (see More Info).

MORE INFO

● There are two ways to make the text fit the width: either make it larger and smaller using *ctrl* *Shift* ⌘ *Shift* with the < and > keys, or increase the tracking (letter spacing) by holding *alt* ⌥ and pressing the cursor keys → and ← to make the spacing looser and tighter.

● The curly brackets added in step 4 are in Times, because most freeware fonts don't go to the extent of including these little-used typographic elements. The bracket is made as a new text box, placed above the existing type; then Free Transform is used to scale it horizontally, making it narrower so it looks more in keeping with the narrow serif font beneath:

This bracket can then be copied and flipped horizontally to make the one on the other side.

ANNOUNCING AN EXTRAVAGANT PRODUCTION
IN FULL COSTUME, OF
HAMLET
Prince of Denmark
FEATURING THE TALENTS OF SUNDRY MEMBERS OF THE ACTING PROFESSION

Hamlet, the troubled prince .... Mr. Geoffrey Beaverwax
Claudius, the king and usurper of the throne .... Mr. Arbuthnot de Vere
Gertrude, his queen, and mother to Hamlet .... Miss Fanny Giggleswick
Polonius, a courtier .... Mr. Jeremiah Foole
Ophelia ⎱ children of above .... ⎰ Miss Fatima Wimsie
Laertes ⎰   ⎱ Mr. Freddy McGinger

TO BE PERFORMED WITH NUMEROUS SCENIC PAINTED BACKDROPS, WITH MANY FANTASTICAL ITEMS NEVER SEEN UPON THE STAGE.
TO INCLUDE THE FAMOUS MONOLOGUE
To Be, or not To Be
AS CONCEIVED BY MR. BEAVERWAX TO THE DELIGHT OF AUDIENCES THROUGHOUT THE CIVILIZED WORLD.
TO BE PERFORMED THREE TIMES DAILY

ANNOUNCING AN EXTRAVAGANT PRODUCTION
IN FULL COSTUME, OF
HAMLET
Prince of Denmark
FEATURING THE TALENTS OF SUNDRY MEMBERS OF THE ACTING PROFESSION

Hamlet, the troubled prince .... Mr. Geoffrey Beaverwax
Claudius, the king and usurper of the throne .... Mr. Arbuthnot de Vere
Gertrude, his queen, and mother to Hamlet .... Miss Fanny Giggleswick
Polonius, a courtier .... Mr. Jeremiah Foole
Ophelia ⎱ children of above .... ⎰ Miss Fatima Wimsie
Laertes ⎰   ⎱ Mr. Freddy McGinger

TO BE PERFORMED WITH NUMEROUS SCENIC PAINTED BACKDROPS, WITH MANY FANTASTICAL ITEMS NEVER SEEN UPON THE STAGE.
TO INCLUDE THE FAMOUS MONOLOGUE
To Be, or not To Be
AS CONCEIVED BY MR. BEAVERWAX TO THE DELIGHT OF AUDIENCES THROUGHOUT THE CIVILIZED WORLD.
TO BE PERFORMED THREE TIMES DAILY

● The words 'children of above' in step 4 are shifted vertically by selecing them and using *alt* *Shift* ↑ ⌥ *Shift* ↑ to raise the baseline.

(7) Adding texture will help a lot here. We won't use the crumpled paper texture used elsewhere in this book: this is a piece of stained paper, placed at the top with its layer mode set to Hard Light so we can see through it. The white background makes the effect far too strong, however.

(8) Changing the color of the background from white to mid-gray solves the brightness problem neatly. We could have set the mode of the paper layer to Multiply instead, but this way it affects the type as well as the background: the brownish, slightly mottled tint makes the type look old and faded.

SHORTCUTS

 MAC   WIN   BOTH

71

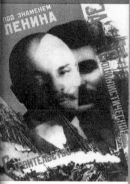

Russian revolutionary

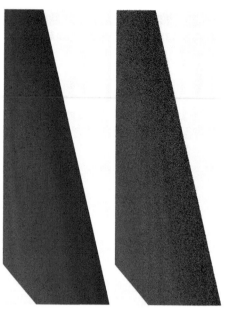

The Russian Revolutionary style of poster design is unmistakeable: strong, bold colors, generally in combinations of black, white and red. The Cyrillic typeface is, of course, a key element in this poster; but what's even more distinctive is the tendency towards strong diagonals, as if the entire poster design has been rotated by around 30°.

The intention of the Constructivist movement, of which the posters were the graphic expression, was that art should be used only for social development, rather than pure decoration. The movement first appeared in around 1914, and with the October revolution of 1917 it gained impetus, especially with the backing of political patron Leon Trotsky. We'll use this 1930 poster by Gustav Klutsis as the inspiration for our own version.

1 We'll begin by copying that red diagonal shape in the back of the original poster. Make a new layer, trace the shape and fill it with red. We'll also set the background to a creamy color, rather than pure white, which will help to give the poster an aged look.

2 Make a new layer, using the red shape layer as a Clipping Mask (press `ctrl` `alt` `G` `⌘` `⌥` `G`) and add some shading to the edge with a soft-edged brush (left). When we change the mode of this layer to Dissolve (right), we get this mezzotint effect.

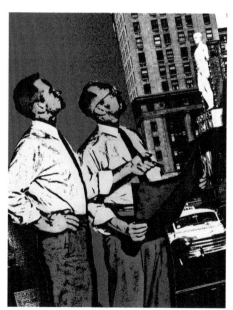

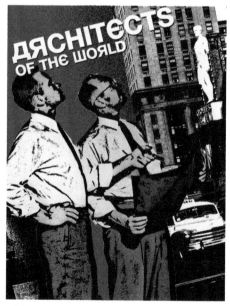

5 The choice of background image depends on the subject of the foreground, of course. Since we're designing an architectural poster here, we can use an image of architecture as our background. The statue on the right, which happened to be part of this image, gives our architects something to look at.

6 The text here is set in the freeware font Kyrilla, which conveys a suitable Soviet feel without being truly Cyrillic. To make it stand out, add a Drop Shadow using Layer Styles: setting the Size to 0 removes the fuzziness, and setting the Opacity to 100% produces the solid black we need.

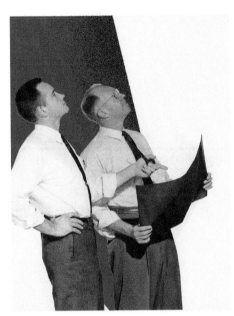

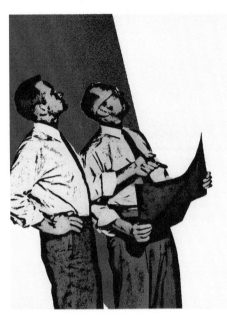

3 Now for the figures. This pair of 1950s architects is perfect for our purposes: the forthright pose, the heavenward gaze, all give the impression of workers who are both anticipating and, quite literally, building the future. Duplicate the layer before proceeding.

4 Use Filter > Sketch > Photocopy to give the duplicated image a distressed, screen printed appearance, then change the mode to Multiply so we can see the original through it. A second copy, filled with the cream color (and set to Multiply) adds the color.

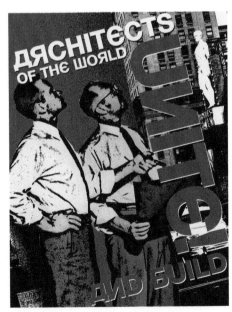

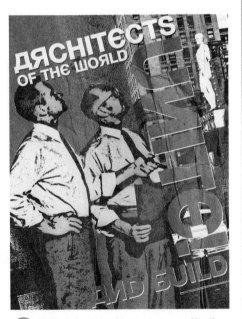

7 This text can now be copied and rotated to make the other two text elements, enlarged as necessary. Here, though, the drop shadow is cream, rather than black; we need to change the mode of the shadow, in the Layer Styles dialog, from Multiply to Normal in order for it to show up.

8 The last step is to add some texture, making the poster look more old and worn. I've provided a photograph of a piece of crumpled paper for this purpose: it's largely gray, with creases and wrinkles. With the mode of this texture layer set to Hard Light, we can see through it to the poster design beneath.

MORE INFO

● Changing the mode of the shading layer in step 2 from Normal to Dissolve produces this stippled appearance. If this is too strong, lower the opacity of the layer. We can achieve a similar effect by setting the mode of our brush to Dissolve before painting with it; the higher the opacity of the brush, the denser the stippled result will be.

● The choice of font here depends on whether you want to be authentic, or to give an overall impression. The font we've used contains characters such as A, E and B that aren't truly part of the Cyrillic alphabet; but they add to the effect, and make the poster more believable. Of course, the only way to make it truly authentic would be to set the whole poster in Russian from the beginning.

● The key to working with a strong diagonal like this is to use just the one angle, and stick with it. The figures, the background, and text, if they're rotated, should conform to this angle. In addition, though, we can place further elements at 90° to the main angle, such as the additional text on this page. But be careful of building in additional angles, which can look messy.

SHORTCUTS

 MAC WIN BOTH

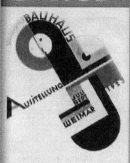

Bauhaus

Founded by the German architect Walter Gropius in 1919, the Bauhaus – literally, Building House – was an art college based in Weimar.

The Weimar Republic, the democratic republic that Germany became after the end of the monarchy and defeat in the First World War, was a liberal state that abolished censorship. This gave rise not only to the decadence against which the Nazis were later to rail, but a fresh and dynamic approach to art and design.

The Bauhaus school of design was a development of German modernism, bringing the geometric shapes of art deco to a new rigorous aesthetic. Bauhaus design informed art, architecture, graphic design and furniture design; many of the most famous pieces of the period – such as the famous Bauhaus chair – are still reproduced today.

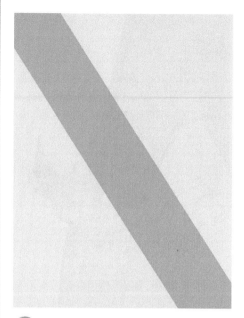

1 Just like the Russian revolutionary posters, a strong diagonal was the key to Bauhaus design. This poster is based on a design created in Cologne in 1928, and uses the same colors and basic layout. To begin, create a filled rectangle, and rotate it.

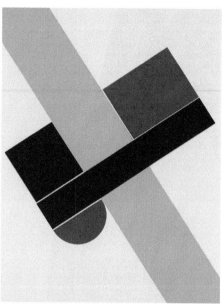

2 This rectangle will determine the angle for all the rest of the components of the illustration. Duplicating the rectangle and rotating it 90° produces the right angle for the other elements, which can then be modified and recolored as needed.

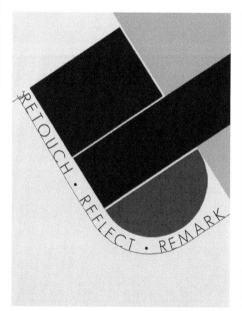

5 It's easiest if the text is aligned left, so we can get the starting point in the right place. Once it's here, adjust the type size using `ctrl` `Shift` `>` `⌘` `Shift` `>` and `ctrl` `Shift` `<` `⌘` `Shift` `<` to make the text larger and smaller, and `alt` `→` `⌥` `→` to add spacing between the characters.

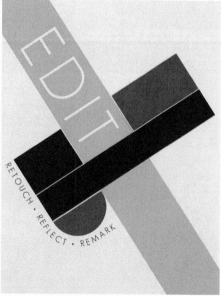

6 For the large text, set it in the same font and then rotate the whole text block to the same angle as the original rectangle. When in Free Transform mode, it's easy to align the type: you just have to make the bounding box line up with the base of the rectangle.

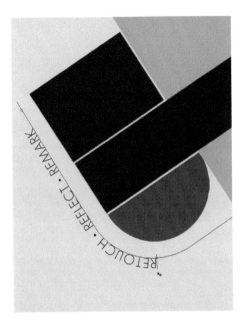

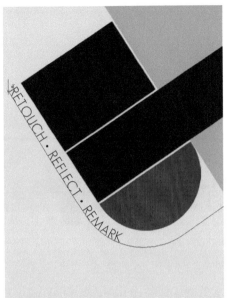

3 To create the curved text, first draw a Pen path following the line (see More Info). Click the Type tool near the path and it will snap the text to it. Type in the text you want: the font used here is Geo Sans Light, which suits the period perfectly.

4 The text will almost certainly appear in the wrong location, and probably upside down. There will be a marker on the left, right or center, depending on how the type is aligned: drag this to change the type position. You can also drag it across the line to flip it vertically.

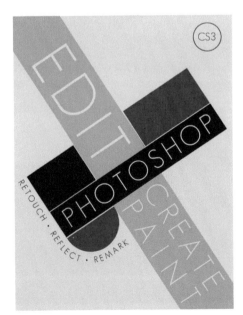

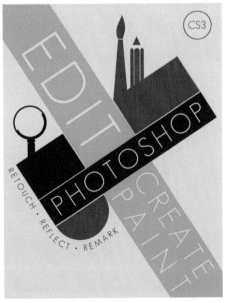

7 The remainder of the type is made by copying the existing text element, reducing it as necessary. The rotated word 'Photoshop' here is at 90° to the other text, and so is easy to place at the right angle.

8 The graphic elements – the brush, magnifying glass and pencil – are best drawn on new layers and then moved into position rising out of the colored blocks. To stay true to the style they should not follow the same angle but rise vertically from the blocks.

MORE INFO

● To rotate the elements by 90° in step 2, and to rotate the text in step 7, you can choose Edit > Transform > Rotate 90°, with either CW (clockwise) or CCW (counter clockwise) depending on the direction you need to go. A quicker method is to use `ctrl T` `⌘ T` to enter Free Transform mode, then hold the `Shift` key as you drag outside the transformation box. This key will make the rotation snap to 15° increments (so that we can easily rotate by 30° and 45°), which means it will click into place once we near the 90° rotation we're looking for.

● Drawing the Pen path in step 3 can be tricky: it isn't easy to follow the curve of the circle it wraps around. The most straightforward method is to use the Shapes tool to draw a circle first (make sure the tool is set to Path mode), and then rotate this circular path. Delete all but the lower left quadrant, then use the Pen tool to extend the path following the angle of the initial rectangle.

● When adding text to a curve, the path will be visible as long as the text is selected. But once you click on another layer, the path will disappear of its own accord.

SHORTCUTS

 MAC WIN BOTH

Art deco

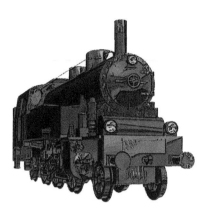

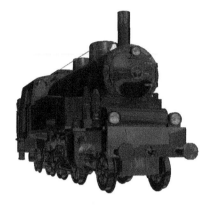

Billboard posters of the 1920s and 1930s highlighted the golden age of travel. In the days before carbon footprints, traveling by plane, train or ship was glamorous and sophisticated, and the posters did their best to convey the thrill of the journey.

The one factor that unites all the posters of the period is the strong perspective and low point of view. These two elements combine to make the subject of the poster appear huge and powerful, looming over us as they make their unstoppable journey between departure point and destination.

Typographically, the art deco period produced an explosion of type: some very angular and graphic, some loose and hand drawn. Art deco took its angular design from the Bauhaus, and turned it into something far more elegant.

1 It can be hard to find suitable starting images taken from a low enough viewpoint. If you're able to photograph your own, that's the best solution. Here, we've used the 3D Layers feature of Photoshop CS3 Extended to pose this 3D model of a steam train. The train model is taken from the Taschen 500 3D-Objects collection.

2 To give the train a hand-drawn appearance, first rasterize the 3D layer to make it a regular layer (I've already done this in the version on the DVD). The Poster Edges filter, found in the Artistic section of the Filters menu, stylizes the image by reducing the number of colors, while adding black outlines to it – perfect for our purposes.

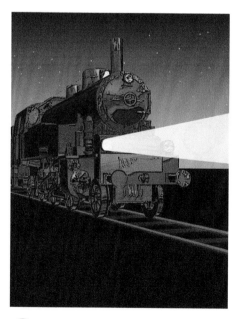

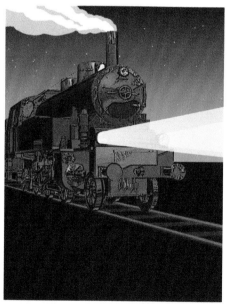

5 To make the headlight beams, first draw the outline of the path using the Pen tool, and turn it into a selection by pressing *Enter*. On a new layer, fill this selection with a pale yellow, then use the Gradient tool with a white foreground color, dragged from left to right, to create the lighter end of the beam near the light.

6 Change its mode from Normal to Hard Light, using the pop-up menu at the top of the Layers palette. This allows us to see the train through it. Duplicate this layer and move it into place for the other light. The steam is painted on a new layer, using a hard edged brush: make it graphic, rather than realistic.

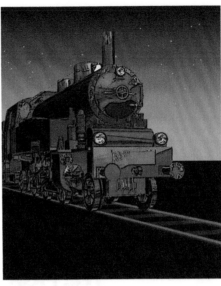

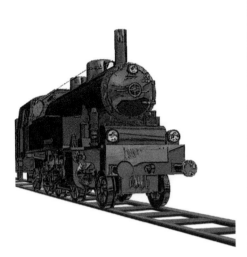

3 The front rail is easily drawn as a straight object, which can be distorted using Free Transform to make it fit the angle of the train; duplicate it for the other rail. A Layer Mask, added to the front rail, allows us to paint it out around the wheels, so they appear to be on top of it. See More Info, right, for details on how to draw the sleepers.

4 Fill the background with black – these scenes are always more impressive at night. Make a marquee selection of the sky area, making sure the horizon lines up with the vanishing point determined by the train angle; use the Gradient tool, set to Foreground to Transparent, to make a glow rising from the horizon. The stars are easily painted with the Brush tool, one at a time.

MORE INFO

● The only tricky action in this illustration is drawing the sleepers in perspective, in step 4. These are created by first drawing a single sleeper near to us, with the top and bottom horizontal and the sides following the angle of the rails. Then Select All, and enter Free Transform using ⌘ T ctrl T. In the center of the bounding box is a center point marker: this is the point about which the transformation takes place. Make the window wider so you can see plenty of gray outside the image area, and drag the center point marker out to the horizon line, aiming for the point where the rails would meet. This is the vanishing point. Now hold ⌥ Shift alt Shift as you drag the corner handle furthest from this marker, and the sleeper will move in perspective towards the vanishing point. Press E to apply the transformation; then press ⌘ Shift T ctrl Shift T to repeat the transformation several times. A row of sleepers will now appear in perspective.

● We could have added grass, hills and trees to this poster to flesh it out; but the stark graphic approach we've taken here fits in more neatly with the design aesthetic of the period.

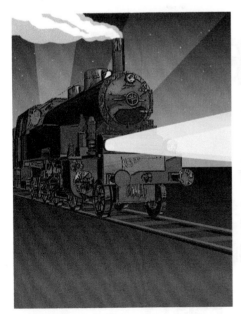

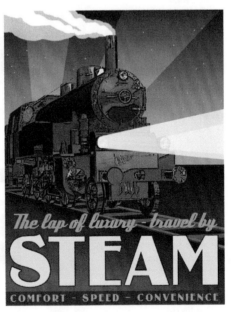

7 Duplicate the gradient over the sky to make a similar one at the base. The angular triangles in the sky were typical of the period: make selections with the Lasso tool, holding *alt* ⌥ to set it to Polygonal mode, and make a new layer from the background gradation to create the extra effect.

8 The fonts are both by Ray Larabie: cursive Deftone Stylus, and Guanine. The shadow on the word 'Steam' has been added using Layer Styles dialog. As a final step, I've added a slight shadow beneath the rails to make them sit more firmly on the ground.

Boxing promotion

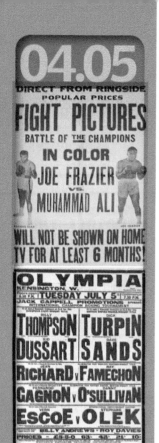

When boxing matches featured big names – and there were none bigger than Joe Frazier and Mohammed Ali – they could fill an entire evening all by themselves. Lesser mortals had to make do with their names alone.

Boxing posters acquired a style of their own, featuring large surnames and much smaller first names or nicknames; the first and last letter of the surname was often enlarged so as to frame the first name within the gap created by the process.

We'll emulate the style of the genre, including reproducing the cheap printing techniques they used.

1 Rather than just going for a pair of standard boxers, let's try something a little different: we can use the format to make a social comment, after all. So here's a businessman in a suit up against a decidedly less heavy challenger. But who will have the edge here?

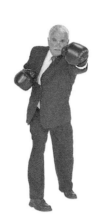
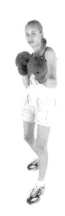

3 The text here is set in two fonts – Headline One and Boris Black Bloxx. When creating the surname text, use ctrl Shift > ⌘ Shift > and ctrl Shift < ⌘ Shift < to make the first and last letters larger and smaller – far quicker than selecting the size from the text size field.

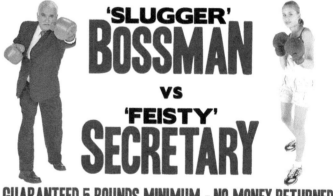

THE FIGHT OF THE MILLENNIUM
'SLUGGER'
BOSSMAN
vs
'FEISTY'
SECRETARY
GUARANTEED 5 ROUNDS MINIMUM - NO MONEY RETURNED

5 When we change the mode of this new texture layer from Normal to Hard Light, we can see through it to the text beneath, and it gives the impression of poorly printed lettering on cheap paper. Note how the Clouds effect works on the black lettering as well as the red.

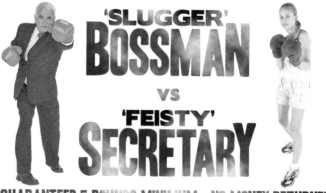

THE FIGHT OF THE MILLENNIUM
'SLUGGER'
BOSSMAN
vs
'FEISTY'
SECRETARY
GUARANTEED 5 ROUNDS MINIMUM - NO MONEY RETURNED

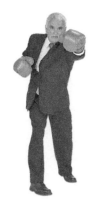

2 Desaturate both layers using *ctrl* *Shift* U ⌘ *Shift* U to produce a grayscale version. If you're designing a poster to be used very large, consider using Filter > Pixellate > Color Halftone, with all the angles set to 45°, to reproduce the kind of coarse dot screen used when printing onto cheap paper.

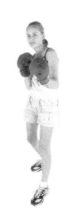

MORE INFO

● In step **4** we need to load up all the text area on a single layer. Hold *ctrl* ⌘ and click on the first text layer's thumbnail in the Layers palette to load it, then hold *Shift* as well as you click on each text block in turn to add it to the selection. If you like, you can fill the selection with a color (on a new layer) so you don't lose it accidentally; but if you're going to apply the Clouds filter right away there's no point, since this will fill any selection automatically.

● The Clouds filter, used to create the texture in step **4**, creates a random mottling effect each time it's used. After the first application, pressing *ctrl* F ⌘ F will repeat the operation in a slightly different way, so it's worth having a few goes until you get the effect you want. For small text, the filter will produce too loose a result; try using *ctrl* *alt* F ⌘ ⌥ F instead. This produces a tighter version of the filter. Again, it can be repeated until you get a good version of the texture.

● The text may need tightening up, but don't overdo it. It's supposed to be set in block letters, so no two letters can overlap each other.

4 Even though the Headline One font is based on an old newspaper style, it's far too clean for this poster: we need to make it look more cheaply printed. Load up each text layer in turn as a selection (see More Info) and make a new layer above the type; set the foreground and background colors to light and dark gray, and run Filter > Render > Clouds to get this mottled effect.

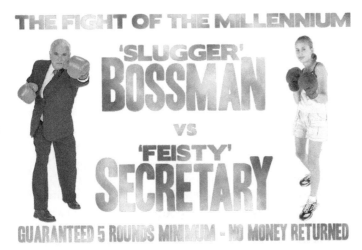

6 This poster really needs to look old in order to work well. So we'll place our standard piece of crumpled paper on top, set to Hard Light mode so the wrinkled appearance shows through on the poster beneath. Here, I've tinted the poster by adding red using the Curves adjustment, to make it look older and more yellowed.

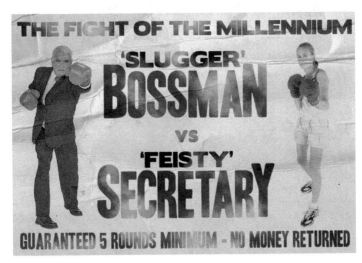

Western movies

From the early days of John Wayne's gung-ho Red Indian slayers to the reinterpretation of the genre in such modern classics as *Brokeback Mountain*, the Western has had a strong hold on our collective consciousness.

The poster style is typified by the font – one of many variations on the elaborate 19th century woodcut, with fancy slab serifs and those trademark pointed bulges half way up the characters. There are many free versions of this font style readily available.

The other factor common to these posters is the color palette, which predominantly features shades of red, gold and brown. This is most often seen in the doomy skies, but is frequently reflected in the coloring of the headline style as well. A big foreground face, of course, sells the film's leading actor.

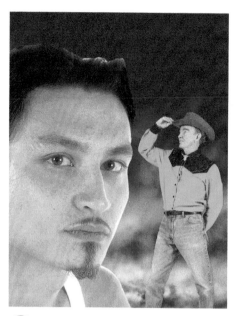

1 Our poster has just three basic elements: the close-up of the man's face; a rather dodgy cowboy with poor dress sense tipping his hat; and that staple of Western posters, the doomy dawn (or is it sunset?) cloudy background.

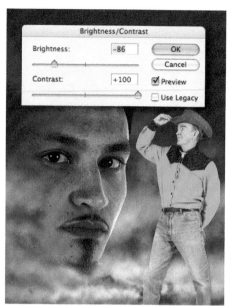

2 We'll start with the close-up. Use the Brightness/ Contrast adjustment to lower the Brightness and increase the Contrast considerably, to boost those skintones; then create a layer mask for this layer, and paint out the side of the face with a soft edged brush.

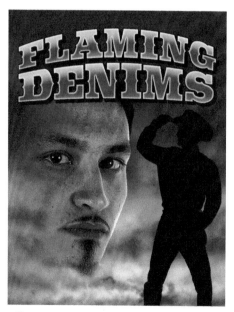

5 Layer Styles complete the text. Here, we use Stroke to make a black outline and Inner Glow for the yellow inline. The Drop Shadow is set to a Spread of 100%, which makes it solid rather than soft edged; at 100% opacity, it's offset from the text to make a solid grounding behind it.

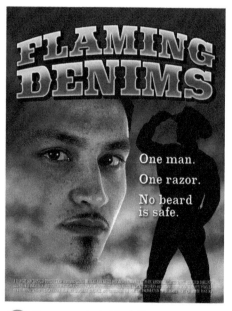

6 The nonsense text at the bottom, simulating film poster credits, is typed in a serif font narrowed to around 40% of its original width to match the style. The standout text is set in white to make it stand out against the background, and a slight drop shadow added using Layer Styles to lift it slightly.

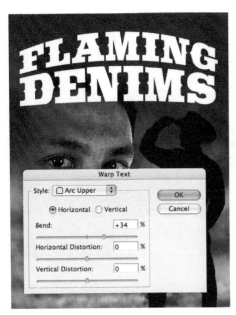

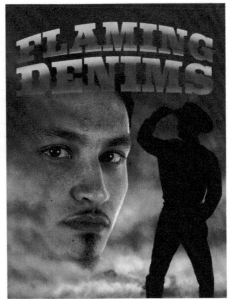

3 The standing figure is simply filled with black to make him an iconic silhouette. The text here is set in the freeware font Saddlebag, and we've used the Warp Text dialog to add a slight bend to it, using the Arc Upper warp style.

4 Fill the text with red, then make a new layer above it, using the text as a clipping layer (so painting on the new layer only shows through where it overlaps the text). The text highlights are now painted in, using colors sampled from the poster background.

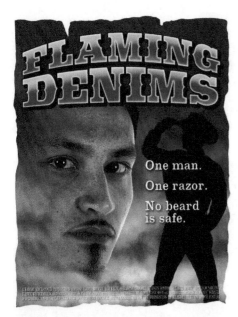

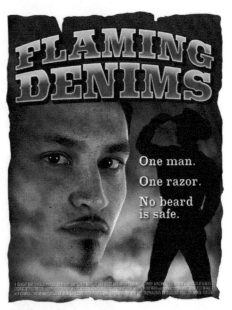

7 The ragged edge is made on a separate layer, above all the rest. Draw this freehand, with the Lasso tool, then inverse the selection using ⌘ Shift I ctrl Shift I and fill the inverted region with white. This technique is far easier than making complex masks for every layer in the document.

8 Finally, make another new, empty layer beneath the mask. Use a soft-edged brush with either a black or a dark brown foreground color, and paint in around the edge of the jagged shape. This adds depth to the poster, and gives it the impression of slightly burnt edges appropriate to the style.

MORE INFO

● When we make a layer mask in step 2, choose Layer > Layer Mask > Reveal All. This creates an empty mask for the layer: painting on it in black hides the layer, painting in white reveals it again. A large, soft brush creates the smoothest transitions.

● The Brightness/Contrast adjustment in step 2 applies to Photoshop CS3, which has had an overhaul of the adjustment tool. If you're using earlier versions of Photoshop then less extreme settings would be required.

● To make the clipping layer in step 4, either choose Layer > Create Clipping Mask, or use ⌘ ⌥ G ctrl alt G as a shortcut.

● At first glance, the standing figure of the cowboy is too posed and artificial for our purposes. But when seen as a silhouette, it adds the sense of a mysterious stranger to the composition, as well as adding a sense of depth and perspective to the scene. It also serves to draw the eye back to the main figure, the direction in which the cowboy is facing.

● This sky serves both as a sunset and as a suggestion of flames – which could be why they're used so often.

SHORTCUTS

MAC   WIN   BOTH

Science fiction

Science fiction posters have intrigued, inspired and occasionally frightened us since the earliest days of film.

There are as many different types of science fiction poster as there are science fiction films, of course; but they do share a number of common elements, and certainly a common feel.

These films are always publicized using posters that have a strong black element to them, in order to express the emptiness of space. Ever since the first *Alien* poster, above, there's been a tendency for widely-spaced lettering.

We can't attempt to show how every kind of sci-fi poster is put together. But we can look at some general principles which may help you in the design of your own posters.

1 There are three starting elements to this poster: the model of a satellite, the photograph of the Earth and the starry background. Each is on a separate layer, and so may be moved around and manipulated at will. In this first example, we can see each element clearly.

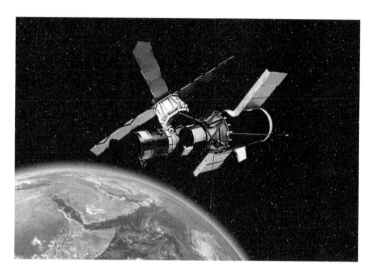

3 We're used to thinking of the Earth as lying beneath us – the normal state of affairs. But when we move the planet to the top of the screen, we create a tension that wasn't there before: this is no longer a satellite hovering above the earth, but a spaceship creeping upon it surreptitiously.

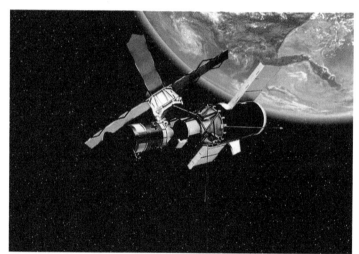

5 We can make the lettering more eerie and atmospheric by adding a glow treatment to it. Here, we've used the Outer Glow section of Layer Styles to make a white glow. In fact, the glow alone is enough: we don't need the actual letters at all. Set the text color to black, and set the layer mode to Screen so it disappears.

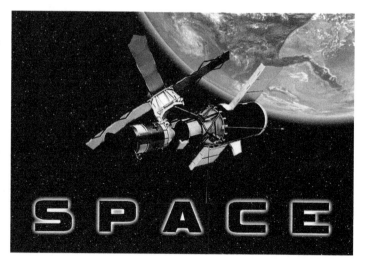

2 A simple question of moving the planet so it overlaps the satellite makes a huge difference to the unity of the image. Rather than being two separate elements, they're now combined in a single image: the satellite is clearly a small object in front of the planet, whereas previously it could have been an enormous space station behind it.

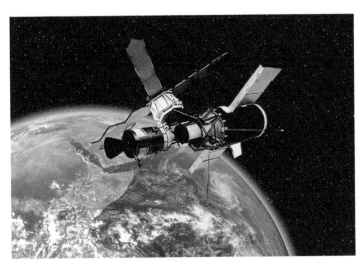

4 Every science fiction movie needs its own font – and there are dozens to choose from. We'll use the rather sedate Ray Larabie font Vipnagorgialla, which works well. The text is spaced out here, using the Tracking control on the Character palette.

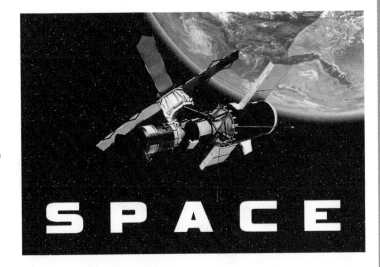

6 We could just stop at the end of step 5, but let's unify our poster still further. Here, we've created a solid layer, filled with pale blue, at the top of the layer stack; set to Multiply mode, it adds a uniform tint to the whole artwork. When the 'In space...' line is added in white above this, it stands out from the rest of the poster.

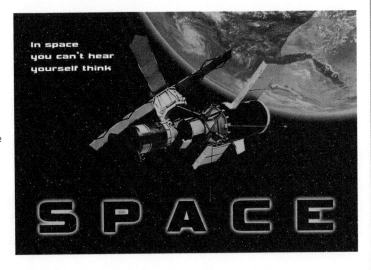

 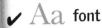
MORE INFO

● The effect used on the text gives a space-like, subtle glow around the letters – be careful not to make this glow too large, or it will simply start to look fuzzy. Because it's a Layer Style effect applied to live text, we can change the font, wording and tracking as much as we like, and the glow effect will be retained whatever we do.

● In step 6, we've added a new layer filled with blue, and set to Multiply. It's now easy to change this color with the Hue/Saturation dialog: this allows us to experiment with different colors (by dragging the Hue slider) and different opacities (by dragging the Lightness slider). Alternatively, we could create a Solid Color adjustment layer at the top of the layer stack, and set that to Multiply instead.

● Placing the planet at the top of the screen, rather than at the bottom, is a technique used frequently in science fiction movies. In almost every eposide of *Star Trek*, for example, when you see the USS *Enterprise* approaching a planet it will be from below, rather than from above. It looks far more space-like that way.

SHORTCUTS

[MAC] [WIN] [BOTH]

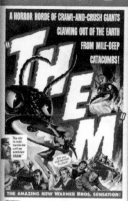

A HORROR HORDE OF CRAWL-AND-CRUSH GIANTS CLAWING OUT OF THE EARTH FROM MILE-DEEP CATACOMBS!

THE AMAZING NEW WARNER BROS. SENSATION!

The 1950s may have been Hollywood's Golden Age, seeing the release of *12 Angry Men*, *Rear Window* and *Singin' in the Rain* – but it's also the decade that produced some of the corniest, cheesiest horror movies ever created.

The posters of the time reflected the mood of the films: brash, gaudy, ludicrous in scale and conception.

You'll notice an anomaly in the poster we're creating here. The title of our imaginary movie is *Day of the 20 Foot Hamster* – but the rodent in our illustration is clearly many hundreds of feet high. This, too, was a feature of the posters of the period: scale was frequently greatly exaggerated in order to pull viewers into the theaters. As, indeed, were the comments that adorned the posters themselves.

1 The text for this film is set in the font Bullpen, designed by Ray Larabie. To achieve the distortion, we first use the Warp Text dialog to set an arc, using fairly small numbers – just a 19% distortion here. The small amount of horizontal distortion adds the beginnings of a sense of perspective to the text.

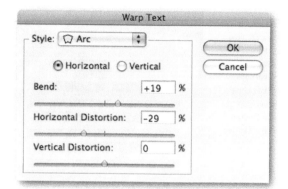

3 The words 'Day of the' are added in a similar way to the main headline. Both sets of text are colored yellow, and the pixels locked so we don't spill over the edge (see More Info); the red is painted on with a large, soft-edged brush (top). Then Layer Styles are used (bottom) to add a hard-edged drop shadow, and an Inner Glow to give the soft stroke around the edge.

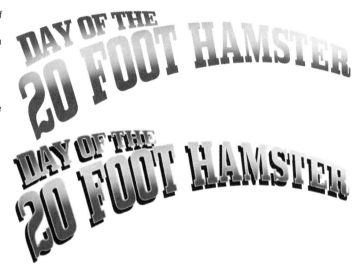

5 To integrate the hamster into the scene, it's important to place some foreground elements in front of it. The best way to do this is to hide the hamster layer, and select a group of buildings from the background layer; make a new layer from these, and bring them in front of the hamster, then reveal the hamster layer again.

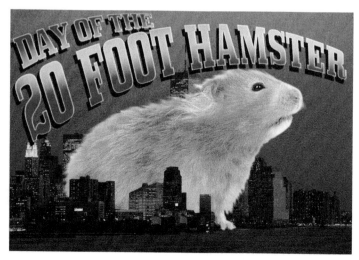

2 When we stretch the text vertically (top) we exaggerate the arc added in the first step – which is why we used such a small amount. To add the perspective distortion (bottom) we first need to turn the text into a regular, editable layer (see More Info). Then, using Free Transform, hold *ctrl* ⌘ as you drag the corner handles to produce a more radial view.

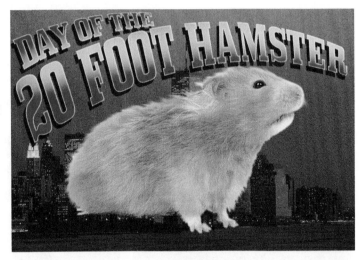

MORE INFO

● We've used the Arc distortion in step 1, as it suits the style of this poster. But it's worth experimenting with different warp methods: remember, the Warp Text effect is live, and can be adjusted at any point.

● When we distort the text in step 2, we need to turn it into regular pixels first – use Layer > Rasterize > Type. Once this is done, however, we lose access to the editability of the text, so be sure to check your spelling first. An alternative method would be to turn the text into a Smart Object, and to apply the perspective distortion to that – but this would entail creating additional layers to hold the painted color.

4 The text stands out far more clearly against a dark background – could this be the reason why key scenes in these movies are so often set at night? The hamster is positioned so that it's clearly the dominant figure in this nocturnal landscape.

● In step 3 we begin with yellow text, and paint the red effect on using a large soft-edged brush. But if we were merely to paint on the layer, the red would be seen over the background as well. The solution is to lock the transparency of the layer, using the icon at the top of the Layers palette; or, as a shortcut, use the / key. Now, when we paint in red on the layer, the red only has an effect where it goes over pixels already present in the layer.

6 Finishing touches include adding more headlines, and adding some color and shading to the hamster layer to make it blend in better with the rest of the scene. The dummy credits at the bottom are the same as those we've used earlier in this chapter. Finally, adding the torn paper layer in Hard Light mode adds a creased, worn look; the color helps to unify all the picture elements.

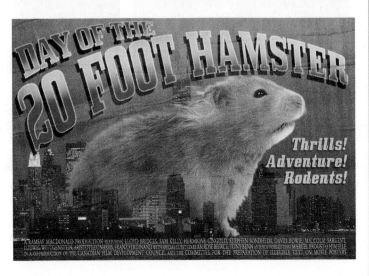

Horror movies

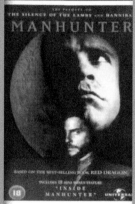

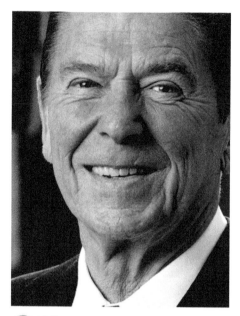

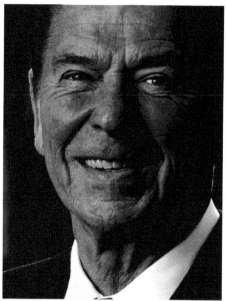

The film *The Silence of the Lambs* was a huge hit for both Jodie Foster and Anthony Hopkins – and the public wanted more of Hopkins' character, Hannibal Lecter. *Red Dragon* was filmed in 2002 – but the film of this prequel had already been made as *Manhunter* in 1986. The posters for the two films are remarkably similar, given the 16-year gap between them: it seems that the horror of a psychotic individual is nearly timeless.

We'll see if we can emulate this style of hard, moody lighting with a horror movie of our own.

1 We'll start with an official publicity photograph of Ronald Reagan, for no reason other than turning this amiable grin into an image of menace will present us with a particular challenge. Our personal political views have no place in a book of this kind.

2 We can darken Reagan's features using the Curves adjustment: open the dialog and drag down in the center of the RGB curve to produce this deeper, stronger effect. At the same time, take out a little green in order to boost the red appearance.

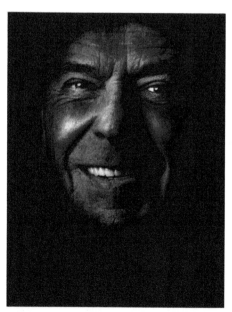

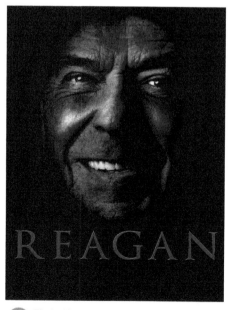

5 We can also use the Dodge tool to add sparkle to the eyes and teeth, which makes them jump out of the picture. Use the Burn tool, set to Midtones, to add strategic darkness within the face: under the eyes, below the mouth, around the cheek, and so on. This will help to make the image look properly shaded.

6 The text here is set in Manfred Klein's font Optimus Princeps, which has precisely the sedate, traditional, elegant look that counterbalances the menace of the image perfectly. A little tracking spaces out the letters: use the Character palette to add spacing.

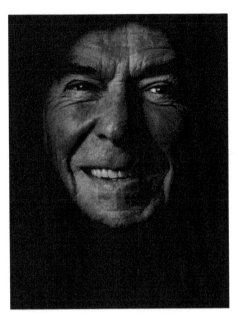

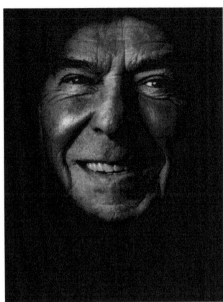

3 Since the image is going to appear on a black background, the easiest way to mask it is to paint in black on a new layer above it, using a soft-edged brush. At present, we're only concerned with painting around the edge of the face.

4 We need to bring out those highlights on the cheek and the brow, to make them shine a little more menacingly. Duplicate the Reagan layer and use the Dodge tool, set to Highlights, to brighten up these areas – but be careful not to brighten it too much.

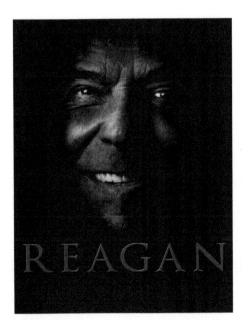

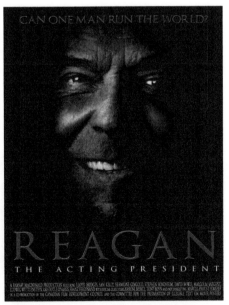

7 Add another new layer, and paint on here in black to make the visible portion of the face narrower. We want to hide those laugh lines around the mouth, to make him look more sinister – and we can also cut down the amount of light on the forehead and cheeks by painting over them.

8 The remainder of the text is added in the same font, with more spacing on the subtitle 'The Acting President' so that it fills the full width of the poster. The nonsense text at the bottom, once again, is there purely to complete the effect. Note how the top text frames the face neatly.

MORE INFO

● Although it's not specifically mentioned in the text each time, I've created a duplicate layer for each adjustment stage of this workthrough. When creating the initial black mask in step 3, it's easy enough to switch between the Brush tool and the Eraser tool to paint the shadow in and out; but when we're adding shading directly to the image using the Dodge and Burn tools, we need to be able to maintain editability. Creating new layers at each stage allows us to experiment without ever damaging our artwork irrevocably.

● We can use the Character palette in step 6 to space out the text. Alternatively, select it all with the Type tool and use *alt* to increase spacing between all the characters.

● Despite adding deep shadows to the face, the image of Ronald Reagan remained smiling right up to step 7, when we add the second black mask. That's because until this stage, we could still see laugh lines around the mouth and eyes – which suggest a far more pleasant character than we want to indicate. Hiding these lines makes the smile look more menacing.

SHORTCUTS

 MAC   WIN   BOTH

DISASTER
HAS A
PASSPORT

Comedy movies

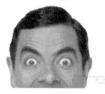

Comedy posters have to make the film look funny. Often, this is achieved mainly through the expression on the face of the main character: and when the character is big enough, like Rowan Atkinson, his beaming face is enough to sell the movie on its own.

There are other common factors that typify the comedy poster. Fonts are usually playful, bold and sans serif, and will frequently have some or all of their letters set at an angle. This accentuates the wackiness of the poster, clearly signaling to the viewer that laughs are in store.

Some comedy movies are parodies, such as *Airplane* and *Police Squad*, in which case the poster will reflect the genre the movie is sending up. But the predominant feel is always bright and airy, making full use of primary colors and plenty of white.

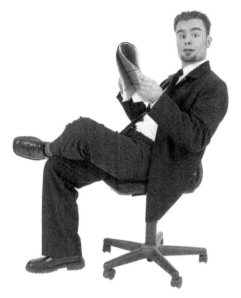

1 The main image is, as always, the key element in this poster. Here's our publicity shot: it shows the lead character with a surprised expression. But he's too far away, and the detail of the chair stand is too fiddly and distracting.

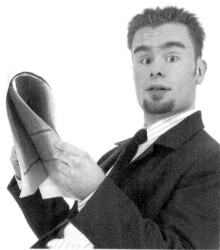

2 Zooming in on the shot helps a lot, and the shape neatly frames the bottom of the poster. It's not a bad arrangement, but it somehow lacks immediacy. The character still looks too detached and too distant for us to engage with him.

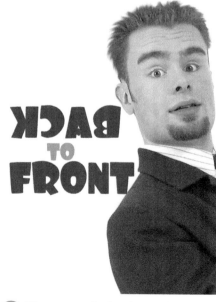

5 It's common practice to make a graphical pun on one or more words in the title, if this is appropriate. If the film were about learner drivers, for example, we might place the letter 'L' in red on a white square so it looked like an L-plate. Here, the word 'Back' is crying out to be reversed – and it is still legible.

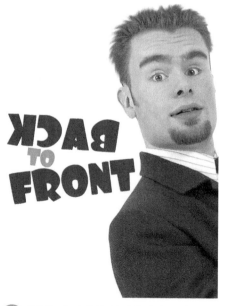

6 Rotating the individual text blocks to wacky angles helps to get across the idea of the film as comedy. Again, this is a common procedure in comedy films. In the poster for *Mr Bean's Holiday*, above left, just the letter 'A' has been rotated: this neatly gives a sense of impending disaster.

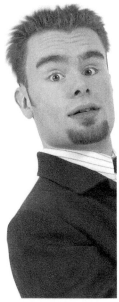
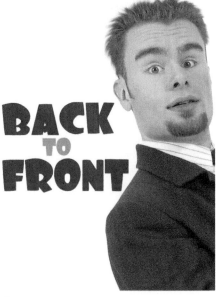

MORE INFO

● The angle at which a figure is placed can have a big impact on the comedic value of the image. In step 3, for example, we could have left the figure upright, simply flipping the original image horizontally:

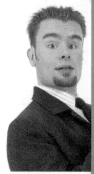

It frames the side of the page well enough, but there's no humor in the pose. In the rotated version, the overall impression is that the man is walking out of shot, and has leant back slightly to look at us because we've just caught his intention. The pose also makes him appear to be in motion – and, without looking where he's going, we can be fairly sure some disaster is about to befall him.

● The word 'back' works when reversed because it's a very short, recognizable word. This wouldn't work with longer words, as they'd be too hard to read.

3 Zooming in to a head shot gives the poster more impact. We have to flip him horizontally so we can fit the text on the left. Rotating the image counter-clockwise makes him lean backwards into the frame, which in itself is a comical pose.

4 The text we've chosen here is Ray Larabie's font Foo, which has a nicely casual, comic look. Set each word in a different text block, so they can be moved around and manipulated independently: for example, we clearly need the 'to' smaller than the other two words.

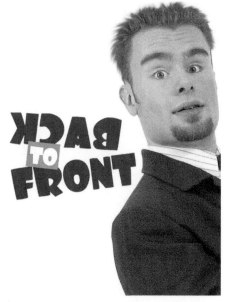
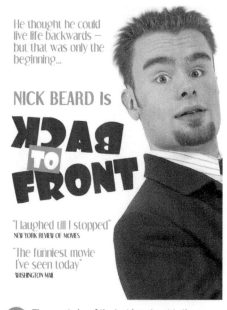

7 To make the title stick together as a logo, it helps to add a unifying element. In this case, this is achieved by making a rotated blue square behind the word 'to', and setting the word in white. Because the square overlaps both words above and below, it links them together visually.

8 The remainder of the text here is set in the font Dream Orphans. It's light and airy, and its quirkiness of letter form has a potentially comic element to it. As with many such posters, the quotes from newspaper reviews help to reinforce the idea that this movie really is funny.

04.11

French art house

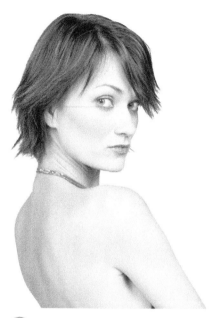

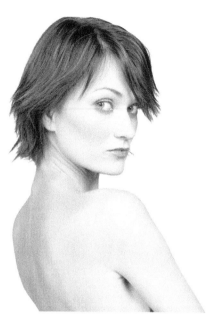

The French and international versions of the posters for the 1986 movie *Betty Blue* are similar – except the French version shows a man and woman at the bottom. Clearly, for the French, the relationship is more important than the girl on her own.

The poster is typical of the genre: a pouting, unsmiling girl; the stark treatment of the image, turning it almost into a graphic element; the dark, moody background.

While we don't have Beatrice Dalle to model for us, we do have an image of a girl who fits the bill well enough.

1 This girl is taken from the photos.com collection of royalty-free images. She's looking over her shoulder at us in a scornful way that well befits the French temperament: and her short haircut is well matched to current French styling.

2 We need to remove that halter neck top from her dress, of course. If there's one thing the French expect from their art movies it's naked women, and to suggest otherwise on the poster would be disastrous for sales. Use the Clone tool to get rid of it.

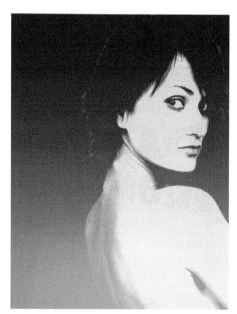

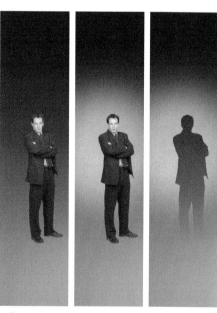

5 The girl looked fine at the end of the last step, and fitted the frame well: her eyes started a good diagonal that ran down the arm to the corner of the image. But by moving her over to the right, we create additional tension: she's now clearly turning her back on us, the viewer.

6 By adding a second figure we get in a suggestion of that all-important relationship issue. This man's in a suitable pose (left). Paint a glow on a new layer behind him with a large, soft-edged brush (center); then delete the man's area from the glow, and hide the man layer for a subtle silhouette effect (right).

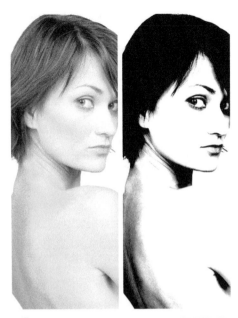

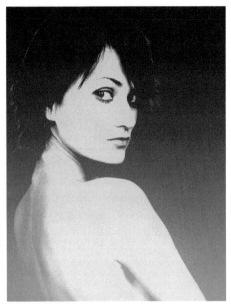

(3) To make the stark version, first use `ctrl` `Shift` `U` `⌘` `Shift` `U` to desaturate the image, taking all the color out of it. Then use the Brightness and Contrast adjustment to increase the contrast significantly (right): see More Info for more on this.

(4) Color the image using Color Balance to add a little blue and cyan to it. Color the background blue, and use the Gradient tool to darken the top; then set the mode of the girl's layer to Screen, so that her hair disappears into the background.

MORE INFO

● In step 3 we use the Brightness & Contrast adjustment to produce this almost black and white version of the grayscale image. In recent versions of Photoshop, however, this adjustment has been changed so that it has a more subtle effect on the image – which means it will no longer produce an effect as strong as we want. To make it behave as it did before, check the Use Legacy button at the bottom right of the dialog. We can now apply a large amount of contrast to the picture, modifying the brightness as required.

● In step 6 we delete the man's outline from the glow layer. The best way to do this, of course, is to use a layer mask. First, hold `ctrl` `⌘` and click on his thumbnail to load as a selection; then make a layer mask for the glow layer, and fill the selection with black. When we hide the man, just his silhouette remains. If we move the glow around, the silhouette will move with it. But if we click on the chain icon between the layer and its mask, we can move the two independently. This can make it easier for us to adjust the position of the silhouette within the glow, as we can drag it while the glow remains in place.

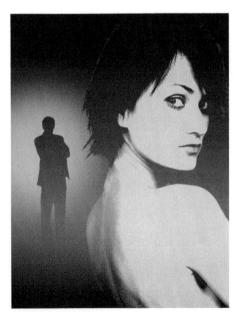

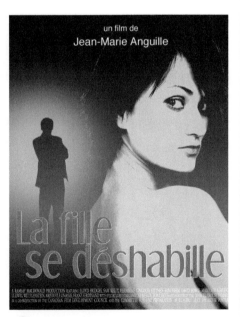

un film de
Jean-Marie Anguille

La fille
se déshabille

(7) In theory, we delete the area taken up by the back of the woman's hair from the glow layer, since the scale indicates that it's clearly behind her. But leaving the glow visible, as we do in step 8, makes it look more natural, as if it's so bright that it's dazzling us enough to shine through her hair.

(8) The text is added in the font Dream Orphans, in a color that stands out well against the blue and black that predominates here. It has a slight shadow, created using Layer Styles: change the mode from Multiply to Normal, and choose white for the color. To avoid fuzziness, set the Size to 0 and the Spread to 100.

Film noir

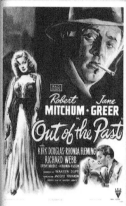

'Film noir' is the French for 'black film' – in the sense of dark themes, dark scenes and an overriding air of gloom. No happy endings to be expected here.

Film noir posters followed a definite pattern, as the two near-identical examples here show. The man was always smoking, and smoking played a large part in the films.

The posters convey the shabbiness of the men and their surroundings, the mock glamor of the women, and the air of desperation that pervades the movies.

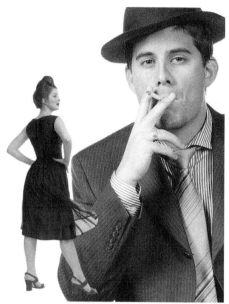

1 Our two characters are in costume and ready to go. She has her billowing dress and her haughty pose; he has his open-necked shirt, his fedora and, of course, the prop he could never last a scene without – his cigarette.

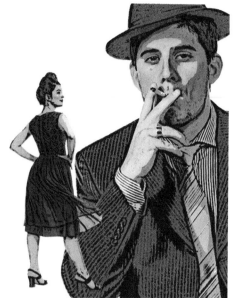

2 Applying Filter > Artistic > Poster Edges to both layers makes them look more hand painted than photographed. Boost their colors with the Hue/Saturation dialog to make them larger than life, and darken with Curves if required.

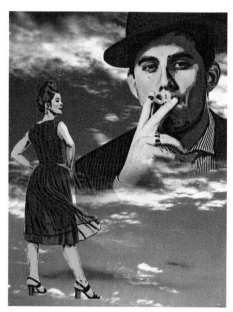

5 We need some sort of background for the top left. Posters of the period often used a painted texture here that didn't represent anything; we can do the job effectively with a photograph of clouds at sunset. Darkening the image considerably makes it look more moody and threatening.

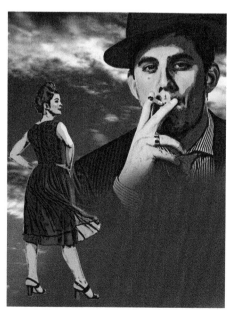

6 To make a clear area in the bottom right, we need to cover up some of that cloud texture. Make a new layer, above the clouds, and sample a blue color from the sky; paint on the new layer with a large soft brush to obscure the sky from this region.

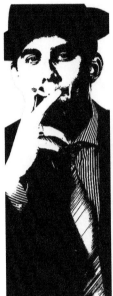
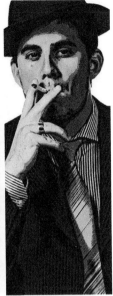
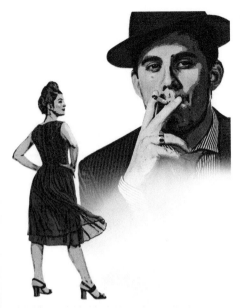

MORE INFO

● In step 3, we change the mode of the layer to Multiply before applying the Threshold adjustment. This is so we can see the end result through it: as we drag the Threshold slider, we can see how much of the face is being shaded. After applying the adjustment, the effect may well be too strong; I've reduced it to 60% opacity here.

● To reduce the size of the quotation marks in step 7, select one of them and use ctrl Shift < ⌘ Shift < to make the type size smaller. It will also appear much lower down, so with the character still selected, use alt Shift ↑ ⌥ Shift ↑ to raise the baseline to line up with the tops of the letters. The easiest way to make the other quotation mark is to copy and paste this one, then replace it with the correct symbol.

● In step 8, we need to add three stars' names in two different fonts. The best way to do this is to set one name, using both fonts, and adjust the leading to fit; then duplicate the text block twice to make the other two names. With the Move tool, hold alt ⌥ as you drag a name to make a copy, then add Shift to move it only horizontally.

3 To make his shadow stronger, duplicate his layer and desaturate using ctrl Shift U ⌘ Shift U. Change the layer mode to Multiply so only the darkest areas are visible, then use Image > Adjustments > Threshold to turn it to pure black and white.

4 We need to make room for our titles, so make a layer mask for the man's layer and paint out on here using a large, soft-edged brush. If we set the Threshold layer to use this as a Clipping Mask, it will be hidden by the layer mask as well.

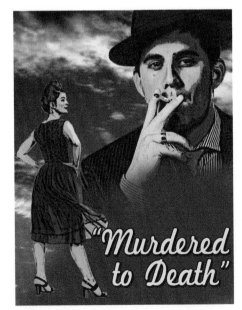
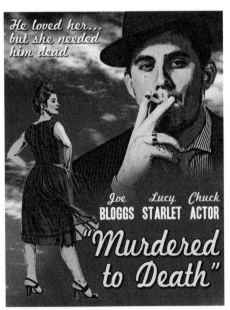

7 The font we've used here is Dieter Steffmann's Marketing Script, which captures the hand lettered style of the time. It was customary to include quotation marks around the title, which is something we'd never do today; make this very small, and raise them so they line up with the letter tops (see More Info).

8 The tag line, top left, can be set in the same font. It's also fine for the first names of the actors – but their surnames need to be bolder, for contractual reasons. Here, the surnames are set in Headline One, a condensed bold face that sits neatly with the script font used for the first names.

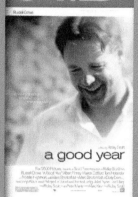

Romantic comedy

'Pleasant, pretty and predictable... one might add piddling' was how the *New York Times* described *A Good Year* upon its release in 1996.

It was certainly a departure for Russell Crowe, fresh from his successful roles as hard-bitten action heroes in *Master and Commander* and *Gladiator*. The poster for the movie had to show the film's star in a different light altogether – not so much to put off the diehard action fans, as to draw in female viewers who might have admired Crowe's physique but who have previously been put off by the amount of gore in his movies.

And so the result was a poster that shows a warm, sunny movie that we know from the start is bound to have a happy ending. As some wag once said: 'Men like films in which lots of people die quickly; women like films in which one person dies slowly.'

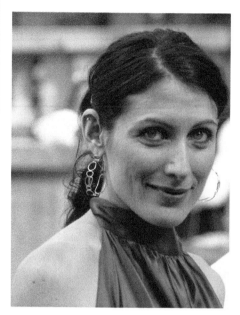

1 This photograph of actress Lisa Edelstein was taken by Christopher Peterson, and is taken from Wikipedia under the Creative Commons licence. Despite the busy background, it's an appealing pose that will do as our starting point.

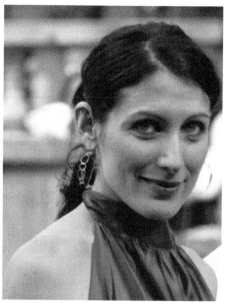

2 The first thing we need to do is to soften the features. The best way to do this is to use the Filter > Blur > Median, which works in a similar way to Gaussian Blur but keeps hard edges crisp. This has taken out the worst of the pores and wrinkles.

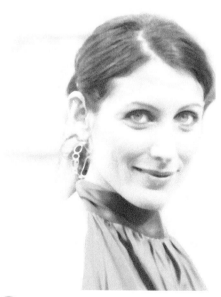

5 We could do a hard cutout of this image, but sometimes it's better just to paint out the background. Make a new layer, and paint on here in white with a soft-edged brush, leaving the head visible. It's worth keeping that faint horizontal behind her, as this stretches the image neatly off the left of the page.

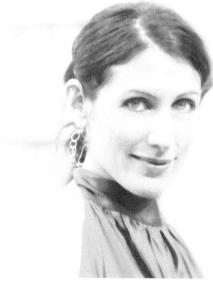

6 It's looking good – but not yet good enough. With the background largely hidden we can concentrate on the face, and the blemishes are more apparent – the bags under the eyes, the lines around the mouth. Use the Clone tool to hide these: see More Info for a neat way of doing this.

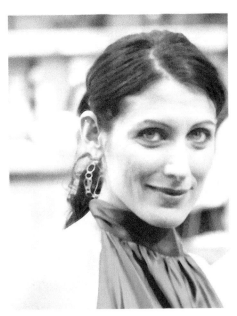

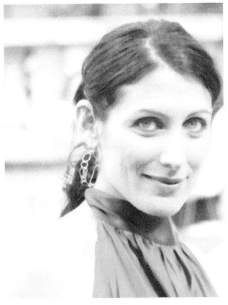

3 It's standard practice when photographing actresses and models to bleach out the image, This hides some blemishes, and also conceals the hard line of the nose, making features look more dainty and refined. Use the Curves adjustment to do this.

4 While we're using Curves, add a fair amount of red and a little green to the mix. This warms up the image considerably, bringing a summery glow to the whole picture. Far more appealing than the blue image we started with.

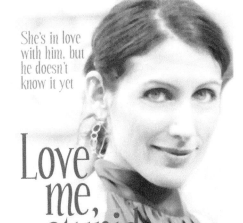

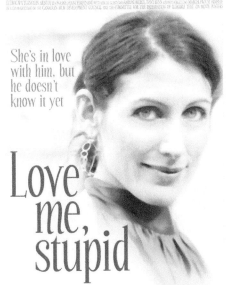

7 The text here is set in the Ray Larabie font Echelon, which has exactly the loose, freeform feel we need for this kind of movie. We've set the smaller text in the same blue as her dress, to tie in with it; but setting the main headline in this color would look weak. Instead, the color is sampled from her lipstick.

8 There was a problem with the image after the previous step: the end of 'stupid' was running into the clothing, making it hard to read; and the horizontal line behind her head interfered with the word 'Love'. Paint out some more of the background on the mask layer to avoid the headline entirely.

MORE INFO

● In steps 3 and 4 we brighten and add color to the image. Rather than working directly upon it, it's always better to use an Adjustment Layer, chosen from the pop-up menu at the bottom of the Layers palette. This allows us to add the Curves adjustment, but in such a way that we can come back and edit it later if the results aren't exactly as we'd like.

● When we paint out around the back of the head, we can use a soft-edged brush to get a wispy, soft focus effect. But we need to remove that dark patch to the lower right of her jaw: it has to go in its entirety, as it's ugly and confusing. Use a very small brush to paint right up to the chin here.

● In step 6, we need to clone out the wrinkles. But it's best to do this on a new layer, in case the effect doesn't work. With Photoshop CS3 and above, there's an option in the Clone tool to sample the current layer and below: previously, we had to sample either just the current layer, or all layers. This means we can create a new layer above the image, but beneath the Adjustment Layer: we can clone over the wrinkles here, without damaging the image beneath.

SHORTCUTS

95

Apocalyptic thriller

THE YEAR
2027:
THE LAST DAYS OF
THE HUMAN RACE
NO CHILD HAS BEEN
BORN FOR 18 YEARS
HE MUST PROTECT
OUR ONLY HOPE

Clive Owen
Julianne Moore
Michael Caine

Children of men

a film by Alfonso Cuarón

The film *Children of Men* presented a future that was bleak, anarchic and violent. In this it was strikingly similar to all the other movies set in a post-apocalyptic world, which are also for the most part bleak, anarchic and violent: *Mad Max*, *Waterworld*, and many more.

The film has a strong visual style that's carried through into the publicity material. Clive Owen gazes at us ruggedly though a broken window: you can tell he's rugged because he hasn't shaved for a few days.

Unusually, I'm going to use this tutorial not to typify a genre, but to reproduce a single example of a film poster. That's because this poster presents several distinct points of interest – the stark photographic treatment, the broken glass, the fuzzy stencil lettering – that I think are of enough interest for us to want to see how they're assembled.

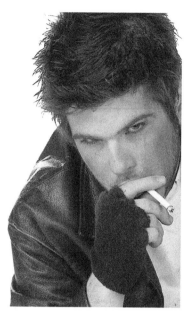

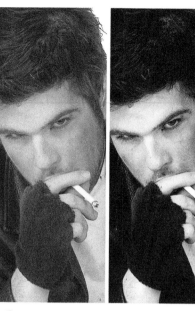

1 This photograph, from the Photos.com collection, has the right kind of anti-establishment rebellion to it, and will make a good subject for the poster. But it's too warm, having been photographed under perfect studio lighting: we need to make it more gritty.

2 Begin by duplicating the layer. Desaturate the duplicated version using `ctrl Shift U` `⌘ Shift U`, to produce a grayscale copy (left); then set the mode of this copy to Hard Light, which produces a stark photographic effect (right).

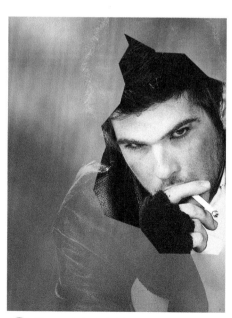

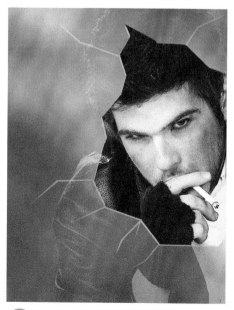

5 If we want this to look like real glass, we need to be able to see through it. Lower the opacity of the layer to around 70%, and use the Dodge and Burn tools to add some highlights to it, to break up the uniformity of the surface.

6 The edge of the glass has to be given some thickness. This is created by nudging the shape of the hole and intersecting it with the original glass – see More Info for details. The cracks are drawn with the Lasso tool, and filled with white on the same layer.

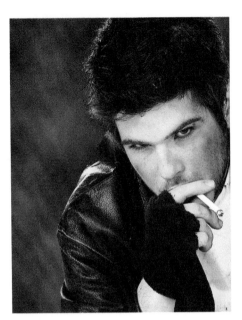

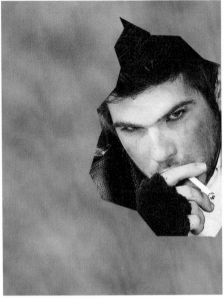

③ Add a little blue to the grayscale version of the photograph, and we get an image that more closely matches that seen on the original poster. To make the background, choose dark blue and black as the foreground and background colors, and choose Filter > Render > Clouds.

④ The 'hole' in the glass is selected using the Lasso tool. Inverse the selection using `ctrl` `Shift` `I` `⌘` `Shift` `I`, and make a new layer: choose white and pale blue as the foreground and background colors, and run the Clouds filter again to make the glass. This filter adds a useful starting texture.

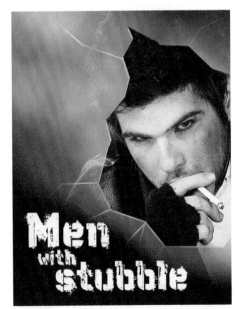

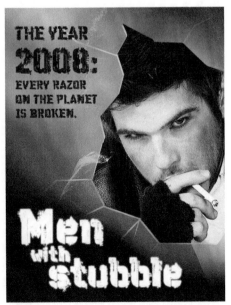

⑦ The font used here is Wunderback Mix, and it's a useful degraded stencil design. Create each letter as a separate text block, so they can be moved around and sized independently. The shadow is painted on a new layer behind the text.

⑧ To make the headline a little softer, add a faint Outer Glow to it using Layer Styles. Be sure to set the glow color to white, rather than the default yellow. The remaining text is set in a deep blood red color to add to the sense of menace.

MORE INFO

● The Clouds filter, used for the background in step 3 and the glass in step 4, produces a random texture. If the first attempt doesn't look right, keep pressing `ctrl` `F` `⌘` `F` to repeat the texture until you get a result you like. You can also press `ctrl` `alt` `F` `⌘` `⌥` `F` for a tighter version of the Cloud texture.

● In step 6, we can create the glass edge as follows. Select the hole in the glass layer with the Magic Wand tool, then nudge this selection a couple of pixels down and to the left using the cursor keys (◄ and ▼). Hold `ctrl` `alt` `Shift` `⌘` `⌥` `Shift` and click on the glass layer's thumbnail in the Layers palette: this key combination produces the intersection of the new selection with the old one, and so in this case will create a selection of just a couple of pixels around the edge. Use the Lasso tool to add the cracks from the corners to the selection, holding `alt` `⌥` to trace straight lines. Then make a new layer, and fill the selection with white: use the Burn tool to add a little shading to it. Lower the opacity of this layer to around 50% for a convincing glass effect.

SHORTCUTS

Psychedelia

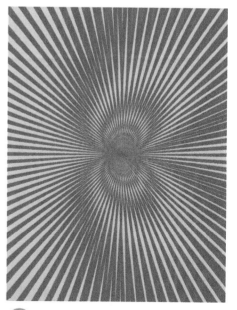

At one time, every student's wall would be adorned with posters. In the 1960s and 70s these were guaranteed to be one of two subjects: either a girl lifting her tennis skirt, or a multicolored piece of psychedelia.

The subjects of these posters varied from Che Guevara to Janis Joplin, but they all had features in common: a dazzling array of colors, and an op art background image.

The colors were produced from photographs by messing around with the plates in the printing process. We'll use a simpler method directly in Photoshop, using a standard adjustment.

We'll also see how to make an eye-popping background of interfering lines from scratch, which we'll place behind our treated image to complete the poster.

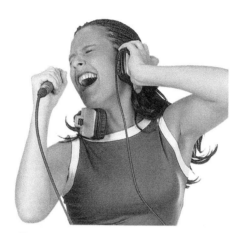

1 In the absence of a platinum-selling rock star, we'll have to make do with this image of a singer from www.photos.com. I've recolored the shirt, which was originally black – we need some color in there to start with.

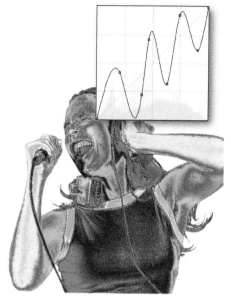

2 To make the psychedelic colors, open the Curves dialog (ctrl M ⌘ M). Click roughly one quarter of the way along the curve, and drag upwards; then click just before the halfway point and drag down. Continue to drag up and down, making this stepping effect. Adjust as necessary – see More Info for details.

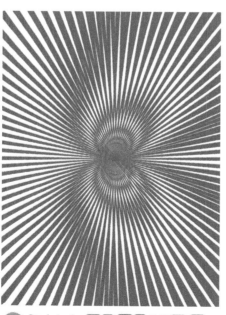

5 Deselect using ctrl D ⌘ D. Hold alt ⌥ as you drag a copy of the finished layer, and the two will interact to make this interference pattern. You'll see that when you drag the copy to the side it will no longer reach that edge; scale it to fit, as necessary.

6 Recolor the new version of the interference pattern using any color that seems appropriate; then color the background using a different color. Here, I've used shades of blue and purple because they match the colors in the treated photograph.

MORE INFO

● In step 2, when you first drag up on the curve the whole image will simply get much brighter: that's what the Curves adjustment is for. It's only as you click more points along it, and drag up and down, that the colors go haywire like this. Depending on your image, the curve you get may not look exactly like this one: experiment with dragging points up and down once you have the basic curve, to see how it affects the image.

● In step 3 it helps to trace with the Lasso tool just outside the Canvas area. To do this, drag the window size so it's slightly larger than the canvas, and you'll be able to click the Lasso in the gray area outside. The click points are numbered:

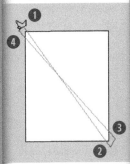

If you don't like holding alt ⌥ while tracing, you could instead choose the Polygonal Lasso from the Toolbar – it's behind the regular Lasso.

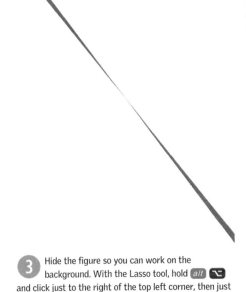

3 Hide the figure so you can work on the background. With the Lasso tool, hold alt ⌥ and click just to the right of the top left corner, then just to the left of the bottom right corner. Click just above the bottom right, then just below the top left: fill with color on a new layer, and you'll get this thin double triangle.

4 Select All (ctrl A ⌘ A) and use Free Transform (ctrl T ⌘ T) to rotate the shape by about 5° and press Enter to apply the transformation. Then press ⌘ alt Shift T ctrl alt Shift T and you'll duplicate the transformation: keep pressing that key combination to rotate in a complete circle.

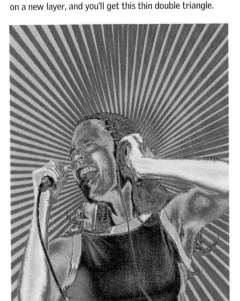

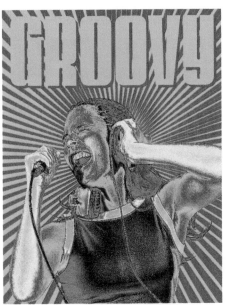

7 With the photograph visible once more, we can see how the psychedelic lines seem to radiate from behind the head. Avoid the temptation to add any drop shadows or outer glows, even though these might improve the image: the technique wasn't available then.

8 This text is set in the Ray Larabie font Velvenda Cooler, and the main color is the same blue as the background. The shadow could have been made using the Drop Shadow in Layer Styles, but it's sometimes easier just to duplicate the font layer and recolor it.

Swinging sixties

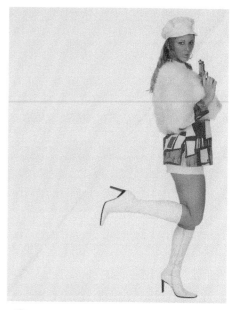

In 1966 *Time* magazine devoted an edition to Swinging London, celebrating as well as fueling the explosion of counter-culture that made the 1960s such a memorable decade.

As well as the psychedelia, the tuning in and the dropping out, the 1960s was the decade of cool. Music was cool, clothes were cool, design was cool; even comedy was cool, for a while.

The 1960s produced an outpouring of visual styles. We've already looked at psychedelia; here we'll examine a design style that used black and white photographs, bold splashes of color, and a wackiness of typography that had never been seen before. And since the 1960s saw the birth of the James Bond movie, we'll mark the era of the spy film with a typically wacky comedy that combines some of the most common themes of the day.

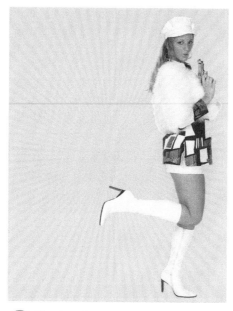

1 It's not easy finding models in appropriately groovy gear for the 1960s, but I came across this one on the excellent photos.com royalty-free site. Her pose is perfect, and will define the layout for the rest of the poster.

2 Desaturating the model using *ctrl Shift U* *⌘ Shift U* turns her to grayscale; changing the mode of the layer from Normal to Hard Light means she'll only darken up the background. As it stands, though, the image has lost some of its power.

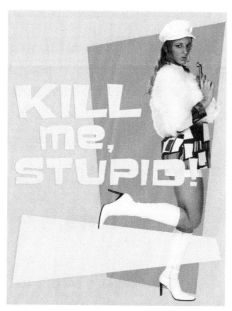

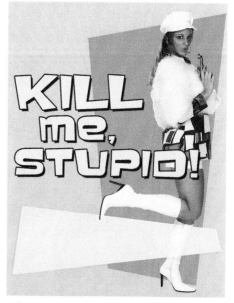

5 The text here is set in Baveuse, which captures the spirit of the 60s well. Each word is set as a separate text block, to make it easier to arrange the words: we could do it using letter spacing and leading, but as there are only three words it's better if we're able to drag them around as required.

6 The stroke is added using Layer Styles, which gives the words more legibility. The drop shadow is also from Layer Styles: set the Size value to zero to avoid any feathering, which would be out of character for the period. Set the opacity to 100% so we get a solid black shadow.

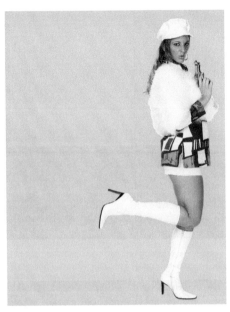

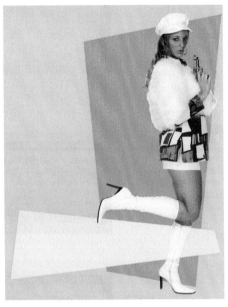

MORE INFO

● In step 4 we create two new color panels, making three colors in all. It's important that the colors all match in terms of density and feel. We've used pastel shades of pink and blue here, whose paleness matches the strong yellow. There's quite a wide range of pastel colors that could be chosen:

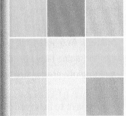

The yellow, incidentally, would be equally at home with stronger hues:

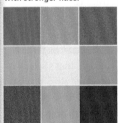

But these colors are not only out of keeping with the era, they're also far too strong to form a background – they'd just leap right out of the page at us, distracting the viewer from the poster's key elements.

3 Duplicate the layer, and change the mode of the copy to Hard Light. Now the white areas, of which there are a lot in this image, are returned to full strength: but the blue background is still seen through the midtones, such as the face and leg.

4 Draw irregular polygons with the Lasso tool – hold *alt* ⌥ to use it in Polygonal Lasso mode. On new layers, fill the selections with pink and yellow, or choose whichever colors you think are appropriate (but see More Info about the choice).

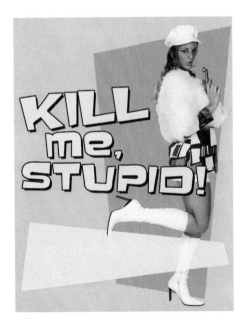

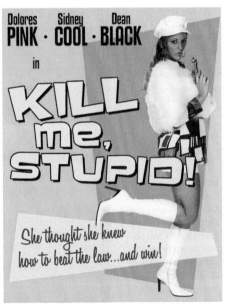

7 To add a little life to the title, and to stress that it's a comedy, rotate the words slightly. This misalignment adds a slight wackiness to the overall effect. Another good reason for setting the text as three separate blocks: it would be impossible to rotate them if it were all one.

8 The names of the stars are set in Kenyan Coffee. Set each group of firstname and surname as a separate text block, then duplicate the text block to make the other names – it would be hard to try to align two lines if it were all one block. The script at the bottom is Honey Script.

SHORTCUTS

MAC WIN BOTH

Motivational

1 We'll begin this poster by drawing a frame to hold thie image. Draw a rectangle with the Marquee tool to the size of the 'window', then inverse this selection using `ctrl` `Shift` `I` `⌘` `Shift` `I` and fill with black on a new layer. Use Edit > Stroke to apply a 1 pixel outside stroke. Here, I've also added a sunset – the first element of the montage.

I don't know who invented the motivational poster. I don't know who buys motivational posters. And above all, I can't imagine how bored and unmotivated office and factory workers would have to be in order to be uplifted by these crass, corny, clumsy truisms.

That said, the genre is ripe for parody. There's a distinct look to these posters that's seen nowhere else: the black frame, the serif white text with oversized first and last characters.

But there's more to these posters than the obvious. They tend to have very high production values, since they're stared at (in theory, at least) for days on end: glossy sunsets, warm glows, and a sense of overall perfection mark these posters out.

3 To make the reflective surface, we can begin by making a copy of the sky layer. Flip it vertically using Edit > Transform > Flip Vertical, and move it down to the bottom so that the reflection butts right up against the original sky. Don't lower the transparency yet – we'll do that later.

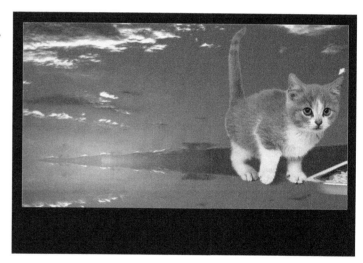

5 Select the reflected sky, kitten, and both parts of the tray, and choose New Group from Layers from the pop-up menu in the Layers palette. We can now lower the opacity of the group as a whole: around 30% produces this subtle sense of reflection in a black surface, which adds an immediate sense of luxury and sophistication to the image.

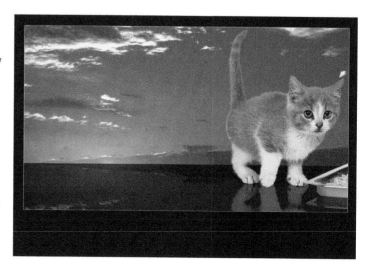

2 The sunset needs to be strengthened to make it more impressive: I used the Brightness and Contrast controls to do this, setting the Brightness to zero and the Contrast to 100 (recent versions of Photoshop only; smaller values before CS2). The cat is placed to fit well within the frame; the litter tray is moved right out of the picture, since it should only be noticed on second glance.

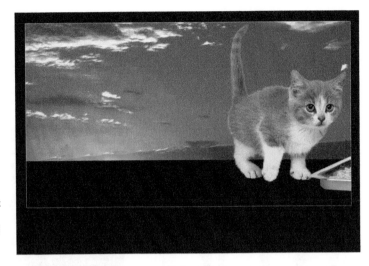

4 The kitten is duplicated and flipped vertically as well. The tray needs special treatment: first, the bottom section (below the rim) is selected, copied to a new layer, then flipped and sheared using Free Transform so that it fits beneath the original. Then the rim is copied to a new layer, and moved without being flipped behind the copied lower section. See More Info for how this works.

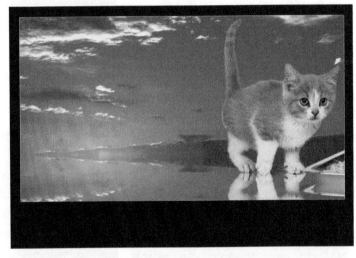

6 The text here is set in Optimus Princeps: it's an elegant and tasteful traditional serif. The first and last characters are enlarged by selecting them and using *ctrl* *Shift* *>* ⌘ *Shift* *>*, then shifted down using *alt* *Shift* ⬇ ⌥ *Shift* ⬇. Finally, I turned a copy of the cat's eyes upside down to make it look down – and to make it look slightly worried.

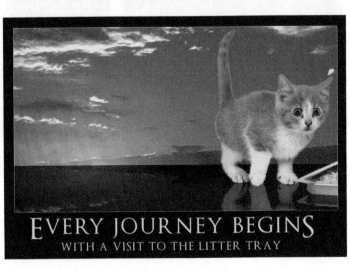

EVERY JOURNEY BEGINS
WITH A VISIT TO THE LITTER TRAY

MORE INFO

● Creating the reflection of the tray is the only tricky part of this job. To begin with, select the bottom of the tray and copy it to a new layer, and flip vertically:

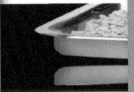

Then enter Free Transform, and hold *ctrl* ⌘ as you grab a side handle to shear it to meet the original:

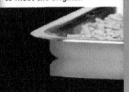

Then select the rim of the tray, and copy it to a new layer. No need to flip this: just drag it down beneath the previous layer:

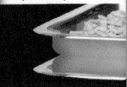

Once the opacity is reduced, any errors will be hidden, and the result will look like a convincing reflection.

SHORTCUTS

 MAC WIN BOTH

Museum exhibitions

Some exhibitions sell themselves. Any showing of Tutankhamun, for example, will draw enough crowds to be a guaranteed sell-out in just about any city in the world. For everything else, it's a hard sell.

Getting the paying public interested in a possibly minor art form requires skill, tact and a good deal of persuasion. We may think of museum curators as dusty, kindly folk who spend their days polishing fossils, but behind them there's the publicist whose job it is to keep these curators in work.

Museum posters need to convey sophistication and elegance. After all, they're appealing to a rather select portion of the community, and the posters need to flatter their sense of intellectual achievement. They also have to include a large amount of information, making the job harder.

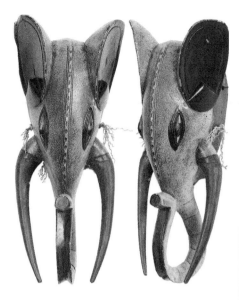

1 Every poster begins with an image. It's been decided that this figure should feature on the posters, but which angle should we use? While it might seem that the head-on view is more immediate, it's also more confusing. The three quarter view is clearer.

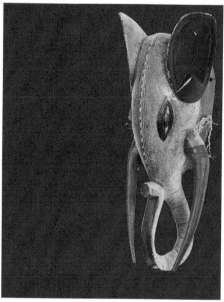

2 A red background is sampled from the elephant's ear, so we know it will be a good match for the original item. We have to place the mask on the right, facing into the page, so that the text can appear in its proper place on the left.

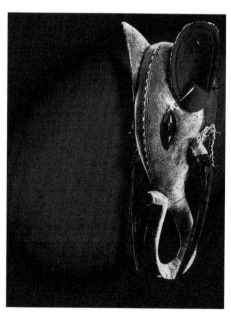

5 The drop shadow helps to position the object in front of the wall. Hold `ctrl` `⌘` as you click on its thumbnail to load it as a selection, then make a new layer behind; use `ctrl` `alt` `D` `⌥` `⌘` `D` to Feather the selection by, say, 8 pixels, and fill with black. Reduce the opacity of the layer, and move into place.

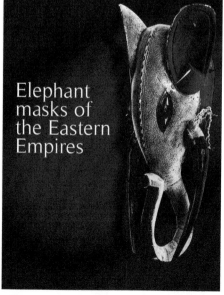

6 The font needs to be authoritative, traditional, and elegant. It's quite a tall order: we certainly can't set this in Times, because it's too staid and clunky. This is called Timeless, and has that extra refinement that makes it a good choice for this job.

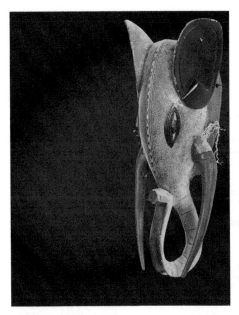

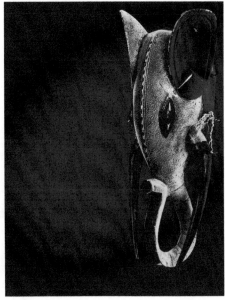

3 The shadow is painted on a new layer behind the mask, using a very large (around 500 pixels) soft-edge brush. This gives the impression of a spotlight being shone on the object in a darkened room, which enhances the sense of mystery and discovery.

4 We can't modify the object, but we can adjust its lighting. Here, the mask has been duplicated, and the mode of the copy changed to Hard Light. This is a little strong, so I've reduced the strength of the copy to 50% which gives a good compromise.

MORE INFO

● In step 5, we add the shadow below and to the left of the mask. Normally, we'd choose to add a shadow on the outside, rather than the inside of a composition; but the mask here is so clearly lit from the right that to put the shadow anywhere else would be confusing.

● To make the National Museum of Antiquities logo, I began with the main words in Optimus Princeps:

NATIONAL MUSEUM ANTIQUITIES

The 'OF' and 'THE' are set in smaller type, placed appropriately in the text:

ᵀᴴᴱ**NATIONAL MUSEUM** ᴼᶠ **ANTIQUITIES**

Tracking on the words helps them to fill the space; the lines accentuate the regularity of the form.

ᵀᴴᴱ**NATIONAL MUSEUM** ᴼᶠ **ANTIQUITIES**

If we wanted to reuse this logo, we could convert the layers into a Smart Object and scale it as a single layer.

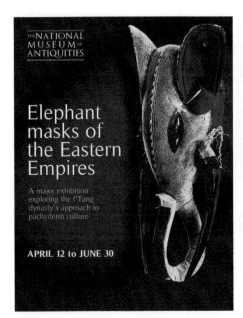

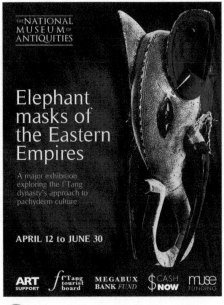

7 Once we've included the exhibition description, the logo of our fictional museum and the date of the exhibition, we're starting to fill up the space. The description can go in a less strong color – here, I've reduced the opacity of the layer to 50% – so that it fades more into the background, strengthening the headline.

8 It's a painful fact that just about every serious artistic endeavor needs commercial sponsorship. Painful for the designer, that is, since they're the ones who are going to have to fit all those clashing logos in at the bottom of the publicity. There's no way around it; just grit your teeth and get on with it.

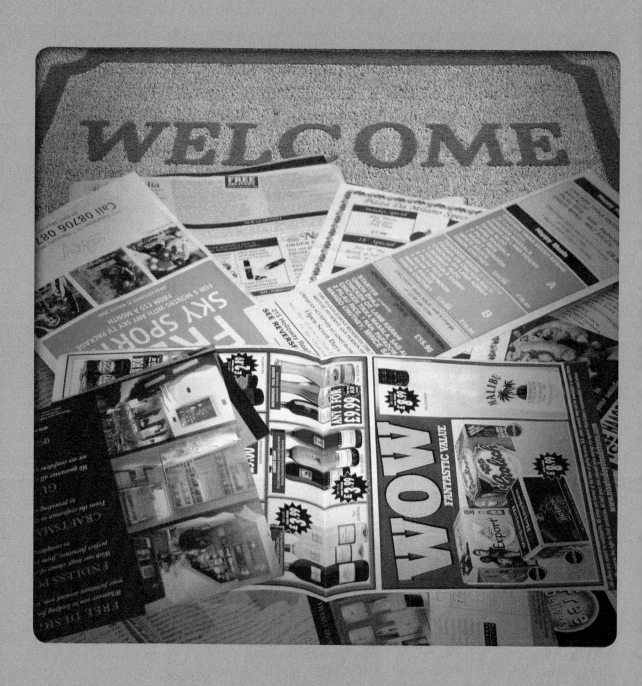

Works on paper

Printed matter assails us today as never before. Even in the age of email and the paperless office, we're besieged daily by junk mail, magazines and newspapers. We're handed flyers in the street, we're sent leaflets in the mail. And every single one of these has been designed to catch our attention, to make us buy into the product it's promoting.

The one thing all these disparate items have in common is that they're printed on paper. In this chapter we'll look at how to design a range of printed material, from medieval manuscripts to ransom notes.

Partly, we'll be exploring the design process, to find out why certain designs work and show how to implement them. But we'll also be looking at how to create the textures we need for parchment and certificates, and how to make flat artwork into a three-dimensional object.

paper

1. a material made of cellulose pulp derived mainly from wood or rags or certain grasses

2. an essay (especially one written as an assignment)

3. a daily or weekly publication on folded sheets; contains news and articles and advertisements

4. a medium for written communication

5. a scholarly article describing the results of observations or stating hypotheses

6. a business firm that publishes newspapers

7. the physical object that is the product of a newspaper publisher

Wordnet Dictionary

Ransom notes

The ransom note, painstakingly assembled from letters cut from newspapers, has a special place in our collective consciousness – even if the vast majority of us have never seen one, and hope never to do so.

There are a number of automated ways of creating ransom notes, such as the font Ransom Threat, shown above; there's also a website, http://contactsheet.org/junk/ransom.html, at which you can enter text to have it turned into a version of the note without your even having to install the font.

The trouble with this approach is that, first, it's hard to believe that hardened criminals making ransom demands would have the time to clip individual letters from a newspaper, when whole words are widely available. And, second, if every instance of a letter looks exactly like every other instance of the same letter, the whole thing is going to look utterly false.

1 We need a crumpled piece of paper for the background for our note – and it's the same piece we've used before, brightened and desaturated. Type the first word as a text block on its own, since we'll need to treat each word separately.

2 Continue to create a new text block for each word in the note, changing font as you go. When all the words have been created, select all the layers and make a new group from them; then duplicate the group and flatten it, so that all the words are on one layer.

5 In some cases, we'll want to add color to the lettering before adding the background. Choose the color you want to add (red, in the case of 'marked') and, with the selection made, press `alt` `Shift` `Backspace` `⌥` `Shift` `Backspace` to fill the lettering with the foreground color.

6 When all the words have backgrounds, and have been suitably rotated, we need to add a shadow effect to give the note a sense of three-dimensionality. Use Layer Styles to do this, but set the distance and the opacity very low: we don't want it to appear as if the scraps are floating above the surface.

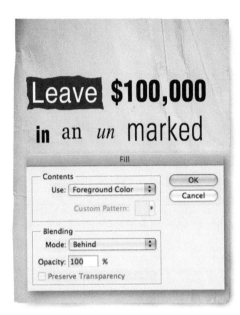

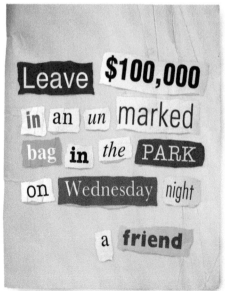

3 Now to turn each word into a scrap of paper. Using the Lasso tool, make a selection around each one, and pick a suitable foreground color (in this case, I've inverted the word first). Press *Shift Backspace* to open the Fill dialog, and choose Behind as the method.

4 Repeat the process for each word in the note. Remember that the bulk of the words will have a white or off-white background. After the background has been put in using the Fill dialog, rotate the selection slightly to make the words more uneven.

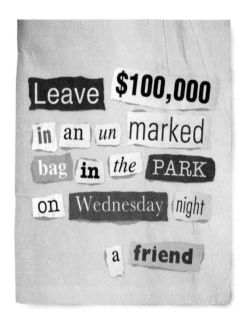

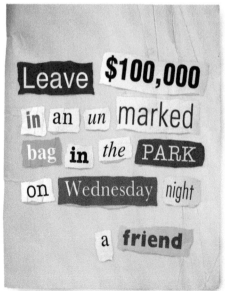

7 To add some texture to the scraps of paper, duplicate the background (the crumpled sheet) and make a clipping layer with the scraps of paper layer. Set the mode of this duplicated version to Hard Light, and darken it slightly. Now, on a new layer behind the scraps, paint some glue in gray with a hard-edged brush.

8 The glue we painted at the end of the previous step needs to be made to look more like glue and less like gray paint. Use Color Balance to add a little red and a little yellow to it, and add a bevel using Layer Styles. You may need to reduce the opacity of the layer if the effect is too strong – it should be just visible.

MORE INFO

● In step 2, we make all the words into a group by selecting the layers and choosing New Group from Layers in the pop-up menu at the top of the Layers palette. Duplicate the group by dragging it onto the New icon at the bottom of the palette, then use *ctrl E* *⌘ E* to merge all the layers into one. There are several reasons for doing this: first, it's easier then to add drop shadows to a single layer, as we do in step 6, rather than adding them to each layer in turn; and second, it's easier to apply the texture to a single layer, as we do in step 7.

● When shown in movies, ransom notes are almost always black and white. They do have a certain power that way – but we've recognized the fact that large words may well be found in glossy magazines, and the likelihood is that headlines in these magazines are more likely to be in color than in black and white. The choice is yours.

● Painting the glue at the end of step 7 adds a subtle touch that most viewers would barely notice; and yet the difference is marked, as it creates a visible bond between the cutout scraps of paper and the background sheet.

Medieval manuscripts

Some illuminated manuscripts were very highly decorated, with extensive use of gold leaf and hand painted imagery. We'll attempt something a little less ambitious for our first foray into the world of medieval parchment: a simple drop capital will do to suggest the form.

Originally, of course, these manuscripts (as the name implies) were painstakingly written by hand. The thick quills were ideally suited to the 'black letter' format of the characters, despite their lack of clear legibility.

With the advent of printing, many texts, such as bibles and other devotional material, continued to be printed using typeset versions of these old-style characters. It wasn't until the pioneering work of such typographers as Garamond that the letterform as we know it today began to evolve.

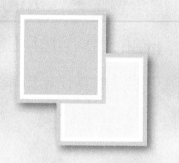

1 The first step in making our manuscript is to prepare the parchment. Creating a convincing texture here is easy, but it does require having the right starting foreground and background colors: aim for dark and light versions of tan, as seen here.

2 On a new layer, use Filter > Render > Clouds to create a texture like this. This filter creates a random texture using the foreground and background colors, so try a few variations until you achieve a pleasing result.

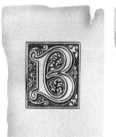
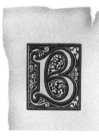

5 To add a little more texture, choose Filter > Texture > Texturizer, and choose Sandstone. The amount of relief should be minimal – you should barely be able to see it here. In this case, a relief setting of just 2 is sufficient. I've also added a Drop Shadow here, using Layer Styles.

6 The drop capital is part of the font Medieval Victoriana. Create the letter you want, then select inside it using the Magic Wand tool; on a new layer, behind the font, fill with yellow. Repeat for the red outline, filling on the same layer; the brown can be painted in by hand more easily.

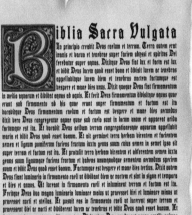

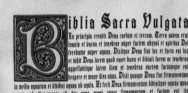

3 The torn-edge effect is easily created by making selections using the Lasso, and deleting them. Make the edges uneven, then take out a few tears that rip into the manuscript itself – but don't go too far, or you'll interfere with your artwork area.

4 Use the Burn tool, set to Midtones, to add a little shading around the edges, going up into the tears as well. It's important to set it to Midtones to achieve this warm effect: set to Highlights and you'll just get a muddy gray result.

7 The text here is set in the medieval style font Cantebriggia. Although there are many Black Letter style fonts available, this one has a slightly uneven, worn feel that makes it look more handwritten. The text used here is from the first chapter of the book of Genesis, in the Latin version.

8 Select all the text layers, and (if you have Photoshop CS2 or higher) choose Make Smart Object from the pop-up menu in the Layers palette. Adding a little Image Warp distortion makes the effect less rigid. On a new layer, I've painted the word Deus in red each time it appears for added effect.

MORE INFO

● The success or failure of the texture creation in step 2 depends on two factors: the random action of the Clouds filter, and the colors used within it. The first is easy; simply keep pressing `ctrl F` `⌘ F` until you get the result you want. For a tighter texture, hold `alt` `⌥` as well. Sample your foreground and background colors from the Swatches palette, if you like, but be prepared to use the Color palette to adjust the values, repeating the filter each time, until you get a convincing effect. Remember, you can use the `X` key to switch foreground and background colors, which makes sampling and defining them much easier.

● Instead of deleting the edges in step 4, you could create a layer mask and use the Lasso tool to select areas on that, filling with black to hide the unwanted portions. If you set black as your background color, you can use the `Backspace` key to fill with this color on the mask; the effect will be the same as if you'd deleted that area on the parchment, except that you'd always be able to paint it back in again later.

● Always work on a copy of the layer before adding shading, just in case.

SHORTCUTS

`MAC` `WIN` `BOTH`

Bank checks

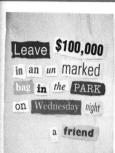

Leave **$100,000** in an *un* marked bag **in** *the* PARK on Wednesday *night* a **friend**

Earlier in this chapter we looked at how to make a ransom note; here, we'll see how to make the check used to pay that demand. (On second thoughts, I have to admit it's likely that kidnappers, like plumbers, prefer cash.)

Checks are typified by the information they all have to contain – the amount in words and figures, the date, the person to whom the check is payable, the signature, as well as the various account numbers, sort codes, and so on. But they also tend to have a background pattern of words, designed to make forgery and alteration that much harder, and that's what we'll begin with here.

Interesting aside: in the 1990s a bank in England came out with checks that were completely black and white. When these were photocopied, the word FRAUD appeared across the copies in unmistakeable letters. Clever stuff, indeed.

1 Start by typing two or three lines of the background texture (top). Here, I've typed National Bank of Toytown three times, with offset word arrangements. This is so that the elements will join together after the Text Warp style Flag is applied (bottom).

3 Make a new background layer, filled with a paler blue than the wavy lettering. Then select bands at the top and bottom, and brighten them: this gives a lighter space where we put the name of the bank (which is no longer the Bank of Toytown, for reasons which escape me) and at the bottom.

5 I've never found a font which accurately reproduces the machine readable numbers at the bottom – so these are hand drawn. You're welcome to take them apart and reuse the numbers; I've included a whole set here, as well as those odd punctuation marks.

7 There are many handwriting fonts available, but they always look just like fonts and rarely like real handwriting. Far better to write your own, on a new layer; or, if you find writing on the screen that hard, write on paper and scan it in.

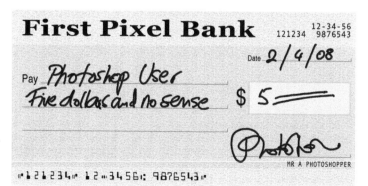

NATIONAL BANK OF TOYTOWN
BANK OF TOYTOWN NATIONAL
F TOYTOWN NATIONAL BANK O

NATIONAL BANK OF TOYTOWN
BANK OF TOYTOWN NATIONAL
F TOYTOWN NATIONAL BANK O

First Pixel Bank

First Pixel Bank   12-34-56
121234 9876543
Date
Pay
$
MR A PHOTOSHOPPER
121234 12 3456: 9876543

First Pixel Bank   12-34-56
121234 9876543
Date 2/4/08
Pay Photoshop User
Five dollars and no sense $ 5
MR A PHOTOSHOPPER
121234 12 3456: 9876543

2 Turn the text into a regular layer by using Layer > Rasterize > Text, then shrink the layer down to tiny size. Select All, and hold *alt* ⌥ as you drag to make a copy; hold *Shift* to make that drag horizontal. After you've made a row from the pattern, duplicate it to fill the canvas, and change the color to light blue.

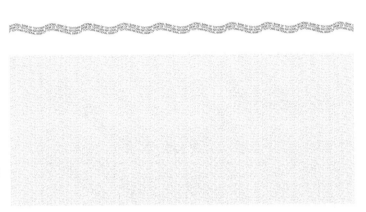

MORE INFO

● The monospaced font Andale Mono, used in step 4, adds a convincing version of the checkbook holder's name and account number. You should already have this font on your system, but if you don't just about any monospaced font should do instead: it simulates the machines that print the information, together with the check number, on each check.

4 All the text elements can be added in, one by one. Although it's conventional to use a plain font such as Helvetica for the words 'Pay' and 'Date', those that vary from check to check – the name, the account number – should go in the fixed width font, Andale.

● In step 8, the addition of the shadow beneath the check makes it very much more realistic. You might be tempted to add a shadow using the Drop Shadow feature of Layer Styles, but this would look unconvincing: as the check is on a slight curve, the shadow would follow this and look false. Instead, the solution is to draw the shadow on a new layer, ignoring the curve of the check entirely: if it were lit from above, this is exactly how the shadow would appear.

6 The horizontal lines are best drawn on a new layer. Draw a marquee selection one pixel high, and fill with black; then duplicate this to make all the other lines. The pale box after the dollar sign is a white box with a blue border, positioned just above the background.

● It is, of course, highly illegal to attempt to forge checks for the purposes of deception, and such a procedure is punishable by a sentence that makes Guantanamo Bay look welcoming. Don't even think about it.

8 Like most paper items, it really only looks realistic when viewed in three dimensions. This has been distorted using the Flag option in Image Warp – see the following pages to find out how this is done.

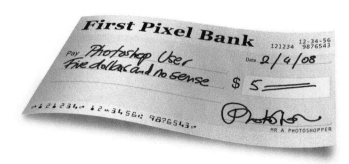

Paper in perspective

Throughout this chapter we'll be looking at creating flat artwork on paper. But paper is a three-dimensional surface: about the only time we see it head on is when we're drawing on it, and even then we'll most likely see it from a slight angle.

Here, we'll look at using warping techniques to distort paper objects so that they can be viewed from a different angle. The Image Warp button appears in Photoshop CS and later; you won't find it in earlier versions of the application.

We're using the Flag Warp method to distort the check in this example. In fact, I used exactly the same method to distort the sheet of parchment, above, which is borrowed from the tutorial on page 110.

1 Begin by pressing `ctrl` `T` `⌘` `T` to enter Free Transform mode. On the Options bar you'll see the Image Warp icon; press it, then choose Flag from the pop-up Warp menu (the default setting is Custom). You'll see this massive distortion, which is the preset Flag amount.

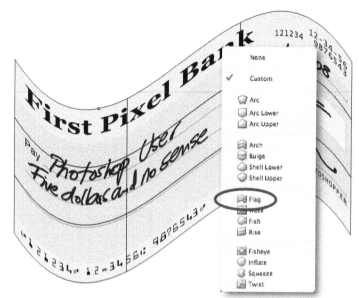

3 To add some perspective, don't press `Enter` yet. Instead, switch back to standard Free Transform by pressing `ctrl` `T` `⌘` `T` once again. Grab one of the corner handles, and hold `ctrl` `alt` `Shift` `⌘` `⌥` `Shift` as you drag it towards the center to produce a symmetrical distortion.

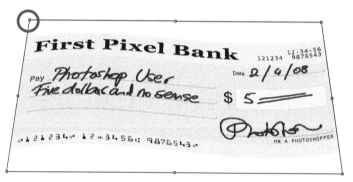

5 This is a convincing shadow method for curved paper, and it depends on the shadow being straight. With the Polygonal Lasso, mark the four corners of where the check would lie if we hadn't curved its surface. Feather using `ctrl` `alt` `D` `⌘` `⌥` `D` (about an 8-pixel feather) and fill with black on a new layer.

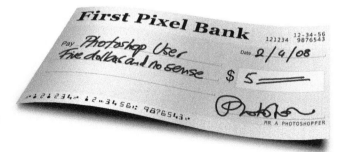

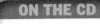
2 There's only one control for this distortion, and it's the tiny handle about a quarter of the way in from the left-hand edge. Grab this, and drag it up to produce a much more subtle distortion, in the opposite direction.

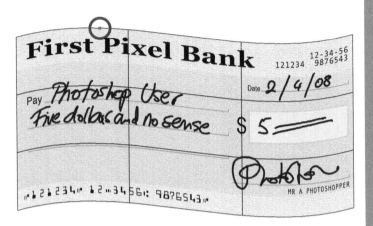

MORE INFO

● Although we can just use Custom Warp and adjust all the handles ourselves in step 1, it's a lot easier to begin with one of the preset methods. Note that the default for the Flag setting is to warp vertically; when distorting the parchment for the introductory image, we need a horizontal distortion. There's a button on the Options bar to change this: click the button to switch between horizontal and vertical warp directions for all Image Warp presets.

● By switching directly from Image Warp to standard Free Transform in step 3, we maintain the quality of the image by applying just one transform procedure, rather than two. It's a useful technique that's well worth knowing.

4 With the basic distortion in place, we now want to view the check more from the side. Release the keys, and hold just `ctrl` `⌘` as you drag each corner handle in turn, until you create a perspective view at the right angle for your work.

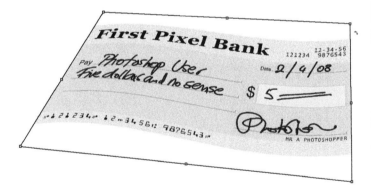

● In step 5, I recommend using the Polygonal Lasso to trace a four-sided shape. Of course, we can just use the regular Lasso tool, holding `alt` `⌥` to give us the Polygonal mode temporarily; when we release the button we'll get the regular Lasso back again.

6 Lower the shadow opacity to around 50%. Finally, we need a little thickness for the paper. Select All, then hold `alt` `⌥` as you nudge the check up two pixels using the `⬆` key. Inverse the selection, pick a pale color from the check and press `alt` `Shift` `Backspace` `⌥` `Shift` `Backspace` to fill the check edge with that color.

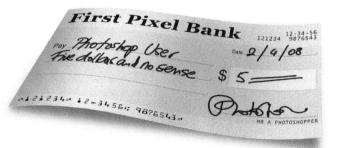

● In step 6, holding the `Shift` key ensures that the color fill applies only to pixels already present within the layer.

Certificates

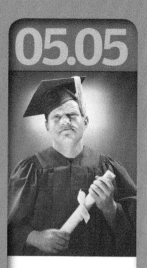

To some cultures it might seem absurd that several years spent in academic study should culminate in a rolled-up piece of paper. The certificate, with its piece of colored ribbon, is no more ridiculous than the mortar board hat or pleated gown.

Certificates are society's way of putting their recognition of someone's worth in a tangible form. Whether it's a school child receiving praise for swimming 100 yards, a student collecting a degree or a physicist receiving the Nobel Prize, the certificate will always share elements in common. There will always be a formality of style, usually an old-fashioned typeface, an intricate border, and frequently a series of decorative elements.

We'll incorporate some of these features into our version of the certificate style, and we'll see how to make them easily.

1 The hardest step is to make the intricate border. Here's one solution: first type a row of 8s in Times Regular. Then use *alt* ← ↖ ← to tighten up the letter spacing, and finally condense it using Free Transform. When this is duplicated and applied around the edge – with a suitable parchment background, of course – the effect is convincing.

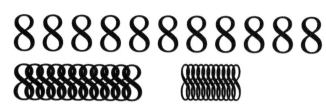

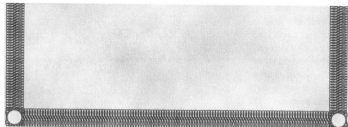

3 The remainder of the text can be set in the same font, except where it's very small (the word 'President'). Adding a slight Bevel using Layer Styles gives the font a raised look, as if the type has been embossed. The dotted lines are no more than a string of full stops reduced to an appropriate size.

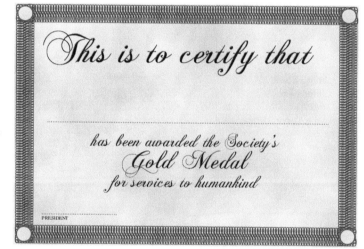

5 We'll add a gold seal to the certificate – but first, we need a red star on which to place it. Use the Shapes tool, and choose the Polygon option. Set the number of sides high – I've used 60 – and set the Indent value (click the arrow to open the dialog) to around 5%, so that the star is barely indented at all. Adding a small amount of embossing using Layer Styles makes it look more three-dimensional.

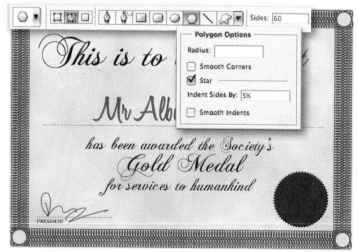

2 There are many script fonts available; we'll use Dieter Steffmann's font Chopin Script. Note that while we might frequently tighten a font's letter spacing, we can't do this with a script like Chopin: the characters are precisely designed to link perfectly from one to the next.

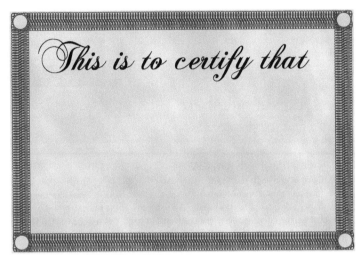

4 We need to use a different font for the recipient's name: it has to look as if it's been written on afterwards. This is another Steffmann font, Honey Script; setting it in a different color helps to make it look separate from the rest of the text. The signature is best scrawled with a hard-edged brush directly in Photoshop.

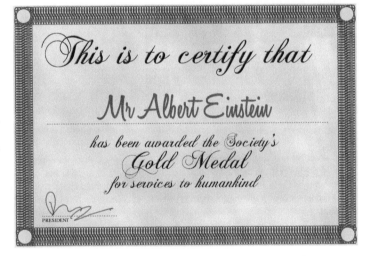

6 The seal placed on top gives the certificate a sense of luxury and authority. This is just a silver dollar, recolored using the Color Balance dialog: add maximum amounts of Red and Yellow to achieve the gold effect, then just a little Green to make it less brash.

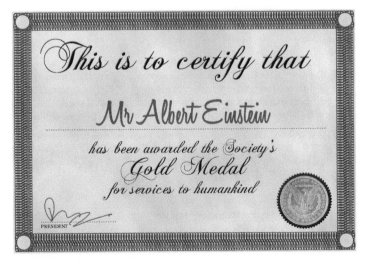

MORE INFO

● The creation of script fonts is a specialist task, even more so than regular typography. The letters each need to flow into the next, as if it has been written by hand – without the author knowing, of course, what order you're going to type the letters in. Look at these few letters:

The letters t, h, o, s and e look unfinished and awkward when seen on their own. But when placed together the effect is almost miraculous:

The letters appear linked together perfectly. Note how the leading tail at the top of the 's' begins inside the 'o', and how the tail on the 't' sweeps up into the loop of the 'h'. It's the same with all well-designed script fonts: even the more informal Honey Script, used for the name, has tails that lead between the characters, greatly strengthening the hand drawn appearance.

SHORTCUTS

MAC   WIN   BOTH

Picture postcards

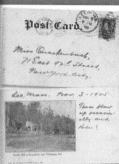

Postcards have come a long way since the earliest photographic examples – such as the one shown above, dating from 1905. Color printing, cheap production and reliable postage have all contributed to the huge explosion of the form.

Postcards have had a long and fairly checkered history. The British postcard artist Donald McGill begain drawing postcards in 1904, and continued to produce his unique brand of saucy, irreverent cards – packed full of double meanings and suggestive phrases – until the 1950s. In 1954 he was prosecuted under the Obscene Publications Act for the production of cards which, today, seem to contain nothing more damaging than mild innuendo.

We'll look at a more traditional form of card, of the kind that can be found in hotel bookstores throughout the world, using the popular four-view format.

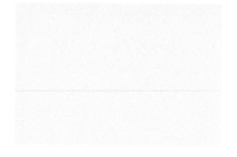

1 Begin by drawing a rectangle, slightly smaller than your canvas area. Make a new layer, and fill this with very pale gray, rather than white. This will help us to see the edges later: viewing a white card against a white background is never easy.

2 To make the four views, we need to make a mask. Draw a rectangle on a new layer about a quarter the size of the card, and fill with black; then duplicate this selection on the same layer to make another smaller rectangle next to it.

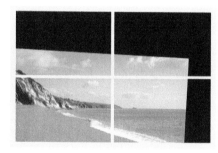

5 Place the first image, and press `ctrl` `alt` `G` `⌘` `⌥` `G` to use the mask layer as a clipping mask. Rotate and scale the image so it fits within one of the quadrants, then delete the area outside that quadrant.

6 Place the remaining images in the same way, rotating and scaling as necessary. Remember to keep the center of the card clear, as that's the position where our title will go.

GREETINGS FROM

8 The words 'GREETINGS FROM' are set in capitals, and distorted using Warp Text. Then, on a new layer behind, make an elliptical selection that matches the top of the lettering, and fill with yellow.

GREETINGS FROM

9 Use the Lasso tool, holding the `alt` `⌥` key to trace straight lines, to select and delete the sides of this ellipse. The cuts should go through the first and last letters, rather than outside them.

GREETINGS FROM

10 Now use the Elliptical Marquee tool to make another elliptical selection, this time lining up just below the bottom of the lettering: delete this area.

GREETINGS FROM

11 Draw circular selections at each end of the banner, the same height as the banner, and fill with yellow to complete the effect.

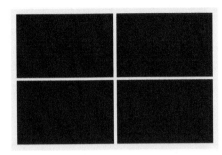
3 Deselect, then stretch the whole layer until it fits the width of the card *with a small border around the edge). This is the easiest way to divide the card into two, and avoids having to bring up rulers and guides.

4 Select both these rectangles, and drag downwards, holding `alt` `⌥` as you do so to make a copy. Leave a small gap between the pairs, then repeat the process in step 3 to scale the group so it matches the size of the postcard.

MORE INFO

● At the end of step 4 we've created a mask which has four quadrants; this means that when we place the images on top, in step 5, we have to trim away the excess that appears in the other quadrants. An alternative method would be to duplicate the rectangle as a new layer, rather than a new selection, in steps 2 and 4: we'd then end up with four separate panel layers, each of which could be used as a mask individually. This way, we wouldn't need to trim the images placed on top, so it would be easier to adjust them later if we need to.

● To make the shadow in step 12, hold `ctrl` `⌘` and click on the thumbnail of the base layer to load it as a selection. Then use `ctrl` `alt` `D` `⌘` `⌥` `D` to feather this selection – a feather radius of around 6 pixels will work well. Make a new layer, and fill this with black; then reduce the opacity of this layer to around 60% for a good shadow effect. By having a straight shadow beneath a curved card, we accentuate the curve and the sense of the card lying on a flat surface. This is a far more convincing approach than merely adding an automated drop shadow using the Layer Styles dialog.

7 The title is here set in Georgia Bold Italic, which you should already have loaded. It's set in red, with a thick yellow stroke created using Layer Styles. The stroke should be large enough so that there are no longer any holes within the letters 'a' and 'e' – this would look ugly.

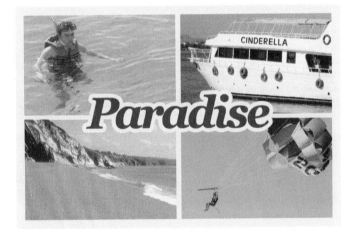

12 To finish the card, hide the background layer and use `ctrl` `alt` `Shift` `E` `⌘` `⌥` `Shift` `E` to make a merged copy. If you have Photoshop CS2 or higher, you can use Image Warp to curl the edges up slightly; otherwise, use a large brush to do this in the Liquify filter. When you create the shadow, though, use the original postcard shape rather than the distorted one: see More Info for details.

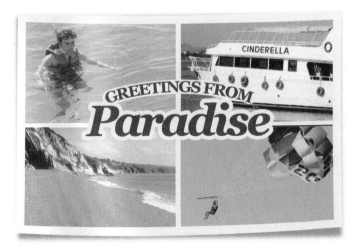

Postage stamps

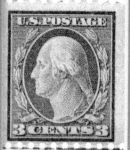

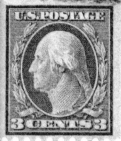

Postage stamps are unique in that their design is virtually identical in every country in the world. There are varying sizes and colors, of course, but the perforation principle and the appearance of an engraving or photograph remain largely the same.

We'll feature Thomas Edison on this stamp, for a traditional, old-fashioned appearance. These days, stamps are just as likely to feature space stations, or Disney characters, in commemoration of some anniversary or other.

The only tricky part here is creating the perforated edges: we've got a quick and easy way to do this, which avoids having to draw a whole string of holes.

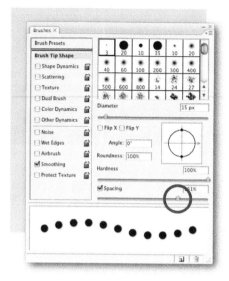

1 Begin by making a gray rectangle on a new layer. To make the holes, we need to modify a brush: open the Brushes palette, and select a small hard-edged brush. Drag the Spacing slider until the spaces between the dots are the size of the dots themselves. I've used a setting of 191% here.

2 Press **Q** to enter QuickMask mode. Hold the Shift key as you click near the top left corner and drag down to the bottom to draw a string of dots. It probably won't fit (left); so use Free Transform to scale the dots to fit the side better (center), then nudge across so the dots are three-quarters over the edge (right).

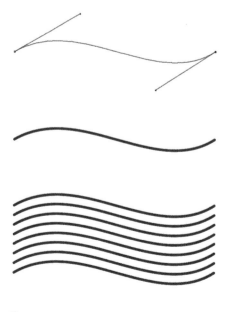

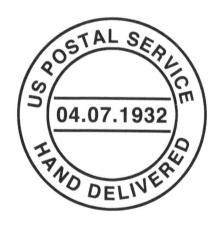

5 To make the wavy lines, first draw a single line with the Pen tool, by clicking and dragging to the anchor points shown here. Then switch to the Brush tool and, on a new layer, press **Enter** with the Pen path still active: it will stroke the path with the brush size. Duplicate the resulting stroke several times.

6 The first circle is drawn with the Elliptical Marquee tool, holding **Shift** to make a perfect circle, then the outline added using Edit > Stroke. This is duplicated for the inner circle. The outer text is added by placing text on paths drawn with the Shapes tool – see page 214 for more about how to do this.

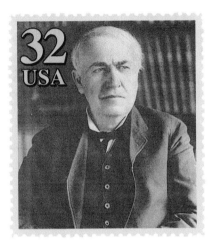

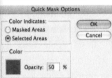
MORE INFO

● In step 2, we use QuickMask to create the holes. The default mode of operation for QuickMask is for painted (red) areas to be masked – that is, not selected. We can change this to operate the other way around by double-clicking on the QuickMask icon at the bottom of the toolbar.

Now, when you leave QuickMask, the holes will be selected, and you can just press *Backspace* to delete them.

● Overlapping the dots at the end of step 2 gives us more loose paper to play with when we're roughening up the edges in step 3. By deleting some extra pieces of edge we make the stamp look more like an object in the real world.

● In step 5, remember to either set the spacing on the brush back as it was, or choose a different brush – otherwise you'll get wavy lines composed of dots. The spacing won't be remembered next time you choose this brush, so if you want to save it you need to create it as a new brush.

③ Still in QuickMask, select the dots and copy them to the other three sides, removing a few dots for the shorter top and bottom. Press **Q** to exit QuickMask, and delete the dots (see More Info). This gives a regular arrangement (left); to make the perforations look hand-torn, erase some chunks with the Eraser tool (right).

④ The figure of Thomas Edison is added on a new layer, set within the stamp border; the price of the stamp is set in white, with a shadow and stroke added using Layer Styles. A Hue/Saturation Adjustment Layer, placed above the assembly, is used with the Colorize button checked to add color to the stamp.

⑦ With the stamp merged into a single layer, rotate it slightly and add a small drop shadow using Layer Styles. (Rotating an item helps it to look more realistic, as if it has been photographed at a slight angle.) Merge the elements of the franking into a single layer, and use Filter > Blur > Motion Blur to add a small amount of blur to it, to give the impression that it's been slightly smudged in the franking process. Finally, add a layer mask to this layer and paint out small areas of it to create a more uneven, poorly inked appearance.

Old newspapers

In the golden era of newspaper publishing, the newsman was king. Enough so for Orson Welles to have a hit on his hands with the classic *Citizen Kane* (above), one of the all-time greats, about the exploits of a megalomaniac newspaper baron.

Orson Welles also went on to make the notorious radio version of H. G. Wells' novel *War of the Worlds*, which was broadcast in the style of a series of news bulletins about Martian invasion in 1938. The realism of the production caused public unrest as gullible homeowners headed for the hills – and it's the combination of these two artistic endeavors that we're commemorating here.

Until recently, newspapers were all in black and white, which gave them a currency and rawness that the advent of color has taken out of them. In this tutorial, we'll stick to black and white.

IT'S WAR!
WORLD WATCHES AS MARS INVADES

$\mathfrak{The\ Daily\ Register}$

IT'S WAR!
WORLD WATCHES AS MARS INVADES

1 The headline needs to fit the space – and omitting to do this is a mistake often made when newspapers are mocked up in movies and on TV. In the plain text version, top, the words are too widespread; we need to bring them closer together (see More Info).

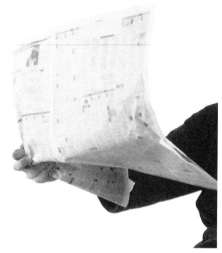

2 This is the newspaper section of the photo we're going to turn into our front page. It's not actually the front page of a paper, but that needn't concern us; the key thing is to hide all the text on the upper half of the paper so we can put our headline there.

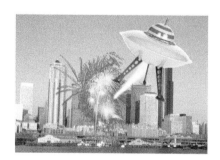

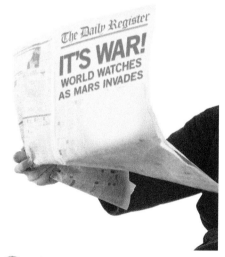

5 The montage for the front page photograph is composed of three simple elements – the city background, the flying saucer model, and an explosion (it's actually a photograph of a firework). No need for too much sophistication here, as it will occupy only a small portion of the final image.

6 Before placing the photograph, we need to make space for it. With the Pen tool, draw a shape that follows both the line of the type and the curve of the edge of the paper. Make a new layer from this, and paint on here using colors sampled from around the edges once more.

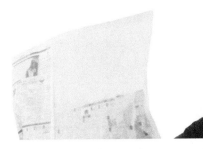

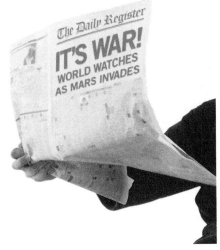

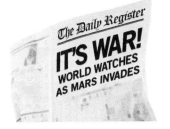

MORE INFO

● The font used here is OldSansBlack, which is a good match for the 'gothic' style of sans serif that was used in newspapers of the time (and variants of which are still used on tabloid newspapers today). It's a solid, no-nonsense typeface that conveys its message clearly and boldly.

● In step 1, we need to tighten up the tracking. We can do this by choosing the Tracking section of the Character palette to bring all the letters closer together; but for the main headline, position the cursor between letter pairs and use `alt` ⬅ `⌥` ⬅ to close up the letter space. The tighter the lettering is, the larger the headline can go – and that's the goal of every newspaper proprietor.

3 Make a selection with the Lasso tool and, on a new layer, paint out within this, sampling colors from around the edge. The headline is turned into a single layer, rotated using Free Transform and then distorted using Image Warp to fit the space.

4 To make the headline blend in with the paper, we need to match the colors of the 'black' elements already on the page. This means tinting it slightly brown and lightening it; a touch of Gaussian Blur helps it to look less artificial.

● To make the headline and masthead in step 1 into a regular layer, the best way is to select all the elements and choose New Group from Layers from the pop-up menu in the Layers palette (or simply press `ctrl` `G` `⌘` `G`). Duplicate this group, and Merge it using `ctrl` `E` `⌘` `E` to turn it into a single layer: that way, we still have the original elements intact in case we should need to edit them at a later date.

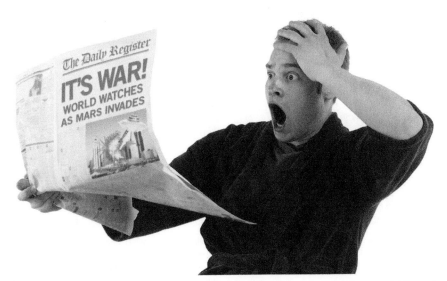

7 Since the mask for the photo placement is on a separate layer, we can position our composite photograph on top of it and use `ctrl` `alt` `G` `⌘` `⌥` `G` to use the mask as a Clipping Mask, so the photo will show up only where it overlaps the mask. This makes it easy to rotate and scale the image to fit: we don't need to be too accurate about our distoriton. Set the mode of the placed photo to Multiply so we can see the mask through it, and add a little Gaussian Blur to blend it in better.

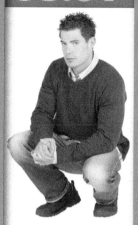

In the early days of recording, album covers were plain paper sleeves with holes in them that allowed buyers to read the label. But in the 1960s the LP brought a profusion of artistic output which made album art as much a part of the record as the music inside.

From Peter Blake's *Sergeant Pepper* cover to Roger Dean's *Yes* fantasies, album art became as collectable as the albums themselves.

The transition from vinyl to CD, of course, meant that album size shrunk from 12 inches to under 5 inches – enough to stem the flow of creative talent at a stroke.

It would be futile to attempt to show how any one album is created. But using a single face, we'll look at some of the styles that are typical of the genre they purport to represent.

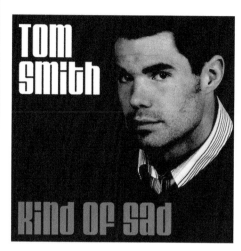

Jazz records have always tended towards the moody and introspective – a reflection of the sentiment of the music they contain. Blue is a popular color, of course, as it directly refers to blues music.

Photographs are generally in black and white, which gives them a raw, newsy quality, as if the addition of color would be just too commercial and too gaudy for the serious music we're about to hear.

Fonts tend to be sans serif, and quirky. This is Velvenda Cooler by Ray Larabie, and it's on the CD that accompanies this book.

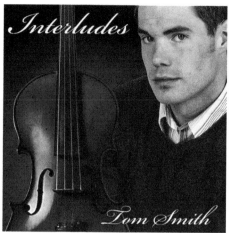

Classical albums need to look serious, of course. But they also need the look of luxury and quality, and we can achieve that by setting our photographs against a deep red background.

The violin leaves us in no doubt as to the nature of the musician featured. The high gloss on it is accentuated using the Curves adjustment, to make it shine even more than it did originally.

This font is Bickham Script, but there are many freely available calligraphic fonts you could use.

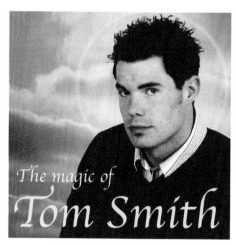

Popular vocal music calls for an unsophisticated approach. This is music for people who don't like their music to be challenging in any way, so the album art needs to reflect this.

The font is Apple Chancery, but there are many such ugly fonts around. The figure is increased in saturation to give him a rosy glow; the halo effect is produced using the Lens Flare filter on a new layer, set to Screen mode, above a photograph of clouds.

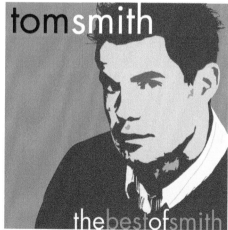

Adult rock uses a wider variety of styles than just about any other form of music. This is a retrospective album, which means the singer is going to be well known. If his face is familiar, we can get away with a graphic treatment and still be sure he's recognizable. This is the Cutout filter applied to the color image, then brightened up slightly.

The stark, stylized look is well set off by a plain background and simple, no-nonsense text.

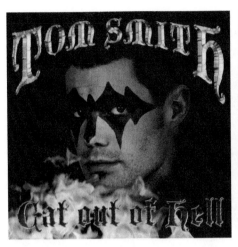

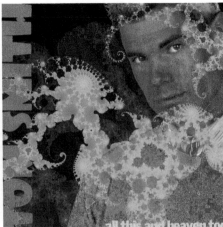

Heavy metal means metal type: it's simply impossible to avoid. The distortion on the top text here is created using the Text Warp control, and the metal effect is added as a Layer Style. It's actually a modification of one of the metal styles on the CD, so you can try it out for yourself.

The face mask is painted in QuickMask on the face layer (see page 227 for more on this technique), and then used as the mask for a new Curves adjustment layer. The coloring on the face is painted on a layer set to Hard Light mode, which allows us to experiment with colors without damaging the original.

Psychedelic music needs wacky colors and trippy special effects. And so this album uses a fractal illustration in both the foreground and the background. These are mathematically created patterns, and are readily available on the internet; there are even Photoshop plug-ins that allow you to create them directly in Photoshop.

The coloring on the face is achieved by using the Hue/Saturation adjustment to rotate the hue value. Because the gray sweater looked dull, I colored it using the Replace Color dialog, boosting the Saturation value considerably.

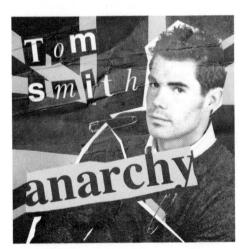

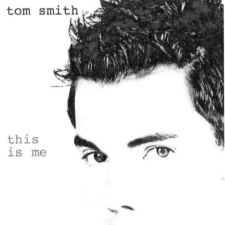

Punk rock was a phenomenon that overwhelmed the UK in the 1970s. The overtly anarchic, rebellious nature of the music led to album covers that looked as if they were put together using scissors and paste – and, in many cases, they were.

The ransom note style of text is utterly in keeping. That gray sweater is far too staid, of course; the best we can do is to tear it in half and hold it together with safety pins, an icon of the era.

Modern folk is a laid back, guitar-oriented style that's best reflected with an understated cover. Our singer is here brightened and contrasted considerably using the Curves adjustment. Placing him at the bottom of the page makes him look shy and retiring, rather than in your face: we can expect soft music from this man.

The typography reflects the laid-back, reserved nature of the imagery. Set in plain Courier, it's so small as to be almost insignificant.

MORE INFO

● In these examples we've had to make do with a bland, uninteresting, expressionless face that's wholly lacking in emotion and interest. I chose this to show how much variety we can produce with the most uninspiring of original photographs. If you're looking to pastiche an album cover, look for images that convey the mood of the music. This might include cigarette smoke for jazz, a screaming face for heavy metal, a beaming smile for popular vocals, and so on. Although we can achieve a lot with graphics alone, a good photograph will make more difference than anything else.

● Typography is of prime importance, of course, as it is with all design projects. But color plays an equally large part in album cover design. The cover has to communicate to the viewer something about the nature of the music, and color – like music – produces and instant emotional response. Consider swapping the blue of jazz with the deep red of classical, for example: neither would work as well. Blue conveys a sense of despair that finds a cathartic outlet through blues music; red suggests the warmth we hear in a well-loved violin.

SHORTCUTS

 MAC   WIN   BOTH

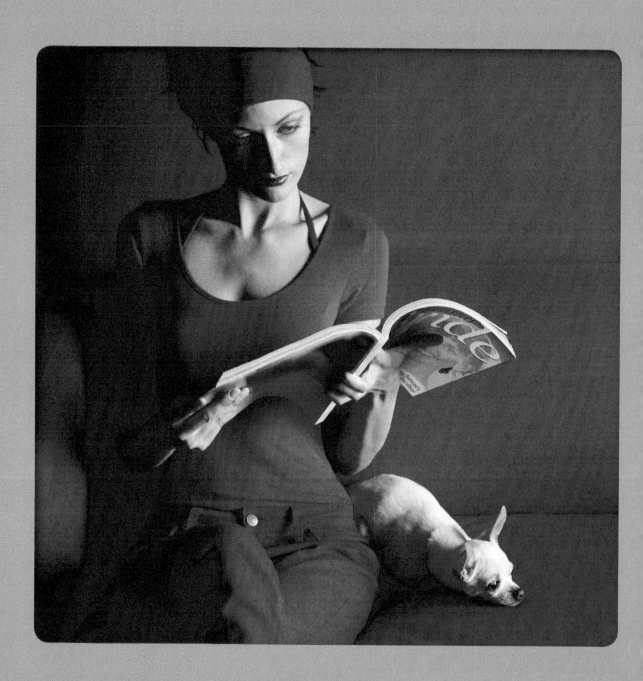

Books and magazines

Book and magazine publishing continues to flourish, despite dire predictions that the internet would kill them both. We may get our news from websites, but we get trusted opinion from magazines. And it can surely be no coincidence that one of the world's top ranking websites is a book store.

In this chapter we'll look at a range of magazine styles, from glamor to weekly news periodicals. We'll see not just how to choose appropriate typefaces, but how to choose and place cover photographs – and when to change the headlines to fit the picture.

Although there are huge numbers of books being published every day, around the world, they fit into well-defined, tried and trusted categories. We can generally tell from a glance at the cover what kind of book we're looking at; the old adage about not judging books by their covers may be a useful proverb, but in the publishing world the cover is all important.

magazine

1. a publication that is issued periodically, usually bound in a paper cover, and typically contains essays, stories, poems, etc., by many writers, and often photographs and drawings, frequently specializing in a particular subject or area, as hobbies, news, or sports.

Dictionary.com

1950s horror comics

The 1950s was the decade that saw a huge explosion in popular comics. Building on the success of Spider-man, Superman, Batman and the rest, comic book artists turned their attention towards a more compelling genre altogether – the horror comic.

Although *Tales from the Crypt* may be the best known of the type, there were many other contenders – with names like *Vault of Horror*, *Weird Science* and even *Maggots*.

With a brash visual style, gory graphics and dripping typography, these comics found a place in the heart of every adolescent boy.

Tales from the Crypt began life as the comic *Crime Patrol*, which dealt with crime stories; the increasing goriness and horror content led to the name change in 1950.

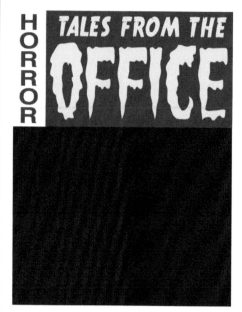

1 Typography is all important here. The main word, 'Office', is set in the Ray Larabie font Green Fuz; the words 'Tales from the' are in True Crimes. The large red panel behind the text is typical of the genre.

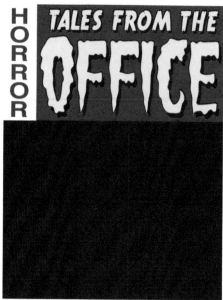

2 We can create an outline for the lettering using Layer Styles: choose Stroke, and change the color from the default red to black. To add the drop shadow, check the Shadow button in Layer Styles: see the More Info panel for more on this.

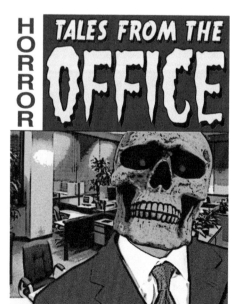

5 To turn the photographs into drawings, use the Poster Edges filter. Make a selection of the bottom half of the image, and use `ctrl` `Shift` `alt` `E` `⌘` `Shift` `⌥` `E` to make a Merged Copy. Here, the Posterization level has been set very low for a stylized, comic book appearance.

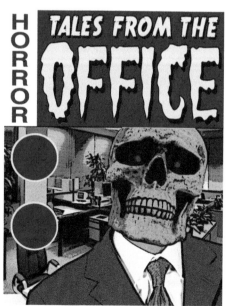

6 We want to place small images within circles on the left. To do this, first create a circular selection and, on a new layer, fill it with color. Add a Stroke using Layer Styles, and set the stroke position to Outside: that way, when the inset image is added, the stroke will still be outside it. Duplicate this layer for the second circle.

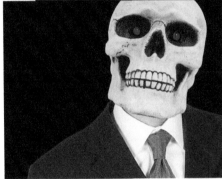

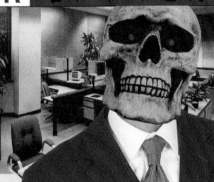

3 The skull has been placed on the body of a man in a suit to make an appropriate foreground figure for our comic front. The fact that the body is real and the skull is a model is not important: we'll treat them later to make the effect more consistent.

4 A typical office background fills the space behind the figure, with a suitable cluttered look. If you have the time, add a few axe-wielding maniacs. I've darkened the skull (and neck) using Curves – see page 238 for more about this adjustment.

7 The two inset elements, the face and the typewriter, are treated using the Poster Edges filter, as we used on the background. Assuming this was the last filter you used, there's no need to bring up its dialog; pressing *ctrl* F ⌘ F will repeat it. The text elements are simply added on new layers.

8 While the pristine state of the artwork might appeal to comic book collectors, we need to make this one look old and tatty for a more convincing result. As we've done several times in this book, add the image of a crumpled sheet of paper, set to Hard Light mode: this adds creases without detracting from the image.

 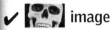
MORE INFO

● The Drop Shadow added in step 2 needs to be hard edged, to give the impression it was drawn with a graphic pen. The Drop Shadow effect in the Layer Styles dialog will, by default, add a soft shadow, since that's currently in vogue. To make this hard edged, set the Size value to 0 pixels. This setting controls the feathering of the edge. The resulting shadow will be an exact duplicate, in shape, of the lettering to which it's attached. Change the Opacity setting to 100% for a solid black shadow.

● When we create the hand drawn effect in step 5, we first create a Merged Copy of all the relevant layers, and work on that. We could, instead, simple merge these layers together – but that would mean we'd be unable to adjust elements later. An alternative technique, if you have Photoshop CS3 or later, is to select the layers and choose Convert to Smart Object in the pop-up menu on the Layers palette. As Smart Objects, we can apply filters to the whole group, and modify the filters' effects later – or even remove them completely. And by double clicking the Smart Object, we can open it to edit its contents.

SHORTCUTS

 MAC WIN BOTH

129

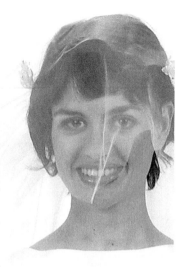

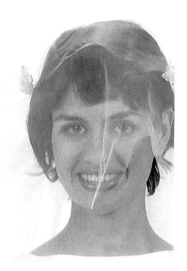

06.02

VOGUE

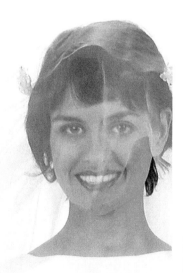

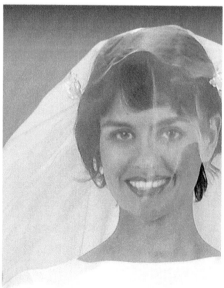

Glamor magazines

While most publications are eager to push the boundaries, glamor titles seem reluctant to break from what's expected of them. It may be that sales pressure is stronger than ever before, but it's hard to imagine Vogue coming up with a cover as radical as the 1957 example above.

Glamor magazines have their own distinct style. The image of a smiling, beautiful girl gazing out at the reader is essential: if the image makes eye contact with you on the news stand, there's a much stronger chance that you'll reach into your pocket for the cash.

Of course, the models who walk into the studios of the magazines aren't anywhere near as glamorous as they are when they appear on the magazine covers. As part of this tutorial, we'll attempt to beautify the rather flawed model we have to work with, to make her suitable cover material.

1 The pose is fine for our cover shot, but this bride needs some attention. She has spots on her face and neck, and bags under her eyes; her bottom lip is a slightly awkward shape, and her nose is too wide. Tricky for a plastic surgeon, maybe, but we can fix it easily in Photoshop.

2 Use the Healing Brush tool to remove the spots. First, hold `alt` ⌥ and click a clear area of skin to be sampled from – the cheek works well. Then paint over each spot in turn: it will appear to clone the sampled area, but when you release the button it will be toned seamlessly into the surrounding skin (see More Info).

5 Although the veil falling in front of this model's face looked appealing, the white streak in front of her mouth, nose and eyebrow is just too strong. Using the Healing Brush tool once again, we can sample a clear area of skin and paint out the highlight in stages.

6 Changing the background to pink adds a bridal flavor. But now we need to make that veil transparent: select it, and use `ctrl` `Shift` `J` ⌘ `Shift` `J` to cut it to a new layer. Then simply color it using Color Balance to match the background.

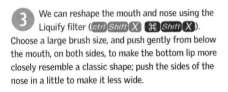

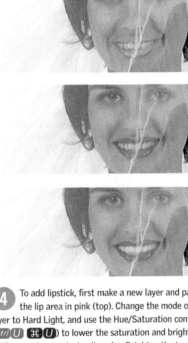

3 We can reshape the mouth and nose using the Liquify filter (*ctrl* *Shift* *X* / *⌘* *Shift* *X*). Choose a large brush size, and push gently from below the mouth, on both sides, to make the bottom lip more closely resemble a classic shape; push the sides of the nose in a little to make it less wide.

4 To add lipstick, first make a new layer and paint the lip area in pink (top). Change the mode of this layer to Hard Light, and use the Hue/Saturation controls (*ctrl* *U* / *⌘* *U*) to lower the saturation and brightness until you get a convincing lip color. Brighten the teeth, as well, using the Dodge tool set to Highlights.

MORE INFO

● In step 2, we use the Healing Brush tool to patch the skin. You might imagine we should use its variant, the Spot Healing tool, instead; this performs essentially the same function, but needs no sample area to be made first. And this is the problem: in attempting to patch without a sample, it frequently draws in unwanted, nearby textures that look quite wrong. The Healing Brush does a far better job.

● The Healing Brush tool behaves in a similar way to the Clone tool. But where we'd always use a soft-edged brush for the Clone tool, with the Healing Brush we use a hard edge: it's surprising, but we get a much cleaner result that way, as Photoshop can match the texture more effectively against a distinct border.

● In step 6, there are any number of ways in which we could have made the new veil layer semi-transparent. We could have changed the layer mode to, say, Overlay, for instance, or reduced the opacity of the layer, or even used Advanced Blending to hide the white. But in the end, it was far simpler just to recolor the layer to match the background.

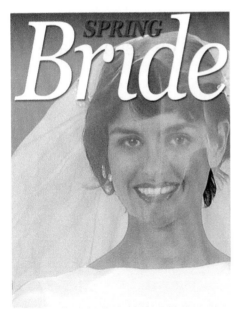

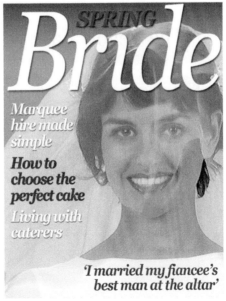

7 The font for our headline is Georgia Bold Italic, which you'll almost certainly already have on your system (it was designed for clear internet use). Add a slight shadow using Layer Styles; here, I've added a layer mask to paint out the dot on the 'i', beneath 'Spring'.

8 The additional headlines need to be written to fit around the shape of the face – it would look clumsy if they covered the face even slightly. The drop shadow helps the text stand out on the left; at the bottom, on a near white background, it's unnecessary.

SHORTCUTS

 MAC   WIN   BOTH

Victorian periodicals

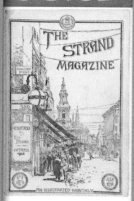

The Strand Magazine was a monthly fiction publication, founded in London in 1891. It is best known as the magazine in which Sir Arthur Conan Doyle first published the exploits of his famous detective, Sherlock Holmes.

That Mr Holmes is a fictional character is a fact that escapes many. The present owners of the house where he was supposed to have lived, 221b Baker Street, are the Abbey building society; they regularly have to reply to letters from people seeking his services.

Late Victorian design followed a fairly set pattern, with squared-up text running around vignetted illustrations on the title pages. It isn't easy to create this effect in Photoshop, however, as its rudimentary typographic features don't lend themselves to runarounds or drop capitals – so we have to do it all by hand.

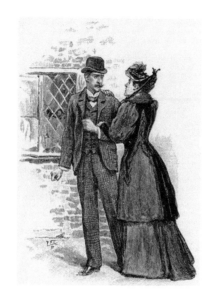

THE ADVENTURE OF
The Yellow Face
BY A. CONAN DOYLE.

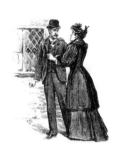

1 This is an original line art engraving from the first publication of Conan Doyle's story *The Yellow Face*, published in *The Strand Magazine*. The paper on which it was printed has yellowed with age; we need to remove that yellowing so we can add our own later.

2 Desaturate the image using `ctrl` `Shift` `U` `⌘` `Shift` `U`, and use Brightness/Contrast to brighten it to get rid of the gray background. The text is set in the Julius Thyssen font Salernomi-J, which has precisely the late Victorian feel we need.

THE ADVENTURE OF
The Yellow Face
BY A. CONAN DOYLE.

5 The drop capital is set in Medieval Victoriana, a popular typeface of the time. To make the body text fit, duplicate the text block and narrow it to make room for the capital. Delete the first letter, and set the first word all in capitals. Change the justification method to full (see More Info for details).

THE ADVENTURE OF
The Yellow Face
BY A. CONAN DOYLE.

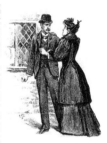

6 We can't flow text between blocks in Photoshop, so we have to make it all fit manually. Look at the words in the first five lines, by the drop capital, then delete these words from the start of the column of text beneath. Move this column up and stretch it to match the width and position of the first paragraph.

THE ADVENTURE OF
The Yellow Face
BY A. CONAN DOYLE.

In publishing these short sketches based upon the numerous cases in which my companion's singular gifts have made us the listeners to, and eventually the actors in, some strange drama, it is only natural that I should dwell rather upon his successes than upon his failures. And this not so much for the sake of his reputations—for, indeed, it was when he was at his wits' end that his energy and his versatility were most admirable—but because where he failed it happened too often that no one else succeeded, and that the tale was left forever without a conclusion. Now and again, however, it chanced that even when he erred, the truth was still discovered. I have noted of some half-dozen cases of the kind the Adventure of the Musgrave Ritual and that which I am about to recount are the two which present the strongest features of interest.

Sherlock Holmes was a man who seldom took exercise for exercise' sake. Few men were capable of greater muscular effort, and he was undoubtedly one of the finest boxers of his weight that I have ever seen; but he looked upon aimless bodily exertion as a waste of energy, and he seldom bestirred himself save when there was some professional object to be served. That he should have kept himself in training under such circumstances is remarkable, but his diet was usually of the sparest, and his habits were simple to the verge of austerity. Save for the occasional use of cocaine, he had no vices, and he only turned to the drug as a protest against the monotony of existence when cases were scanty and the papers uninteresting.

One day in early spring he had so far relaxed as to go for a walk with me in the Park, where the first faint shoots of green were breaking out upon the elms, and the sticky spear-heads of the chestnuts were just beginning to burst into their five-fold leaves. For two hours we rambled about together, in silence for the most part, as befits two men who know each other intimately. It was nearly five before we were back in Baker Street once more.

"Beg pardon, sir," said our page-boy, as he opened the door, "There's been a gentleman here asking for you, sir."

Holmes glanced reproachfully at me. "So much for afternoon walks!" said he. "Has this gentleman gone, then?"

"Yes, sir."

"Didn't you ask him in?"

"Yes, sir; he came in."

"How long did he wait?"

THE ADVENTURE OF
The Yellow Face
BY A. CONAN DOYLE.

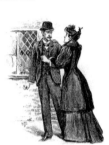

3 Our text is the original Sherlock Holmes story, set in Salernomi-J as well. It's all set as justified type, and all but the first paragraph are indented by 6 points as is the custom for printed books. See More Info for details on alignment and indentation.

4 We need to reduce the size of the text block to make room for the illustration: click in it with the Type tool, then grab a side handle and pull it in to make a much narrower column. We'll have to break this into several text blocks before we're finished.

THE ADVENTURE OF
The Yellow Face
BY A. CONAN DOYLE.

THE ADVENTURE OF
The Yellow Face
BY A. CONAN DOYLE.

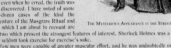

THE MYSTERIOUS APPEARANCE IN THE STREET

7 The text beneath the illustration, running the full width of the page, is placed in the same way: duplicate the text block, make it wider, then delete the words up to the point at which they appear in the text block above. It's a clumsy solution, but the only way to do the job in Photoshop.

8 The illustration caption is set in a new text block, in small caps using the Character palette – see More Info for details. Finally, a scan of a sheet of yellowed paper is overlaid on top of the whole page in Multiply mode, giving it an antique feel that matches the background in the original scanned illustration.

 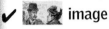
MORE INFO

● Text can be set ranged left, centered or ranged right. It can also be 'justified', in which the words on each full line are spaced out to fill the width. With the standard method, the last line of type is ranged left:

For our first paragraph, and for the last paragraph of the narrow block of text, we need the last line to be stretched full out so that it runs onto the next, which appears in a subsequent text block. So we choose this justification method from the Paragraph palette:

Note that this does not appear on the Options bar at the top of the screen.

● There are two ways of setting text to capitals: All Caps and Small Caps. In the former method, text is all set in capitals:

In the second, used for the caption and for Conan Doyle's name, only those letters typed as capitals are set large; the rest are in capitals but at the size of regular text:

SHORTCUTS

 MAC   WIN   BOTH

News periodicals

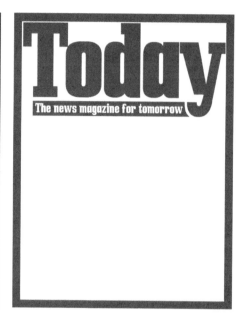

One of the signs of a successful, assured magazine is the degree to which it can cover its masthead (the title at the top) while still achieving instant recognition. These examples of *Time* and *Newsweek* are typical of the amount of cover-up that can be achieved. But while the *Newsweek* cover is almost illegible, clever positioning means all the letters of *Time* can still be read.

We'll invent our own news magazine, using some of the conventions that make the real thing so distinctive in the market place. We'll also look at choosing images to fit on the cover, and fitting headlines.

1 Some news and current affairs magazines opt for a chunky border – *Time* and *National Geographic* are prime examples. *Newsweek* chooses not to, but frequently suggests a border as in the example to the left. This newsy font is called Bullpen.

2 We have to make our page furniture fit the title. Here, the descender of the letter 'y' could prove awkward in a layout; and so we'll square off the masthead by adding a reverse block which contains the subheading.

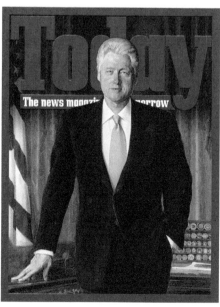

5 We can enlarge the portrait to make Clinton bigger in the frame. There's a limit to how big we can comfortably go, though: it's important to keep his hand within the frame, as cutting it would be awkward. This is also a good time to add a little darkening on a new layer behind the masthead, to make it stand out.

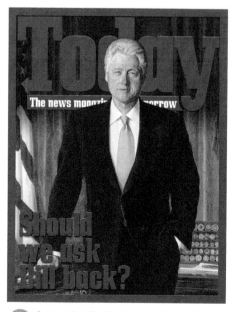

6 Our main headline for this story discusses the hypothetical situation of Clinton running for a third term in office. But placed on the bottom left – the standard position for a news headline – it obscures his hand, and looks clumsy. This position simply fails to be in tune with the image.

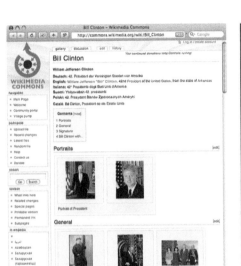

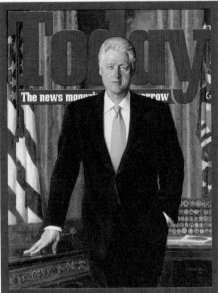

3 Our picture of Clinton is selected from Wikimedia Commons, so we know it's OK to use. There's a good close-up of him, but he's facing right to left; this would look weak on the cover, so we'll choose the full-length portrait instead.

4 When we place the picture on the cover of our magazine it's a good fit. Selecting Clinton's head and shoulders and copying it to a new layer means we can move this portion in front of our masthead: we can still read the word 'Today' behind the head.

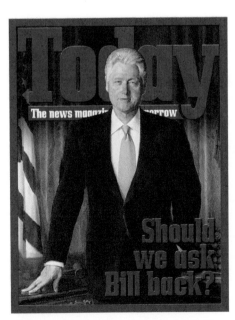

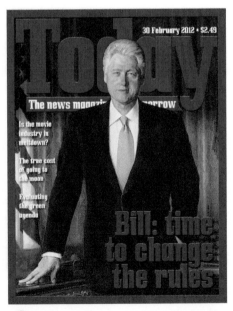

7 Moving the headline to the right means we have to align it right, so it lines up down the right-hand side of the page. Now, however, we have another problem: that question mark makes the bottom line look as if it's indented. If we're going to range the text right, we're going to have to change the words.

8 Our new headline fits much better: note how the words are chosen so that none of the ascenders and descenders interfere with each other. The 'g' of 'change' and the 'l' of 'rules' dovetail neatly together. The additional text elements help to make this magazine look more like the real article.

MORE INFO

● In step 2, we need to make the curve of the slug (the name for the red block) match the curve of the letter 'y'. To do this, first use the Rectangular Marquee tool to make a selection (on a new layer) to the right height – matching the height of the turn at the bottom of the tail. Then hold `ctrl` `⌘` and click on the Today layer's thumbnail to load it up as a selection; use Select > Modify > Expand to make this selection 8 pixels bigger, then delete this area from the slug.

● The choice of portrait in step 3 is simple for us: we only have a few to choose from. For a picture editor with many thousands, it's harder to choose. But the premise of not using images facing right to left will always apply.

● In step 5, we have two layers selected – the background image and the cutout head and shoulders – that we want to manipulate together. We can't place these in a group, since we need to have one in front of the masthead. Instead, select both layers and choose Link Layers from the pop-up menu at the top of the Layers palette. Now, they'll move and scale together, and can be treated as if they were a single layer.

SHORTCUTS

MAC   WIN   BOTH

Pulp fiction

The posters for Quentin Tarantino's 1994 movie *Pulp Fiction* were based on the crime novels of the 1950s, which were cranked out by the bucketload to cater for the growing public taste in crime, romance and a bit of gore.

The style is brash, sensational and highly suggestive. The hard boiled characters created by such masters of the form as Raymond Chandler and Erle Stanley Gardner were frequently larger than life figures, often with the motives of cartoon characters brought to life – and the graphics have to reflect this.

The term comes from the cheap wood pulp on which early magazines such as *Adventure*, *Spicy Detective* and *Weird Tales* were printed. When later turned into books, the same cheap approach meant that the books were often printed on the same rough, raw paper.

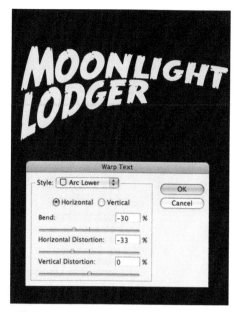

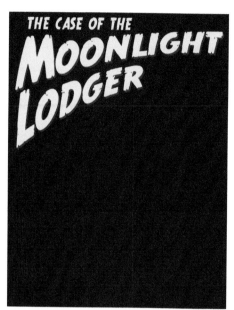

1 We'll start with a black background, so we can see our yellow type more clearly. This font is, appropriately, True Crime. Use the Warp Text dialog to apply a Lower Arc style, with a negative bend so that the text bends up rather than down – and add a little horizontal distortion.

2 As is often the case, the Warp Text controls only get us halfway there. This text also needs to be skewed and rotated to make it better fit the space. The red drop shadow is added using Layer Styles: change the mode from Multiply to Normal so we can see it, and set the Size to 0 for a hard-edged shadow.

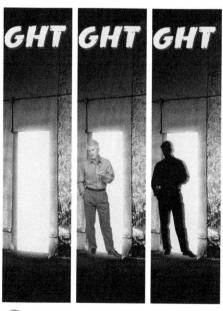

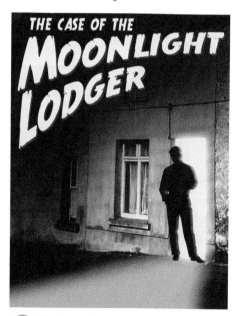

5 To make the doorway, use the Lasso to select the area and, on a new layer, fill with yellow; add an Outer Glow using Layer Styles. The figure is scaled to stand in here. We need to paint him black, leaving just a fine rim on the light side: see More Info for details.

6 The glow on the ground is easily made. Make a selection using the Lasso tool, then use ctrl alt D ⌘ ⌥ D to feather the selection – about 20 pixels should do it. Then fill this selection with yellow on a new layer.

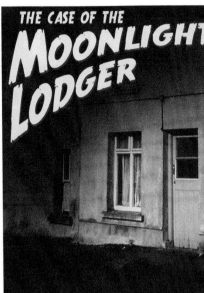

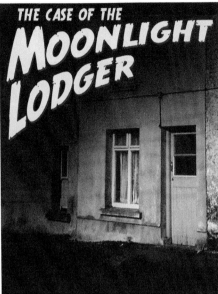

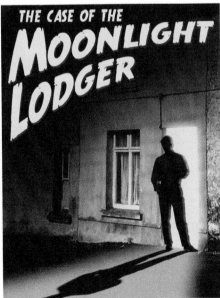

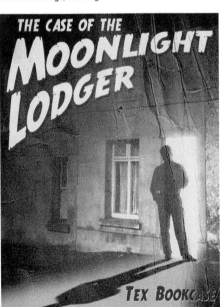

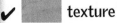
MORE INFO

● In step 5, we want to fill the man with black while leaving a faint rim around the edge that's still lit by the open doorway behind him. To do this, duplicate the layer. Set black as the foreground color (you can use **D** to set the default colors), and press *alt* *Shift* *Backspace* ⌥ *Shift* *Backspace* to fill the layer with black (adding the *Shift* key prevents the whole layer from filling). Use Filter > Blur > Gaussian Blur to soften the edges slightly – around a 2 pixel blur should work well. Make a Clipping Mask with the original man's layer (press *ctrl* *alt* *G* ⌘ ⌥ *G*) and the shadow will only show up where it overlaps the man's original figure; nudge it to the left by a couple of pixels to leave the soft edge.

● When adding the crumpled paper texture in the final step, I've also added a little red using the Curves dialog. When this layer's set to Hard Light mode so we can see the design through it, the red has the effect of giving a sepia-like tint to the underlying layers. This gives the impression of a book that's not only been well thumbed, but which has been left in the sun too long and has started to fade.

③ All we really need is a doorway for our figure to stand in. This downbeat urban dwelling will do fine: it isn't glamorous, but we're only going to see a suggestion of it in the finished image. But it is set in daytime; we need to turn this to night.

④ We can use the Curves adjustment to lower the overall brightness of the image, and to add some blue – this is what gives it a night-time flavor. In addition, we need to darken it considerably behind the title. Add a new layer, and paint the shading in black on here with a large, soft-edged brush.

⑦ To make the shadow, duplicate the man's layer and soften the edges using Gaussian Blur. Flip it vertically, and distort the shadow so it follows the perspective set by the glow from the doorway, getting a little wider as it nears us.

⑧ THe author's name uses the main title colors, inverted. I've added the usual crumpled paper texture to give the impression of age; but in this case, I've used Unsharp Mask to make the crumpling more extreme, so it has a stronger effect.

Thrillers

You can tell how successful an author is by the position of his or her name on the cover of the books. If it goes above the title, they've made it.

There are other criteria as well, of course. Gold blocking, especially if the text is embossed, means they're worth the effort of getting a special die made to stamp the cover as it's being printed.

Gold blocking has also come to mean 'thriller', and you'll see the technique used on the novels of many of our foremost exponents of the genre. Of course, a good murder weapon and the odd bloodstain doesn't hurt.

In this tutorial, we'll make a Layer Style that will create a gold blocking effect on live text. Which means even if we want to change the title or the font of the book later, we can do so: the style will move with it.

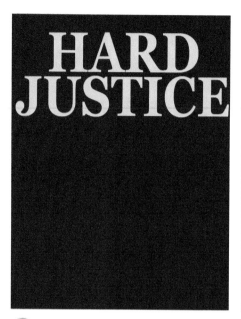

1 Begin with the title. Since this is going to end up in gold, we'll set it in yellow on a black background. The font used here is Georgia Bold, which you should already have on your computer as it's a standard font.

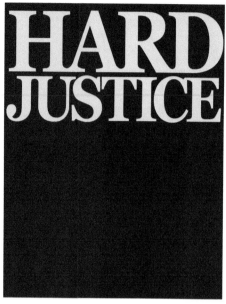

2 For more impact, we need to make the two words the same size: select the word HARD, and use `ctrl` `Shift` `>` `⌘` `Shift` `>` to make it bigger. We also need to tighten up the letter spacing, since the default is too loose: see More Info for how to do this.

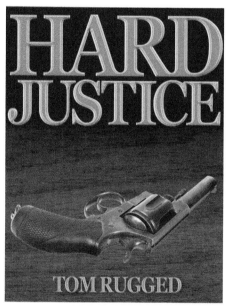

5 The gun fits the shape of the cover well – it's worth placing the author's name so we don't interfere with it. It might have been better if we were able to find a photograph of a gun pointing towards the reader, rather than away, but this will work well once we've added the blood.

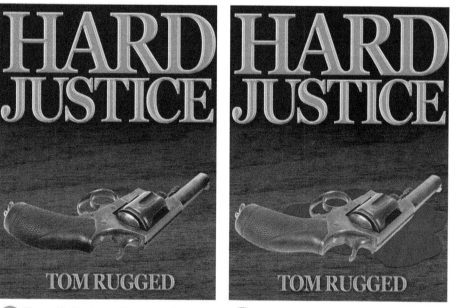

6 The blood, such as it is, is painted on a new layer behind the gun. As it stands, it's wholly unconvincing: all we're after at this stage is to create the basic shape. Use a hard-edged brush, and paint with large, looping curves. Remember that we're looking at this table in perspective!

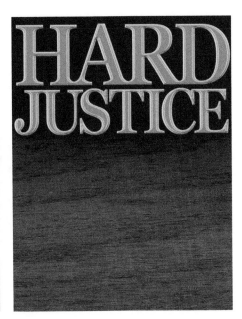

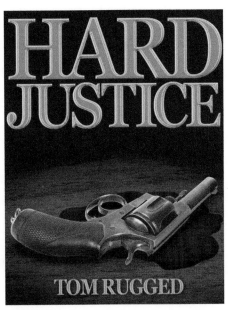

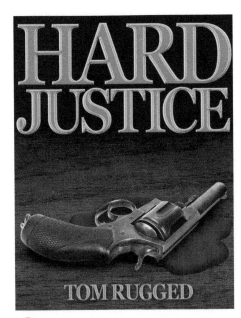

ON THE CD

✔ image
✔ texture
Aa font

3 With the text set, we can create the gold blocking effect. This gold style is created using Bevel and Emboss, as well as Satin – and the style is saved in the document on the CD. See page 236 for more on how to create metallic Layer Styles.

4 We're going to show a murder weapon on this cover, so we need a surface for it to lie on. This scan of a piece of wood has been distorted to make it appear in perspective, and will do just fine. A black to transparent gradient helps the title to stand out.

7 To make the blood look more realistic, use the Burn tool set to Highlights to darken the edges. Make a new layer and paint a shadow beneath the gun, giving it some grounding. Here, I've also increased the contrast on the gun, using the Burn tool to darken the bottom edge where it meets the shadow.

8 When we change the mode of the blood layer from Normal to Hard Light we can see through it to the wood texture beneath, and it looks far more part of the image. We can also create a spotlight effect, focussing attention on the gun, by making a new layer and painting a soft shadow in an ellipse around it.

MORE INFO

● We need to tighten the letterspacing in step 2 – it's called 'kerning' when it's applied to pairs of letters. Position the cursor between each pair, and use *alt* ⌥ ← to close up the space, and *alt* → ⌥ → to open it up. It's OK if the serifs overlap slightly, as at the bottom of the A of Hard, and between the J and the U of Justice; but it would be a mistake if, for example, the curve of the C of Justice touched the I.

● When we create the author's name at the bottom, we can hold *alt* ⌥ as we drag the layer style from the title onto the new layer, and it will be duplicated here. But we'll need to reduce the scale of the bevel and of the satin offset, since the wording is very mush smaller here.

● The Satin effect, added in step 3, overlays blurred and inverted copies of the layer in order to create the satin look. We can use the Contour setting to change the appearance radically: experiment with some of the presets to see the difference. You can even create your own contours, by drawing on the curve to alter it: the changes you make will be shown, live, on the lettering.

SHORTCUTS

 MAC   WIN   BOTH

Chick lit

Will Write for Shoes

HOW TO WRITE A CHICK LIT NOVEL

CATHY YARDLEY

Far from being the derogatory term it once was, Chick Lit – novels aimed at young women and commonly sold in airports and rail station bookstalls – has become a force to be reckoned with. So much so that there' s now a book on how to write the stuff, with the cover set in – of course – a typical Chick Lit style.

It's a visual style that's typified by pale pastel colors, with pink predominant in the mix (the ultimate chick color). Text tends to be frothy and bubbly, often with a hand drawn flavor. Images – almost always of women – show the target audience, frequently treated in the standard glamor mode that bleaches out the nose and any wrinkles to produce a sanitized, ethereal, almost ghostly result. And, of course, there's the obligatory TV show recommendation, without which sales can't be guaranteed.

1 The font we've chosen for this cover is called A Yummy Apology. A curious name, and a curious font altogether: when clicking in it with the Type tool, the cursor appears several spaces to the left of its actual position. Make each word as a separate text block.

2 The font is very spaced out, so we need to tighten it up. Place the cursor between each pair of letters (you'll see the cursor issue when you do this) and use *alt* ← ↰ ← to bring each close to the one next to it. I've also raised the 't' here – see More Info.

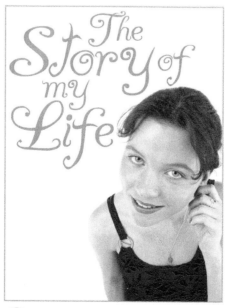

5 This arrangement is much better: the text is more balanced, and it's impossible to read the title incorrectly. Arranging the words in a title such as this is one of the longest processes in designing the book cover: it took me about a dozen different versions before I came up with this one.

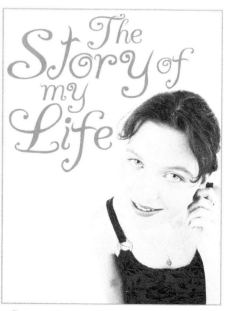

6 The image is brightened considerably using the Curves adjustment, which gives it that bleached-out look. I've also used Curves to increase the amount of blue in the image, which makes it blend in better with the lettering.

MORE INFO

● This font has many peculiarities – not least, the fact that the lower case 't' is facing the wrong way and is set below the rest of the characters. It's a lot more legible when we raise it to line up with the rest of the word. To do this, select the letter and use *alt* *Shift* ⬆ ⌥ *Shift* ⬆ and *alt* *Shift* ⬇ ⌥ *Shift* ⬇ to baseline-shift the selected characters up and down. But make sure you select the right letter – it's particularly tricky with this font.

● The Curves adjustment added in step 6 is quite radical, making significant changes to the image. Best to do this using an Adjustment Layer, so we maintain editability. With the image as the current layer, choose Curves from the Adjustment Layer pop-up menu at the bottom of the Layers palette, holding *alt* ⌥ as you do so: this will open the Adjustment Layer dialog, allowing you to use the underlying layer as a Clipping Mask. Now the adjustment will apply only to the image layer; and we're able to alter it at any time, should we find that the bleached effect or the colors no longer suit our needs.

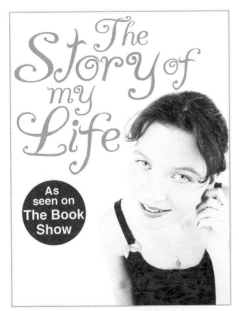

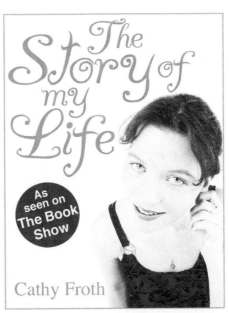

3 We now need to give the words relative prominence. 'Story' and 'Life' are the key words here: the others can go much smaller. This is one reason why we made the words individual text blocks: it makes dragging them to a different arrangement possible.

4 When we bring our photograph onto the cover, we need to rearrange the text to fit around it. This arrangement works fairly well; but there's a danger of the words being read in the wrong order here. There's also a clumsy space above the head.

7 To make the Book Show badge, first make a new layer, draw a circle and fill it with red. I've chosen red to match the dress; pink would have been a possibility, but it would not have stood out as well. The text has to be aligned and sized by eye.

8 Rotating the text on the badge gives it more dynamism, almost as if it had been stuck onto the cover as an afterthought. The author's name is set in the same color as the main title, to tie the two together; but it doesn't need to be in the same font, since this would be overkill on the froth.

CHURCHILL'S
HISTORY OF THE
ENGLISH-SPEAKING
PEOPLES

ARRANGED FOR ONE VOLUME BY
HENRY STEELE COMMAGER

If the author is big enough, then his or her name will sell the book on its own. The rule certainly applies to history books as well as fiction: and when the author is Winston Churchill, a sedate cover is all that's needed.

Most historians don't enjoy such an exalted position in our consciousness, however. And so we have to make their books tantalizing, intriguing and entertaining – at least as far as the cover goes. The stuff inside is entirely up to them.

In this example we'll look at a hypothetical book that attempts to encapsulate a complete history of the world. Even though the subject may sound like it encompasses everything, we need to make it catch the reader's imagination: we can do this with the promise of revelations and a certain amount of gore.

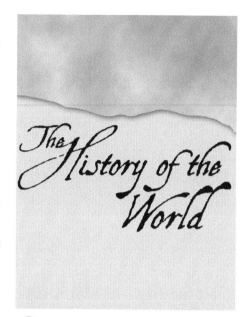

1 The font we'll use for this example is Aquiline Two, designed by Manfred Klein. When we set the words on the page (top) we can see a conflict between the ascenders of 'World', and the descenders of the line above. Offsetting the word 'World' helps to avoid this: we can't rewrite the words, but we can move them.

2 The background is beige stripes on a cream background, hinting at laid paper and therefore suggesting a quality of writing. At the top is a piece of the parchment texture we made earlier in this chapter, darkened and shaped with a layer mask, and with a drop shadow added to make it stand out.

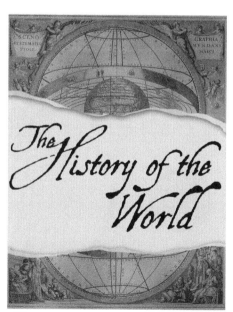

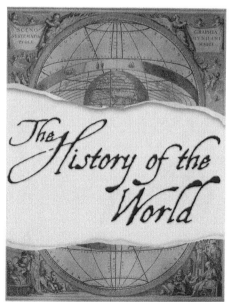

5 The image of the globe is circular. But when we duplicate both its layer and the parchment layer beneath it, we can separate the two halves and redraw the tears to suit the new location. The impression is of history being revealed beneath the surface.

6 To give the text more body, place all the headline layers in a group; then duplicate the group, and flatten it. We can now work on it as a single layer. Coloring the text red suggests blood and intrigue; the embossing, with Layer Styles, makes it more tactile.

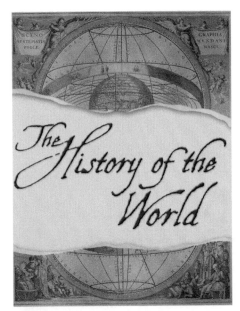

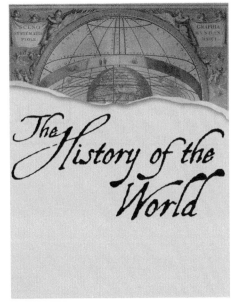

MORE INFO

● The parchment used in step 2 has been darkened up considerably from its original appearance earlier in this chapter. We could use darker foreground and background colors to achieve this effect: but it's easier to take the original paper and darken it using the Curves adjustment instead.

● The double-tear technique we use in step 4 is a useful one for torn paper of all kinds. When we tear a sheet of paper we don't just rip through the face of it, we reveal the fact that paper is a three-dimensional material: we may have torn off the upper layer, but we reveal the subsurface when we do so. Try it yourself – you'll never manage to tear a sheet of paper at exactly 90° to the surface. This method is easy to control, as it uses two layer masks that can be adapted independently for the best results.

● The author's name in the final step has a drop shadow to make it stand out from the background. Set the distance to 0 – we don't want the text to look as if it's floating above the surface. This drop shadow is essentially the same as an outer glow, set to Multiply instead of Screen.

3 This antique map has been neatly framed by the original artist, so it makes sense to include it to the exact width of the book cover. It uses the parchment layer as a clipping mask, so it only shows up where the two layers overlap: it makes a fitting top to the cover, and is appropriate to the title.

4 With its mode changed to Multiply, the map takes on the texture of the parchment layer beneath, giving it an old, varnished appearance. Add a layer mask to this layer as well, and paint it out just above the line of the bottom of the parchment: this accentuates the tearing effect, creating a more natural looking edge.

7 The blobby ends of the 'l' and 'd' of 'World' were a little ugly in the original font, as were the descenders of the 'y' and 'f' – and the 'e' of the first 'The' needs to run into the 'H' of 'History'. We can clean up all these points by erasing them on a layer mask.

8 Adding the author's name at the bottom is essential, of course – unless she's big enough to go at the top instead. Either way, white text will stand out best against this dark background; but to help it along, at a slight shadow with Layer Styles.

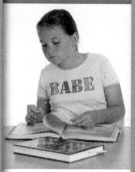

Even in the days of CD-ROMs, Playstations and high speed internet, children still love reading books – and the more profusely illustrated, the better.

It used to be that children's encyclopedias were dull, wordy, worthy tomes with the odd black and white line drawing of a Viking if you were lucky. They'd stretch to a dozen or more volumes, bought by hopeful parents and, by and large, left moldering on the bookshelf, untouched and unread.

Today's reference books for children are bright and colorful, crammed full of photographs and detailed illustrations.

We have to get across the idea of our book as a reference work that will be informative, entertaining and enjoyable to read. We mustn't clutter the cover so much that it looks overwhelming; a few choice items will do to depict the contents.

1 Unusually, I've chosen to set this book title in plain, boring old Times Regular. Why? Because the book has to look authoritative to parents, and this is the most traditional font we can use for this purpose. But by coloring it in two different primary colors, we convey the idea that the book has a sense of fun, as well.

My first Encyclopedia

3 We can now place the rest of our page furniture. The subtitle explains what's in the book; the publisher's name and logo (both fictitious – my apologies if there really is a publisher called Educational Trust Books) are centered above and below the main panel. The text is set in GeoSans Light, by Manfred Klein.

EDUCATIONAL TRUST BOOKS

My first Encyclopedia

Fully illustrated with 5000 drawings and photographs

5 There's space for two more objects: but what should they be? One to appeal to a boy, and one for a girl, perhaps. And maybe they should also represent science or technology, and nature. The motorbike and baby fulfil these conditions: they also neatly fit the spaces in the corners, breaking into the frame to make the book appear to have more content than it can handle.

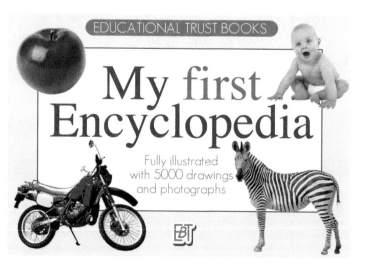

EDUCATIONAL TRUST BOOKS

My first Encyclopedia

Fully illustrated with 5000 drawings and photographs

2 We're going to place objects around the outside, so we need a frame to hold the words. The easiest way to do this is to first fill the background with our chosen color, then duplicate it. Fill the copy with white, and use Free Transform to scale it: if you hold *alt* ⌥ as you drag a side handle, it will scale proportionately around the center. The stroke is added using Layer Styles – see More Info.

My first
Encyclopedia

4 Adding the objects takes some thought. To give an idea of the scope of the book, it helps to have an immediately recognizable first and last: so an apple and a zebra spring to mind as clearly representing A and Z. We have to reset the subtitle now, to move it clear of the zebra.

EDUCATIONAL TRUST BOOKS

My first
Encyclopedia

Fully illustrated
with 5000 drawings
and photographs

6 The book appeared finished at the end of the previous step, but there was some awkwardness about the frame. It lines up too tightly with the belly of the zebra, and there's an awkward corner where it sticks up behind the baby's shoulder. By changing its shape slightly we avoid these problems, making the images fit in more comfortably.

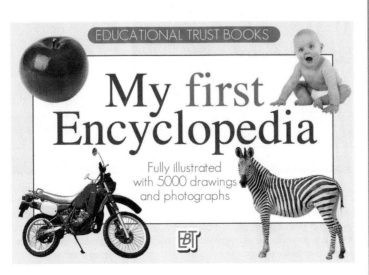

EDUCATIONAL TRUST BOOKS

My first
Encyclopedia

Fully illustrated
with 5000 drawings
and photographs

MORE INFO

● In step 2, we could add the stroke simply using Edit > Stroke, and applying it directly to the layer. The problem here would be that if we then scale the panel, as we do in step 6, the stroke would be uneven; by making the panel taller, we also make the stroke thicker at the top and bottom than it is at the side. When we apply it as a Layer Style, it will remain a 3pt stroke (or whatever figure we choose) however much we move the panel around.

● When defining a stroke in Layer Styles we can choose to place it inside or outside the object. Normally, we'd want it outside, to make a sort of halo; but when we do so with our flat panel, it creates a rounding effect as we can see in this greatly magnified view:

Setting the stroke position to inside, however, gives us a sharp, crisp corner:

It's normally only with thick strokes that we need to worry too much about the placement.

SHORTCUTS

 MAC WIN BOTH

Textbooks, old and new

The teaching of science has changed dramatically over the last few decades – and the design of the accompanying textbooks has kept pace with the new approach.

The textbooks I used at school are nothing like the ones my children work with: the whole approach now is to intrigue as well as to educate. The books I used, on the other hand, seemed designed to generate the maximum amount of boredom in the shortest possible time: learning was clearly going to be a chore, rather than a pleasure.

In this tutorial we'll look at the elements that make up a couple of textbooks, one from a few decades ago and one from the present day. These are both fictional covers, of course, based on design trends.

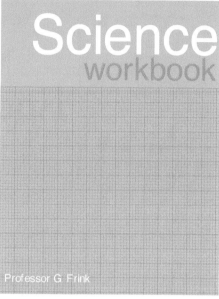

1 Blue for science, orange for history, purple for literature... subjects had an almost subliminal color coding in the 1960s and 1970s. The graph paper background strengthens the science message. It's fiddly to draw, so I've put it on the CD for you.

2 You can't get duller than Helvetica, so that's the neutral, uninspiring font we'll use for our headlines. The splash of color is designed to clash badly with the blue, and even the name is chosen to be as off-putting as possible.

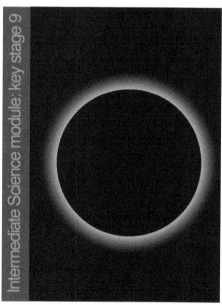

5 There's some key information which has to go on the cover – but we don't want it to interfere with the design. Setting it in a band up the side makes it easy to spot, but keeps it quite separate from the cover image: this is information for the teacher, which is not designed to be noticed by the children.

6 For the eclipse, make a circular selection on a new layer, and fill it with black. The glow is added using the Outer Glow section of Layer Styles: adjust the color of the glow and the size until you get an effect that looks good to you. That's really all it takes to make an eclipsed planet or moon!

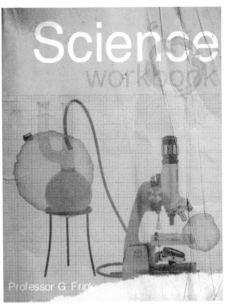

Intermediate Science module: key stage 9

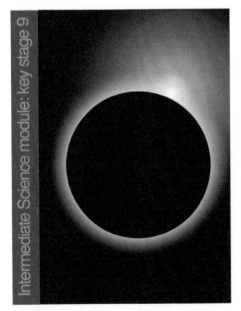

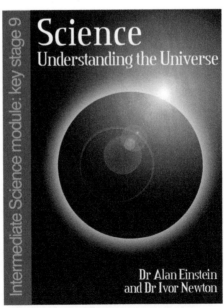

3 Two scientific objects – one for physics, one for chemistry – adorn this cover. They're converted to black and white by desaturating them (full color printing was far too expensive then) and their layer mode set to Multiply so we see through to the background.

4 Our usual crumpled paper, set to Hard Light, adds the creases; the tear is a real scan of torn paper. The coffee stains are painted on a new layer (see More Info). At least, I assume they're coffee stains.

7 Make a new layer, filled with black and set to Screen mode. In this mode the black in invisible, so we see nothing. Choose Filter > Render > Lens Flare, and move the flare just above and right of center (see More Info on this). The sun is behind the planet, so that's where we put the Lens Flare layer, right?

8 Wrong. Moving the Lens Flare layer to the top keeps the sun behind the planet: the flare is an optical effect, not a physical presence. These two elements combine to make an intriguing, powerful cover. The text is set in Credit Valley, which is authoritative while being slightly quirky.

MORE INFO

● In step 4 of the first project, we degrade the book through adding crumpled paper and painting on stains. There are many ways to draw these: here's a simple one. First, select a wiggly outline, roughly circular, with the Lasso tool, and fill with brown:

Using the slider on the Layers palette, change the Fill (not Opacity) to 30%:

Open the Layer Styles dialog, and apply an Inner Shadow. Set the color to brown, and the mode to Normal (not Multiply):

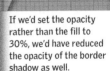

Now, when we place it on a background, we can see through it:

If we'd set the opacity rather than the fill to 30%, we'd have reduced the opacity of the border shadow as well.

SHORTCUTS

Mystic and inspirational

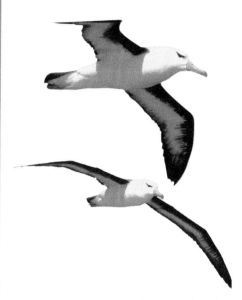

I have a friend who, feeling his life was not running according to plan, turned to self-help books. His interest became an obsession. Last time I saw him, he was reading a self-help book about how to give up reading self-help books.

Whatever you think about the genre, there's no doubt that the need for a mystic, alternative or spiritual approach to managing our lives is of supreme importance to a large section of the population. And these people have to be marketed at just like any other interest group: the marketing may be more low key, but the sell is just as hard.

We'll look at how to put together a typical inspirational text, using elements that are common in the field. We'll also explore the particularly tricky issue of relevant typography for this genre.

1 Every book cover starts with an idea. The idea here is to use a bird to represent freedom and peace. We have a pair of seagulls to choose from: but which is best? The lower one, flying towards us, will have more cover impact.

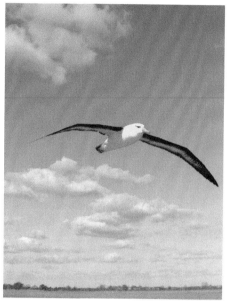

2 Given the fact that we're using a seagull, we clearly need some sky behind it. Dawn and dusk make for dramatic skies, but we're not selling drama – precisely the opposite. A bright, sunny day with fluffy clouds is the right choice here.

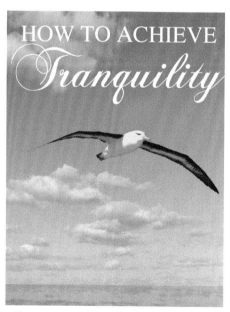

5 Choosing the typeface for this cover is a difficult task. Should we be elegant, informal, playful or relaxed? Here's one possibility: Times Regular and Chopin Script. The script font is attractive, but that first letter is hard to read. This, in itself, is a good enough reason for turning to a different font.

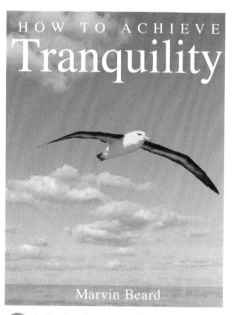

6 Setting the whole cover in Times is one approach: it's detached, inoffensive, traditional. But it doesn't really speak of tranquility. There's a formality here that's potentially off-putting: we're aiming at an alternative culture, after all. Still, the font works well for the author''s name at the bottom.

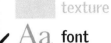
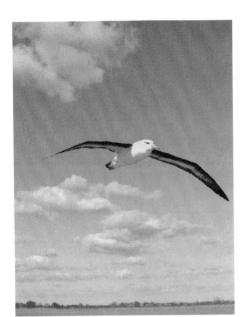

3 Having scaled and rotated the seagull to the correct angle, we need to address the way it blends into its surroundings. Changing the layer mode from Normal to Hard Light allows us to see the sky blue color through the wings, producing an instant match.

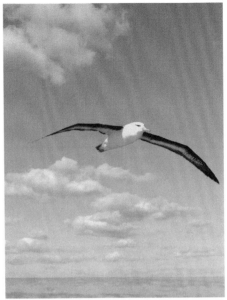

4 That piece of ground at the bottom damages the image. Here's a quick way to replace it with sea. Select the bottom portion of sky with the Rectangular Marquee, and make a new layer from it. Then flip the layer vertically, darken and drag to the bottom.

MORE INFO

● In step 7 the 'How to Achieve' text looks too wide. The reason is that the first and last letters beneath, 'T' and 'y', both have stresses that are inset from their outer edges: in the 'T' it's the large vertical stroke, and in the 'y' it's point at which all the strokes come together. When we arrange type, we have to look at the optical alignment rather than being strictly mathematical about it. Here's a simpler example of the same phenomenon. In the first example, the top line is exactly the same width as the next: and yet it looks too wide:

FIRST LINE
BACK

The reason is that although the serif at the top left of the 'B' sticks out, the stress is that strong vertical. So that's the position we have to line up with:

FIRST LINE
BACK

There's no equivalent vertical stress on the 'K' at the end, so we just balance the beginning 'B' instead.

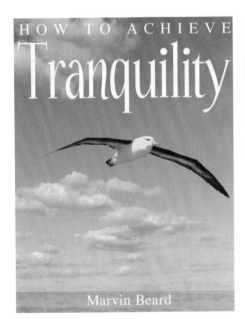

7 This is Echelon, a font by Ray Larabie. It's a much looser, friendlier serif, that speaks of relaxation – a far better choice altogether. But note how the top line, 'How to Achieve', looks too wide: even though it's the same width as the main title word, it seems to overhang it. See More Info for the reasons why.

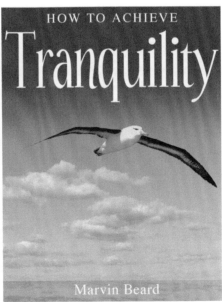

8 Reducing the size of the 'How to Achieve' line, and tightening the loose letterspacing, means it balances the large word 'Tranquility' rather better. The cloud in the previous step interefered with the lettering; here, I've added a blue to transparent gradation, on a new layer, to strengthen and simplify the lettering area.

Philip Pullman

His Dark Materials

The award-winning trilogy:
Northern Lights, The Subtle Knife and
The Amber Spyglass in one volume

Adolescent fiction

The supernatural has always played a strong role in children's fiction. From the Narnia of *Lord of the Rings*, through the fantasies of the *Wizard of Oz*, to the magical world of Harry Potter, children have been enthralled by the mystical element in fiction.

Frequently, the story will center around a single object with special powers: a ring, a chalice, a compass. The object is nearly always gold, partly because it reads well on the page and partly because it looks good on the cover.

We'll base our version of the genre on an orrery, a scientific instrument for showing the relative motion of the planets. With its celestial connotations it already carries the right sense of mystery and wonder. By adding a couple of special effects we can make a routine image of this device into something wonderful.

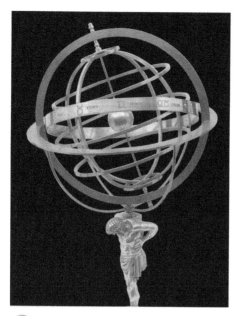

1 Our photograph of the orrery shows it supported on the shoulders of Atlas, who himself stands on a plinth. We don't need any of these extra details, so we'll chop the device off at the bottom to remove the visible support.

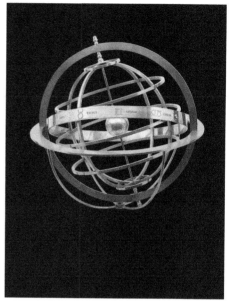

2 Now apparently floating in space, the orrery becomes a more interesting object in its own right. To make it even more impressive, use the Brightness/Contrast dialog to boost the contrast considerably.

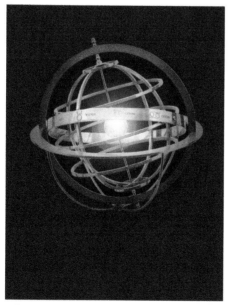

5 The red glow in the middle of the orrery is impressive – so let's make it even more so. Make another new layer, behind the orrery, and set the Gradient tool to create a radial gradient. Sample a red from the Lens Flare layer, and drag from the center to make an additional red glow on the new layer.

The Secret of the Orrery

The Secret of the Orrery

6 We need quirky but traditional looking text for our headline. This is the Ray Larabie font Euphorigenic, which has these descending capitals as standard. Set in one text block, the S and O overlap in an uncomfortable way; placing the words 'of the' on two lines in a separate block helps avoid this problem.

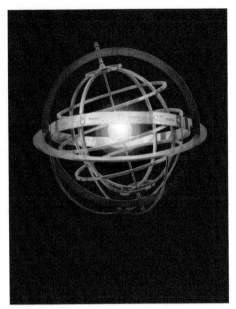

3 We want to add an extra glow to the sun in the center of the device. Make a new layer, fill it with black, and choose Filter > Render > Lens Flare. Drag the center marker so the flare comes directly towards us to create this glowing effect.

4 If we were to change the mode of the new layer to Screen, the black would disappear, leaving us with just the glow. Changing the mode to Hard Light, however, produces a shading effect from the black as well that's far more impressive.

MORE INFO

● What really makes this cover work is not the gold text but the enticing, beautiful image of the orrery itself. And yet the object we started with was a pedestrian, rather dull photograph. Just about any image can be made to look more magical through added lighting effects and boosted contrast: we don't need to spend hours arranging complex lighting in a photographic studio when we can produce a better effect directly in Photoshop.

● The arrangement of the text in step 6 is crucial to the legibility of the cover. As designers, though, we don't have the luxury of being able to change a book title to suit our layout; we must always modify the size and arrangement of the type in order to fit in with the individual demands of the text.

● Because we've applied the gold effect to the type as a Layer Style, we can continue to adjust the text after we've applied it. It helps tremendously to be able to see the text fully styled in this way: the letter spacing looked too loose in the original, but works well when the gold style is placed onto it.

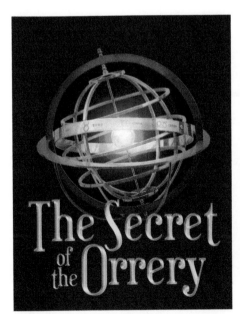

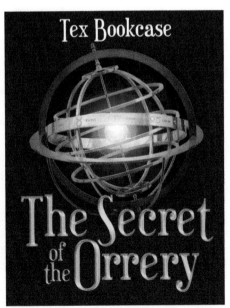

Tex Bookcase

7 The brassy, metallic style on this text is created using Layer Styles. See page 236 for a tutorial on how to create metal in this way. The style used here is saved within the file on the CD, so you can adapt it for use in your own projects (and you can, of course, apply it to any font).

8 The author's name is added in the same font, but without the gold effect so it stands out more clearly at the top. Because the orrery touches the letter S in the main title, there's a potential conflict here: so I've added a Drop Shadow to the text style to darken the region immediately behind this letter.

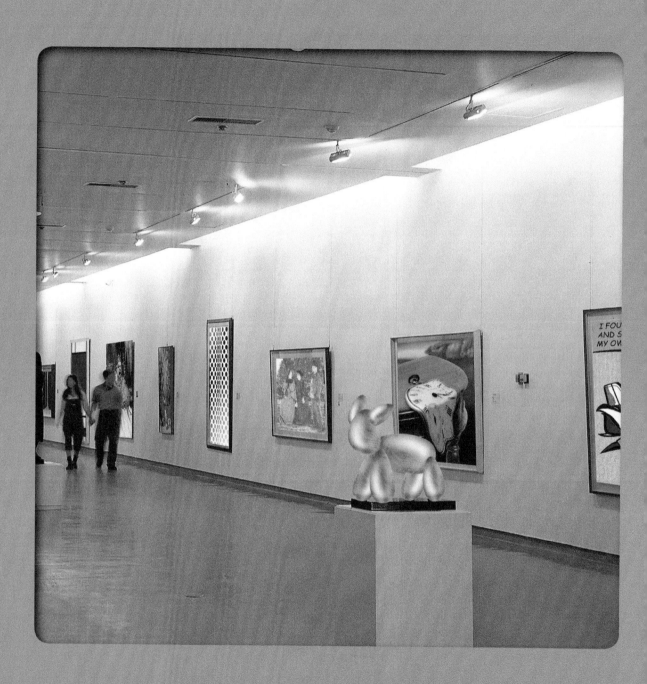

Great works of art

We're surrounded by works of art in a way that people never before have been in history. It leaps out of book covers, beams down from billboards, and assails us through advertising.

These days even the least visually literate of viewers will recognize a couple of dozen famous paintings, starting – of course – with the *Mona Lisa*, and working through the history of popular art.

But how are these works created? And do we need to mix oil paints in order to reproduce them? We'll look at how to simulate a range of artistic styles, from the ancient to the contemporary.

It would be presumptuous of us to think that we could paint like Gainsborough, or imagine like Warhol. So in this chapter we'll only look at those artists whose work lends itself to being replicated in Photoshop: you won't see a tutorial on how to do a Da Vinci drawing here, because if you could draw like that you'd have no need of Photoshop to begin with.

art

1. the products of human creativity; works of art collectively; 'an art exhibition'; 'a fine collection of art'

2. the creation of beautiful or significant things; 'art does not need to be innovative to be good'; 'I was never any good at art'; 'he said that architecture is the art of wasting space beautifully'

3. a superior skill that you can learn by study and practice and observation; 'the art of conversation'; 'it's quite an art'

4. photographs or other visual representations in a printed publication; 'the publisher was responsible for all the artwork in the book'

Wordnet Dictionary

Thomas Gainsborough

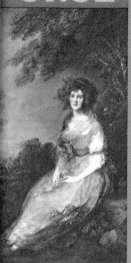

Thomas Gainsborough (1727-1788) was the foremost English painter of portraits and landscapes. More often than not, the subjects of his portraits owned the landscapes they stood in front of: favored by the landed gentry, Gainsborough had little interest in social realism.

In fact, realism played very little part in his work, except for the fine detailing in the foliage and distant views: his subjects were always meticulously posed in stylized, artificial arrangements. His subjects tended to be dukes and earls, and he was the favorite painter of King George III (yes, the mad one).

As well as making a straightforward photograph look like an oil painting, we'll add a canvas texture to complete the effect.

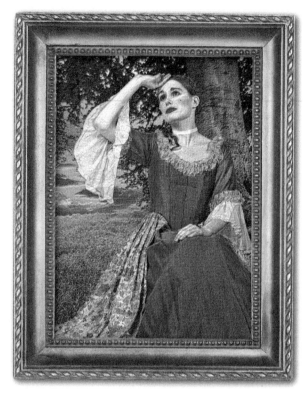

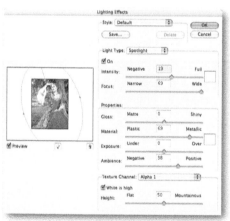

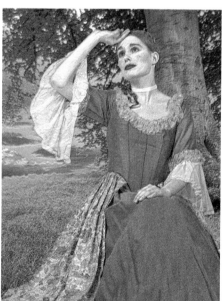

3 Now return to the RGB composite, using the Channels palette, and open the Lighting Effects filter (found in Filters > Render). We don't want to use the spotlight effect here, so make sure the Intensity setting is low, and the Ambient setting high enough so that the preview looks like our original. From the pop-up menu at the bottom, choose Alpha 1 as the Texture Channel. This will form the basis for a bump map, giving the appearance of depth to the image.

4 Once we press OK in the Lighting Effects dialog, we can see the result: the flat artwork now appears to have depth to it, giving the illusion of thick oil paint on the background.

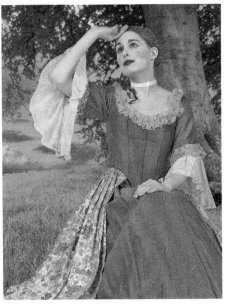

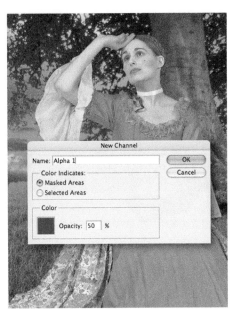

1 Here's our starting image: a bucolic maiden from the Photos.com collection, placed against a new background. The layers have been flattened together so that we can work on them as a single unit. The first thing we need to do is to get some texture into the picture.

2 To make the texture, first select all and copy; then make a new channel, using the pop-up menu in the Channels palette. When the new channel opens, choose Paste (⌘ V / ctrl V) and the image will appear in grayscale in the new channel.

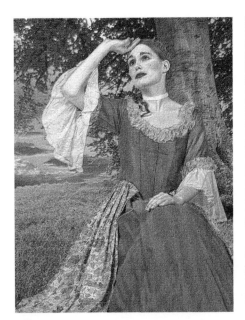

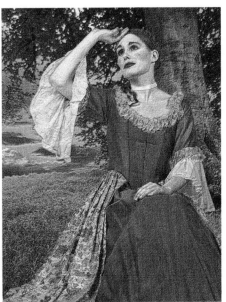

5 Now for some canvas texture. Choose the Texturizer filter from the Filters > Texture menu, and pick Canvas from the pop-up menu. Don't go for too strong an effect here, as it will look artificial: the canvas should be just about visible in this painting, rather than swamping the image.

6 Finally, we need to boost the contrast in this picture. There are many ways to do this in Photoshop, and the simplest is to use the Brightness/Contrast adjustment. Since version CS3 this has been reworked so it's non-destructive: previously, it could cause blown-out highlights that couldn't be fixed.

MORE INFO

● The Lighting Effects filter, used in step 3, is capable of producing dramatic three-dimensional effects. We'll look at some of its capabilities elsewhere in this book. For now, all you need to be concerned about is the Height slider, which raises or lowers the apparent depth. It's hard to see the results in the tiny preview window, though; the only solution is to guess at a setting and see if it looks right. If not, then Undo and use ⌘ ⌥ F / ctrl alt F to reopen the dialog for the filter.

● If you want to simulate a painting that's not painted on canvas, but still want it to look old, then don't apply a Canvas texture in step 5. Instead, take a look at the Craquelure filter, which adds a simulation of a broken, cracked surface. Again, be careful not to overuse this one: begin with the lowest settings and increase gradually until you get the effect you want.

● Nothing helps an oil painting look authentic as much as a gilt frame. The frame used here is on a separate layer, with a drop shadow applied using Layer Effects; the shadow also appears on top of the painting itself, adding a sense of depth to the whole.

SHORTCUTS

155

J. M. W. Turner

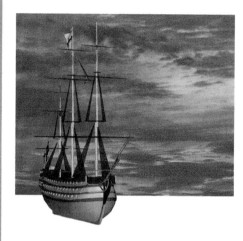

Joseph Mallord William Turner (1775–1851) was a prodigious English landscape painter who was accepted into the Royal Academy of Art at the age of just 14.

Although he started conventionally enough, painting landscapes and the occasional portrait, he soon became obsessed with natural events – sunlight, storms, rain, and especially the sea, whose raw power intrigued him. He was particularly interested in disasters, rushing to witness the burning of the Houses of Parliament in 1834 so he could commemorate the event on canvas.

Turner is best known for his seascapes, which explore light and shade in a way no painter had before: his work, far in advance of its time, prepared the way for the French impressionists who were to follow.

We'll explore his techniques through a homage to *The fighting Temeraire tugged to her last berth to be broken up*, above, which Turner painted in 1839.

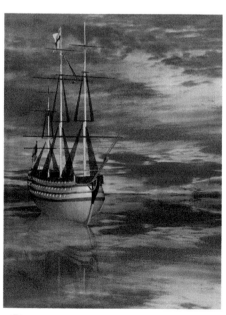

1 The sky is one I photographed; the ship is a 3D model, imported into the Extended edition of Photoshop CS3. If you don't have the Extended edition, it's not a problem – I've provided the ship image as a regular layer on the CD.

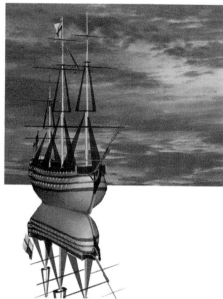

2 The reason I chose a 3D model rather than a photograph of a ship is that it gives us the ability to create a better reflection than we could achieve by simply flipping the ship vertically. Even so, it took a while to achieve a suitable angle of view.

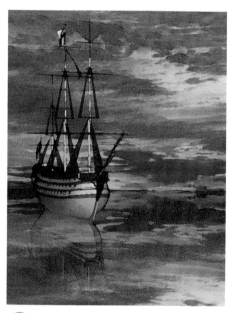

5 In order to make the reflected ship look more real, add a Layer Mask (using Layer > Layer Mask > Reveal All). Painting in black on this mask will hide the ship; painting in white will reveal it. Try to achieve a soft fading away as the ship reflection nears the bottom of the canvas.

6 To apply our filters, first make a Merged Copy of the image using *ctrl alt Shift E* ⌘ ⌥ *Shift E*. The first effect is Filter > Artistic > Watercolor: I used the maximum Brush Detail and Texture values of 14 and 3 respectively, with the Shadow Intensity set to 0.

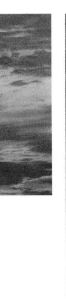

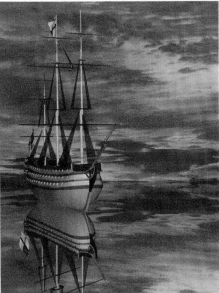

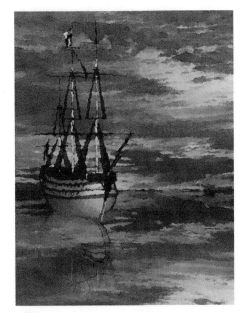

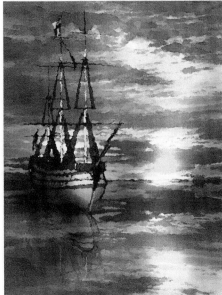

3 We need to make that sky more colorful. Make a new layer, above the sky (and behind the ship), set to Color mode. Paint on here with a large, soft-edged brush, in tones of blue, yellow, red and orange, to add some of Turner's exotic colors to the image.

4 To make the sea, all we need to do is take a copy of the sky and flip it vertically. I've added some black shading with the Gradient tool just below the horizon line, to mark a clearer distinction between the sea and its reflection.

7 The second filter to be applied is Filter > Brush Strokes > Spatter. The values used here depend on the image you're working on, and the size at which you're working; I used Spray Radius and Smoothness values both set to 9.

8 To make the image come alive, we need to beef up the lighting. Make a copy of the layer (so we can return to the original if we make a mistake) and use the Dodge tool, set to Highlights mode, to brighten the area around the sun; then use the Burn tool, set to Midtones, to darken the side of the ship that's in shadow.

MORE INFO

● In step 6, we make a Merged Copy of our artwork. This is necessary so that we can apply our filters to the image as a whole, rather than to each layer individually. Up until this point, the ship model and the photographed sky looked quite out of keeping with each other; applying the filters to both helps to unify them into a single image.

● We've applied the Watercolor and Spatter filters as two separate steps here, in order to show how each one affects the image. But we could apply both at the same time: when in the Filter Gallery dialog, click the New Document icon at the bottom right to add an additional filter, and then change it to the one you want. The advantage of this approach is that we can see the effect of both filters simultaneously, allowing us to modify their appearance in concert with each other until we get the right effect.

● The effectiveness of the Dodge and Burn tools in step 8 depends very much on the mode to which they're set. Here we use Highlights for the Dodge tool, but Midtones for the Burn tool; these modes have the strongest effect on color for each tool.

Georges Seurat

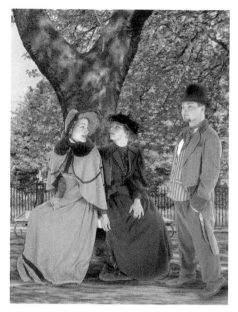

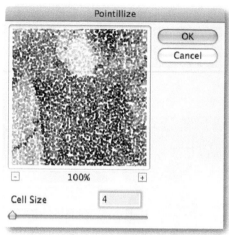

Georges-Pierre Seurat (1859–1891) was the founder of the neo-impressionism art movement. The painting above is a detail from *Sunday Afternoon on the Island of La Grande Jatte*, probably his most famous work.

Seurat was the foremost exponent of pointillism, a technique involving creating a picture from many thousands of tiny dots, rather than naturalistic brushstrokes. The intention was that the viewer's eye would do the job of mixing the colors, rather than the artist doing it on his palette: the result is a rich, dense effect that's full of tiny detail, creating a detached, other-worldly impression in the viewer.

1 Here's a suitable scene: two Victorian ladies sitting on a park bench, while a gentleman strolls past. I've put this together from four separate sources, but of course there's no reason why you should copy the period dress precisely.

2 The first step is, naturally enough, the Pointillize filter – found under Filter > Pixelate. The only control here is the size of the resulting dot: a value of 4 is a good starting point. Work on a copy of your base artwork, as we'll need the original later.

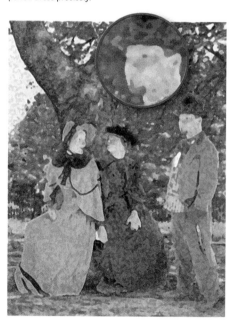

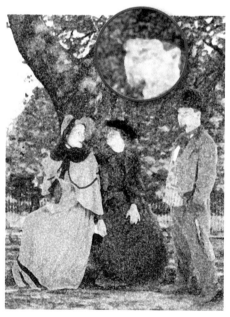

5 The Pontillize/Gaussian Blur combination worked well enough, but we were left with an image that had altogether too much white space behind the dots. We need a way to tie it together better, and to unify the image. Working on a copy of the original background, apply the Sponge filter (Filter > Artistic).

6 With the Sponge-filtered version placed on top of the layer stack, we can't see the original Pointillized version beneath it. But if we change the mode of the layer from Normal to Hard Light, using the pop-up menu at the top of the Layers palette, we can see through to the Pointillized layer beneath.

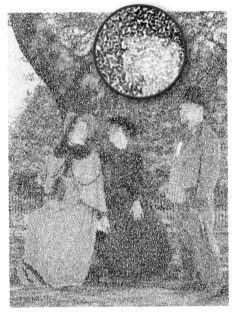

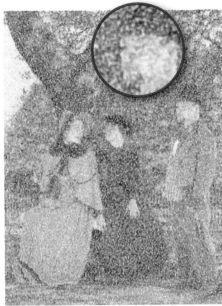

3 This is the result of applying the Pointillize filter. It's not a bad start, but the result is very harsh: these dots look like they've been created by a machine, rather than painted with a soft brush, as the inset shows clearly.

4 The simple remedy is to apply a little Gaussian Blur to the filtered image (Filter > Blur). A value of around 1 pixel will do fine – we only want to soften the edges. You can raise or lower the amount in 0.1 steps, so experiment with different settings.

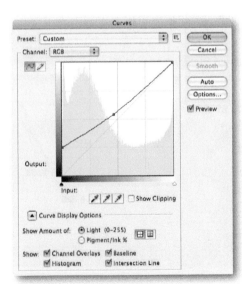

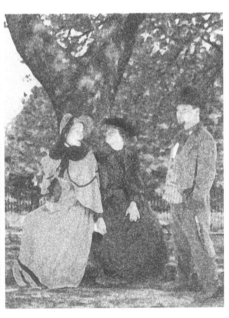

7 The result of combining the two filter effects produces a good result – but it's rather too strongly contrasted. To recapture some of the pastel feel of Seurat's originals, we need to brighten the darkest tones. Open the Curves dialog, and raise the left-hand edge of the curve to brighten the shadows.

8 Here's the finished result: a softly speckled, low contrast image that matches the feel of the pointillist originals.

ON THE CD

✓   image

 texture

Aa font

MORE INFO

● The technique used here, combining multiple layers using different filters while using Hard Light mode, is a good way to build up a complex effect. Because each effect is on a separate layer we can experiment with different 'light' modes – Soft Light, Overlay, and so on.

● When simulating an artistic style like this, it helps to copy the style of the composition as well as the detail in the brushwork. If you're photographing your family for a similar treatment, try to arrange them in a manner that suits Seurat's observational, serene and rather distant approach to his subjects.

● The choice of cell size when using the Pontillize filter in step 2 depends very much on how you're going to present your work. If it's going to be displayed on a website, then what you see at 100% will be what you get. But if you're working for high resolution print, you'll need to raise this figure to avoid simply seeing a messy result. Even in this book, the CMYK print screen used to reproduce the images on glossy paper inevitably clashes with the pontillist effect and hides it to some degree.

SHORTCUTS

MAC WIN BOTH

Paul Cézanne

Paul Cézanne (1839–1906) was the French post-impressionist painter who, perhaps more than any other, changed the style of painting in France from the 19th to the 20th century.

Both Matisse and Picasso described Cézanne as 'the father of us all', acclaiming him for his pioneering work in taking the impressionist style prevalent at the end of the 19th century and preparing the ground for the cubist movement that was to follow.

Although Cézanne painted many figures and landscapes during his career, he returned time and again to still life paintings featuring bowls of fruit. It's this aspect of his work that we'll attempt to emulate on these pages.

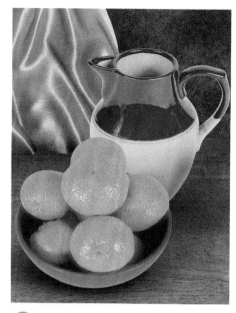

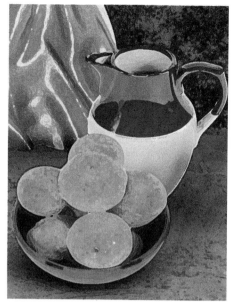

1 I've put this image together from a variety of sources: the fruit bowl, jug, table, curtain and background are all separate layers. But whether you make your own composite or start with a single photograph, you'll need one layer to work on. Use `ctrl` `alt` `E` `⌘` `⌥` `E` to make a Merged Copy.

2 We'll need a couple of separate filter effects to make this image work, so let's start with the basic brush strokes. Duplicate the Merged Copy you're working on, and choose Filter > Artistic > Dry Brush to create the initial effect. Choose a medium sized brush, with high texture and detail values.

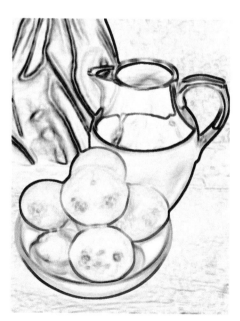

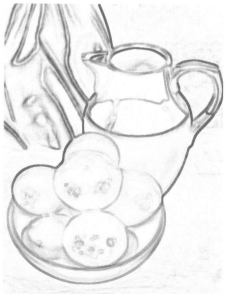

5 The last step neatly outlined all the edges in our document. But we want to turn those edges to blue; as the second step in the process, choose Image > Adjustments > Invert (or use `ctrl` `I` `⌘` `I`) to invert the image.

6 Now to change all those lines to blue. Open the Hue/Saturation dialog (`ctrl` `U` `⌘` `U`) and check the Colorize button: this will change all the hues to a single color. Drag the Hue slider until you get a strong blue result.

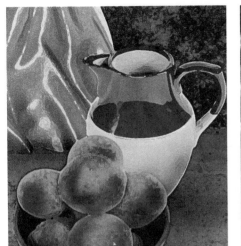

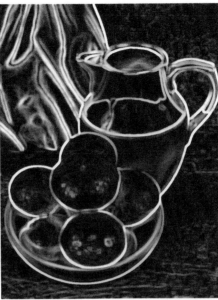

3 To bring a little more life into those oranges, use the Burn tool set to Midtones. This both darkens them and adds saturation, turning the rather insipid orange we started with into a strong, burnt umber.

4 One of Cézanne's recurring habits was to outline the elements of his compositions in blue. We can automate this process with a three step approach. First, take the copy of the original composition (the one you didn't apply the Dry Brush filter to) and apply Filter > Stylize > Glowing Edges.

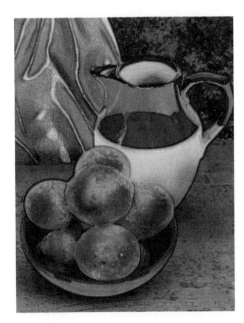

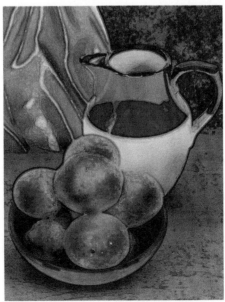

7 When we change the mode of this second layer from Normal to Multiply, all the white disappears and we're just left with the blue outlines, neatly running around all the contours of our composition.

8 The last step is to paint a little additional color into the image. Make a new layer, set to Color mode; with a soft-edged brush, paint blue into the shadows to replicate the shadow effect used commonly by Cézanne and his contemporaries.

MORE INFO

● Both the Dry Brush filter (step 2) and the Glowing Edges filter (step 4) appear in Photoshop's Filter Gallery list, from which we can add multiple filters at once. But the Filter Gallery feature doesn't allow us to modify filter effects to the extent of inverting, colorizing and changing layer modes; that's why we need two separate layers to perform the task. Using multiple copies of the same layer, each treated differently, is a common Photoshop process that gives us more control and flexibility.

● In this workthrough we've attempted to copy the work of Cézanne as closely as possible. But there's no need for you do take this approach: if you find other combinations of filters, or diffferent filter settings, produce a better result, then go for it. What matters in the end is the quality of the finished image.

● In this example we're working with Merged Copies of a multi-layer file. But if you have Photoshop CS3 or later, you can group all the layers ready to apply a Smart Filter to the lot. This means you'll still be able to disassemble and move or replace elements of the composition later.

SHORTCUTS

 MAC   WIN   BOTH

161

Henri Matisse

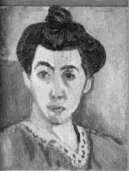

Henri Matisse (1869–1954) was a printmaker and sculptor as well as a painter. Initially his work was considered so outlandish that he and his kind were labeled 'Fauves' – wild beast, in French.

The Fauvists rejected the pastel hues and representational values of the Impressionists, preferring strong colors and vigorous, almost aggressive brushstrokes.

Initially, as with so many art movements, the result was an outcry: as one French critic put it, 'a pot of paint has been flung in the face of the public.'

Matisse formed a close friendship with Picasso, and the two saw themselves as artistic rivals.

Reproducing his style of painting is difficult, because so much of his work depended on his use of color and texture: but we can look at how to simulate his painting *Portrait of Madame Matisse*, above.

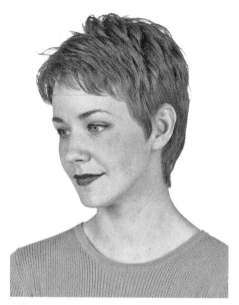

1 Here's a suitable subject for our painting, cut out on a separate layer. Too many portraits show the subject grinning at the camera, and this isn't a style which Matisse would choose: he far preferred a melancholy expression.

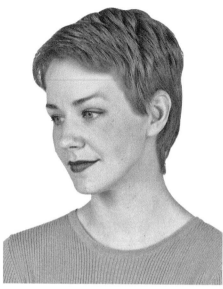

2 The hair has to look painted, rather than naturalistic, so cut off the loose fringes on top with the Eraser tool. We can also use the Smudge tool to smooth out those loose strands of hair that are falling on the forehead – don't worry about the resulting blurring.

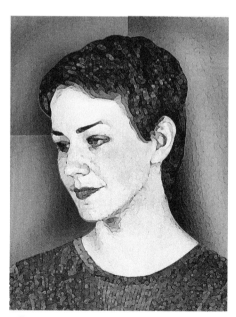

5 Next, apply the Paint Daubs filter (Filter > Artistic once again). Choose a small brush size with medium Sharpness in order to get this detailed, almost three-dimensional oil paint texture.

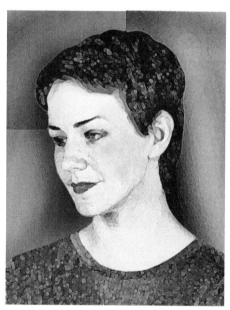

6 The texture we produced following the Paint Daubs filter is all very well, but the result is just a little too sharp to be believable – it looks too crisp to be a painting. Use a small amount of Gaussian Blur (Filter > Blur) to smooth it out: around a 1 pixel radius should be sufficient.

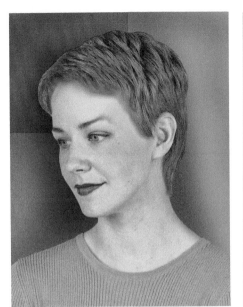

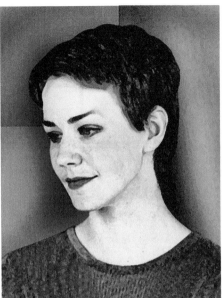

3 Our simple background is made from panels of solid color, matching Matisse's original. The added shading isn't to create naturalistic shadows, but to give the texture process, which we'll look at next, something to work with.

4 We need a couple of filters to generate the oil paint texture. First, make a Merged Copy of both layers by pressing `ctrl` `alt` `Shift` `E` `⌘` `⌥` `Shift` `E`. We'll begin with Fresco (Filter > Artistic), which adds a posterizing quality to the image.

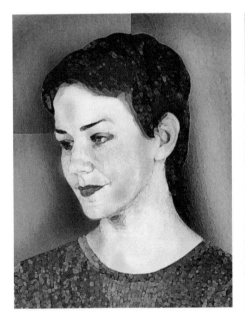

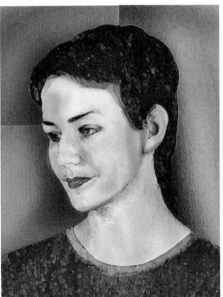

7 Now to add some colors to this – the key to making the effect work. Make a new layer, and set its mode to Hard Light. Now, when we paint on the layer, our colors are translucent: we can still see through to the figure beneath. Choose oranges, yellows and greens for the skin, and save your blues for the hair.

8 It often helps to create a second Hard Light layer half way through the coloring process. Here, we've used the second layer to add detail around the chin line and eyebrows, to add more color to the side of the face, and to change the color of the clothing.

MORE INFO

● In steps 4 and 5 here we first add the Fresco filter, then go on to add the Paint Daubs filter on top. We could do this in a single operation: every time we open the Filter Gallery, we're presented with the option of applying any of the Artistic or Sketch filters. At the bottom right of the dialog is a 'new document' icon, which allows us to add an additional filter effect. Now, we can see how the image looks with two or more filters applied. We can change their order by dragging them, and adjust the settings until they look good together.

● In step 4 we made a Merged Copy of the two layers, rather than merging them together. It's a good idea to keep your original layers intact for as long as possible, just in case you need to make any changes later on.

● This is the kind of image you can keep working on for as long as you have the patience. Try using the Smudge tool to clean up ragged texture, and keep refining those Hard Light layers with different color choices until you get the result you want.

SHORTCUTS

 MAC WIN BOTH

Piet Mondrian

The work of the Dutch painter Piet Mondrian (1872–1944) is among the most difficult examples of modern art for the casual viewer to get to grips with.

One of the foremost members of the De Stijl movement, Mondrian's stark, non-representational, paintings – he called them merely 'compositions' – take abstraction to a level rarely seen before or since. Thick black lines separate sparse rectangles of color, as paintings are reduced to the pure play of form and color: modernism taken to extremes.

Although Mondrian's work has been reproduced everywhere from coffee mugs to wall cabinets, it's a mistake to assume that he was striving for perfect flat lines and shapes. The brush strokes are an integral part of the work, and it's that quality of surface texture that we'll aim for in this version of a painting he created in 1921.

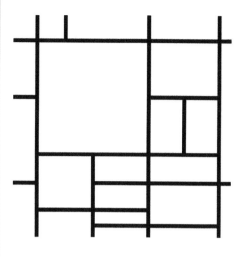

1 The black lines that make up the work are the starting point. Create one vertical line as a marquee selection first, then duplicate it around the canvas to make all the other lines. That way, you'll be sure to make all the lines of uniform thickness.

2 Creating the texture is a multi-step process. Make a new layer, and set the foreground color to pale brown and the background color to white. Apply the Clouds filter from the Render section of the Filters menu, to create this random pattern of light and shade. Each time you use the filter it will produce a slightly different effect, so experiment until you get a pleasing result. I've enlarged a section of the view over these three steps so we can see the texture more clearly.

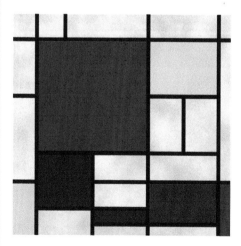

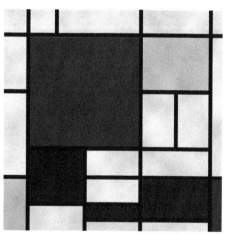

5 To make the colored rectangles, make a new layer behind the black lines. Draw rectangles with the Marquee tool – no need to fit them accurately, as long as the edges are behind the thick black lines. Pick a foreground color, and use ⌫ ⏎ alt ⏎ to fill the selection with the chosen color.

6 We now need to add texture to the colored rectangles as well, otherwise they look too flat and computer-generated in front of that textured canvas. This is simply achieved by changing the mode of the color layer from Normal to Multiply: in this mode, the colors darken up the texture beneath, so we can still see it clearly.

ON THE CD

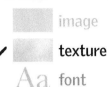

image

✓ **texture**

Aa font

MORE INFO

● In step 1, we created all the black lines by copying sections of one line around the canvas. Make the three vertical lines that extend all the way from top to bottom first; hold ⌥ *alt* as you drag a filled selection to duplicate it, adding *Shift* to constrain its movement to just vertical or horizontal. Use Edit > Transform > Rotate 90° to make the horizontal lines. Where the lines don't reach all the way to the edge of the canvas, hold ⌥ *alt* as you drag over the unwanted area with the Marquee tool to remove it from the selection. The remainder of the lines can be copied from existing horizontals and verticals.

● Although we're basing this on an original Mondrian painting, there's no reason why you should follow this pattern exactly: feel free to make your own composition in this style. Although it may look like child's play, it's harder than it might seem to create an image that contains the balance and grace of Mondrian's work.

● The texture we've created here can be used as the background for many painting styles. If you want to add it to an image, change the mode of this layer to Multiply and place it at the top of the layer stack.

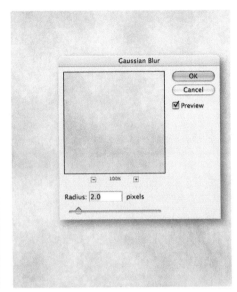

3 The next step is to add some noise. Choose Add Noise from the Noise section of the Filters menu, and pick Gaussian rather than Normal noise for a more natural, varied effect. Make sure it's monochromatic noise (we don't want any stray colors creeping in here) and choose a low setting of around 10%.

4 The noise in the previous step made the whole effect too bitty, so let's add some Gaussian Blur to soften it. The setting should be enough so that the noise is smoothed overall, withhough losing sight of it altogether. When this is done, move the texture layer behind the lines layer.

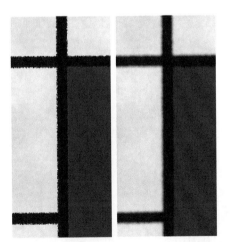

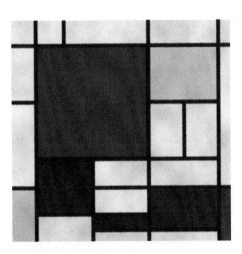

7 Let's now address those black lines: as they stand, they're just too perfect. To make them appear painted, first apply the Diffuse filter, found in Filters > Stylize. This produces the effect shown on the left in the enlarged view, above. Then apply a little Gaussian Blur to the layer, which softens the edges (right) and creates a far more hand-painted appearance.

8 Here's the finished painting. The background texture and the softening of the thick black lines combine to create a work that looks as if it has been painted by hand, rather than created entirely on a computer.

SHORTCUTS

 MAC WIN BOTH

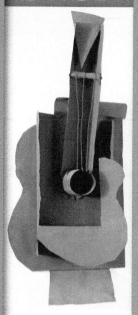

Pablo Picasso

Pablo Picasso (1881–1973) was perhaps the most famous and influential painter of the 20th century. His painting *Les Demoiselles d'Avignon*, painted in 1907, brought cubism to the attention of the world.

Picasso was a supreme draughtsman as well as being a consummate stylist. It would be absurd for us to attempt to reproduce one of his paintings here, as only Picasso can paint a Picasso.

But he also created sculptures, such as his 1912 model *Maquette for Guitar*. We may not be able to paint like him, but we can pay homage to the master by reproducing his cardboard and string model in a public space.

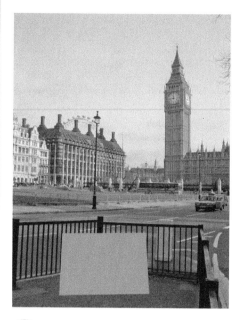

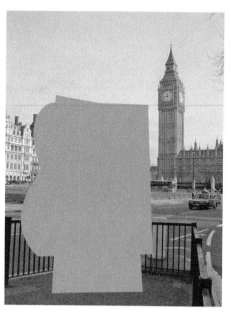

1 Just like Picasso's original model was built from several sheets of cardboard, so we'll use an equal number of layers to make our version of it. We'll begin with the base stand: trace the shape on an empty layer with the Polygonal Lasso tool, and fill with mid gray.

2 Because the next shape has a curve on the side, we'll need to draw a path with the Pen tool to capture it correctly. Use *ctrl Enter* *⌘ Enter* to turn the path into a selection, then fill with gray on a new layer once again.

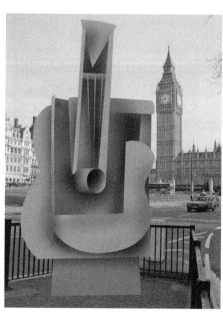

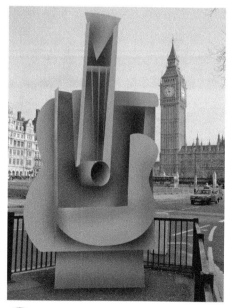

5 Here's the finished sculpture, made up of individual layers and shaded. As it stands it looks far from photorealistic – more like a plastic model awaiting the addition of color and texture. We'll add the texture shortly; first, we need to make it fit better into its environment.

6 Paint a shadow on a new layer at the bottom, so the object sits on the ground. We now need to load all the layers as selections. Hold *ctrl* *⌘* and click on the thumbnail of the first layer; then hold *ctrl Shift* *⌘ Shift* and click on each subsequent layer's thumbnail to add that to the selected area.

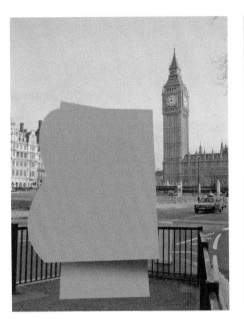

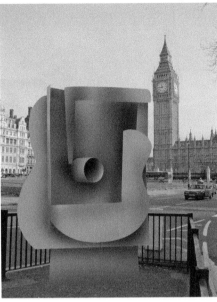

3 We'll now need to add some shading to the layer beneath to make it stand out. Using the Burn tool set to Highlights, paint a shadow on the first layer, cast by the layer we've just drawn. This helps us to see the two layers clearly.

4 Continue this process of making new layers and shading the layers beneath as we go along. The shading helps to define each layer as a separate object, as well as adding texture to the layers.

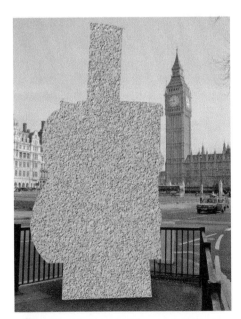

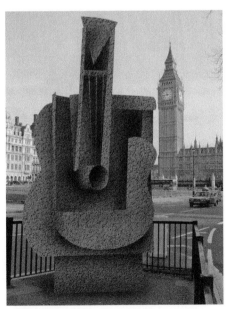

7 With all the layers loaded up, we should have a selection that matches all the layers in the construction. Make the Texture layer visible, then inverse the selection and press *Backspace* to delete everything outside the selection area.

8 The texture we added in the previous step completely obscures the image, so we need to make sure we can see our hard work beneath it. Changing the mode of this layer from Normal to Multiply means that it only darkens up the layers beneath, producing this rough metal appearance.

ON THE CD

 ✔ image

 ✔ texture

Aa font

MORE INFO

● In step **1** we need to fill a selected area with a mid gray color. We could go through menus to do this – but there's a quicker way. With gray as the foreground color, press *alt Backspace* *⌥ Backspace*; this will fill any selected area with the foreground color. If you want to fill an area with the current background color, use *ctrl Backspace* *⌘ Backspace* instead.

● In step **7**, we first load up the pixels on a layer by holding *ctrl ⌘* and clicking on that layer's thumbnail in the Layers palette. If we simply repeat this on another layer's thumbnail, we'll load that as a selection instead; but as with all selections, holding *Shift* as we click adds the new selection to the old one.

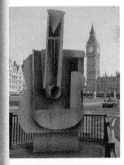

● We don't need to stick to a metallic texture: anything can be added onto this base. Here's a wooden effect.

SHORTCUTS

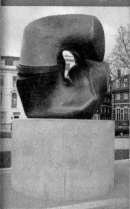

Henry Moore

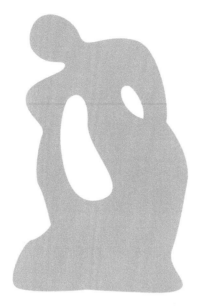

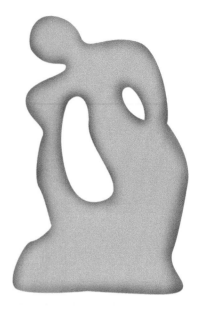

The British artist Henry Moore (1898–1986) is best known for his large figurative abstracts, either carved in stone or cast in bronze.

He usually depicted figures, returning frequently to his favorite subject of 'mother and child'. Moore's work abstracted human anatomy to basic constituent parts, often featuring holes inside his figures: the use of these hollow regions within his work became a sort of trademark.

Moore almost always depicted women, whether nursing children or, commonly, reclining on a plinth.

Rather than producing a slavish copy of a single Moore work, we'll produce an original sculpture based on his ideas. It's a mother and child composition, in which the child is represented by the hole within the mother's torso.

1 Begin by drawing the outline of the figure on a new layer. While it is just about possible to paint this with a hard-edged Brush, the only way to achieve smooth lines is by using the Pen tool, turning the path into a selection and filling with gray.

2 Add some basic shading around all the edges with the Burn tool, set to Highlights. You don't need to be too exact here; we just want to create the initial impression of some rounding at the edges. Use a small, soft-edged brush to achieve the effect.

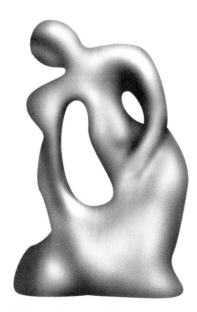

5 To add highlights we can use the Dodge tool. We can also access this tool temporarily while using the Burn tool, by holding down the *alt* ⌥ key: this makes it easy to switch between the two tools. Use the two to build up light and shade, increasing the overall contrast of the figure.

6 With the basic figure complete, we need to add texture on a new layer. The easiest way to create the effect of a bronze surface is to set the foreground color to a warm yellow and the background color to brown, and use Filter > Render > Clouds: choose. Repeat with *ctrl* F ⌘ F until you get the desired effect.

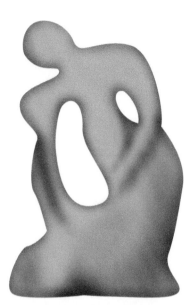

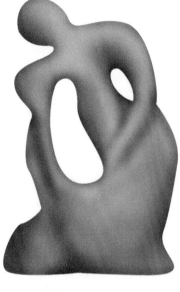

3 Now use the Burn tool once again to sketch in some of the contours within the piece. We'll build up the suggestion of an arm on the right, and add some shading around the base for the sake of realism. Use a low pressure and build up the effect gradually.

4 Now for the lighting. If we imagine that the light source is at top right, we need shadows placed bottom left: so use the Burn tool once more to paint in shading on the sides of the model that fall away from the source of the light.

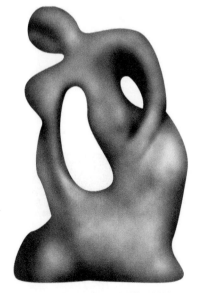

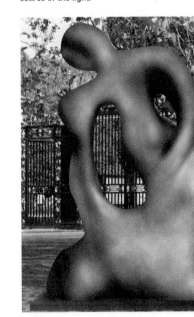

7 To make the texture show up only where it overlaps the figure, make a Clipping Mask by pressing *ctrl* *alt* *G* *⌘* *⌥* *G* or holding *alt* *⌥* and clicking between the two layers in the Layers palette. When we change the mode of the texture layer to Hard Light, we can see the shading beneath.

8 As with all isolated objects, the effect works best when placed in a realistic setting. Here, placing the sculpture in a park scene makes it look far more convincing.

MORE INFO

● This exercise makes use of the Dodge and Burn tools to a high degree, so it's worth looking at how to use these tools effectively. For best results, invest in a pressure-sensitive graphics tablet: Dodge and Burn are much easier to control when you can vary the pressure. If you don't have access to one, then set a low pressure – around 30% or so – and build up the shading gradually, using your mouse or trackpad. Remember, you can change the pressure at any time using the number keys on your keyboard: use 2 for 20%, 5 for 50% and so on, up to 0 for 100%.

● The Clouds filter, used in step 6 here, creates a random texture that's a blend of the foreground and background colors. Because it's random, we don't always get the effect we want first time; repeat the process by pressing *ctrl* *F* *⌘* *F* to apply the filter again. For a tighter texture, press *ctrl* *alt* *F* *⌘* *⌥* *F* instead.

● Because we're applying the texture on a separate layer, we can continue to adjust the lighting of the sculpture beneath using Dodge and Burn. Remember, too, to adjust the brightness of the texture layer itself if it doesn't look quite right.

SHORTCUTS

MAC WIN BOTH

René Magritte

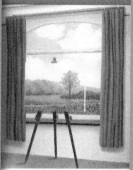

1 There are two starting elements in our montage: a blank canvas on an easel, and a square-on view of a window. It would, of course, be possible to photograph a canvas in front of a real window, but the lighting issues would be severe. Magritte would have placed the canvas directly in front of the window, but we'll exaggerate the effect by moving it slightly to one side.

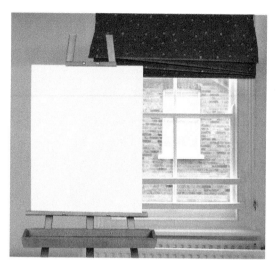

The Belgian painter René Magritte (1898–1967) was one of the foremost surrealist artists. He may not have had the technical skill of Dali, but he more than made up for this with a fervent imagination that had the ability to delve deep into our collective psyche. More than any other surrealist, Magritte's work strikes a chord with the viewer.

La Condition Humaine is a theme that he returned to again and again, painting numerous variations on this theme: a canvas in front of a window or an open doorway. At what point does the view through the window become the view as depicted on the canvas? It's often hard to spot the join – and that's deliberate. The view through the window is itself, of course, just another painting of the scene.

We'll reproduce Magritte's technique in a photographic manner, while staying true to the style of the original.

3 Now for a new view. Magritte always used pastoral scenes, so we'll follow suit. We couldn't use the original view through this window, unless we went to the trouble of leaning out of the window first to photograph it. By placing the landscape on a layer behind the window layer, the layer mask allows us to see through the glass areas to the view beyond.

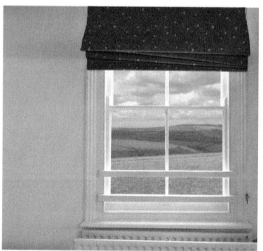

5 Duplicate the background layer by holding `alt` `⌥` as you drag a copy of it above the canvas layer, then press `ctrl` `alt` `G` `⌘` `⌥` `G` to make use the canvas layer as a clipping mask for this duplicated background. Now, it will show up only where it overlaps the canvas. Notice how that thin white edge we left on the right hand side marks the point where the canvas ends.

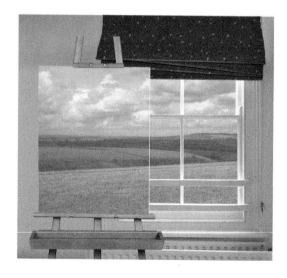

2 The first thing to do is to take out the original view. Having hidden the easel layer, the best way to remove the view is to make a layer mask for the window layer. Select the individual panes with the Lasso or Pen tools, then fill with black on the layer mask to hide these regions.

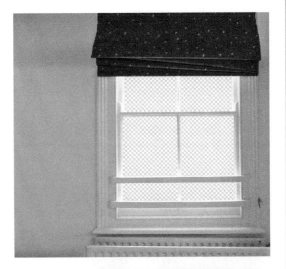

4 To carry this view onto the canvas, first select the canvas area on the easel – a simple matter using the Magic Wand tool. We need to show a slight edge on the window side, however: this is what makes the illusion work. Since the canvas is vertical, we can use the Rectangular Marquee tool to remove a thin slice from this selection. With the whole canvas selected, hold alt ⌥ and drag the marquee over the right-hand edge of the canvas to remove it from the selected area. Then use ctrl J ⌘ J to make a new layer from the resulting selection. I've hidden the original easel layer here to show just the new canvas layer.

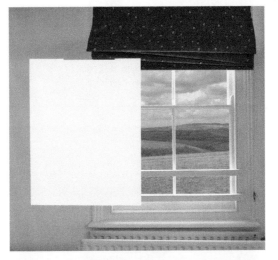

6 All the versions Magritte painted of this subject had both the window and the canvas more or less straight on in the scene. And it's not hard to see why: when we attempt the same technique with an angled window and easel, the horizon line in the view fights with the diagonals made by the tops and bottoms of the easel and window, destroying the effect.

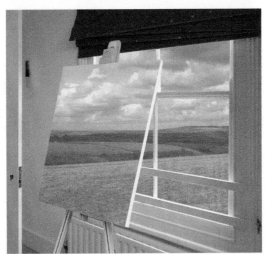

Salvador Dalí

Dalí's painting *The Persistence of Memory*, of which a portion is shown above, is one of his best-known pieces.

Salvador Dalí (1904–1989) was a great showman, and an accomplished artist; there are many who claim his work to be frivolous and meritricious, cashing in on the surrealist movement without truly being a part of it.

Whether or not we like or even approve of his body of work, there can be little doubt that it has had a profound influence on the art of the 20th century, and has invaded the popular consciousness in a way few have managed.

Of the dozens of possible Dalí paintings I could have chosen to emulate, I picked this one as being the most suitable for recreation in Photoshop – and because it's an instantly recognizable example of his work.

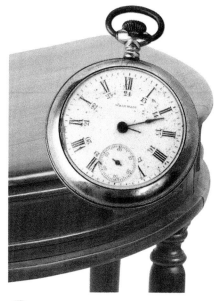

1 We'll start with just two elements – a pocket watch, and a table to bend it over. The image we'll end up with is more photographic than Dali's oil paintings, but will capture the style of his work.

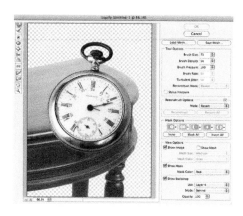

2 The key to melting the watch is to use Photoshop's Liquify filter, chosen from the top of the Filters menu. You can also choose it with `ctrl` `Shift` `X` `⌘` `Shift` `X` as a shortcut.

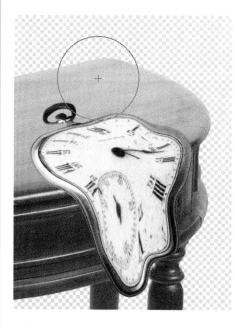

5 With the basic distortion complete, we can carry on to make the perimeter of the watch more lumpy. Lower the brush size – you can use the `[` and `]` keys, or hold the `Shift` key as well for bigger jumps – to get more control. Try to make the rim around the face a more or less even thickness all the way around.

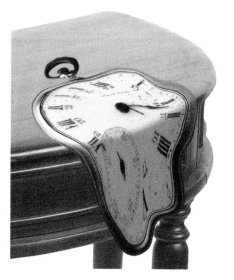

6 Press `Enter` to exit the Liquify filter. We now need to darken the watch where it hangs over the table. In Dali's original, this portion was brighter; but as our table is clearly lighter on top, we need to copy this lighting approach. Select the bottom portion and feather it by about 8 pixels, then darken with Curves or Levels.

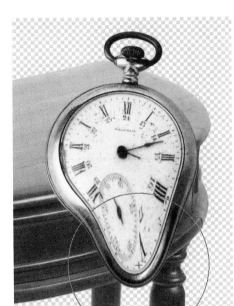

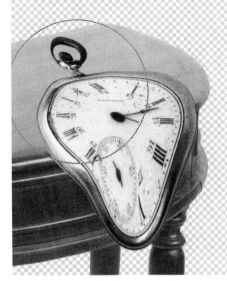

3 We'll use the Forward Warp tool – the default tool in Liquify – to do all the work here. Choose a large brush size, about the size of the watch face, and start to smear the watch down into shape.

4 Now, with the same size brush, smear the top half of the watch to the left so that it appears to lie in the plane of the table. Getting these angles right is the key to making this effect work convincingly.

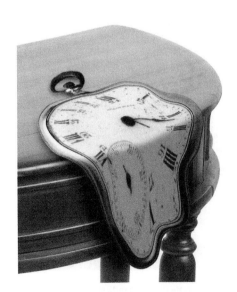

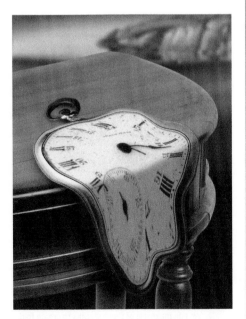

7 To make the effect more convincing, we need to add a shadow behind it. Make a new layer just above the table layer, and press `ctrl` `alt` `G` `⌘` `⌥` `G` to make a clipping mask with the table layer. Now, when we paint in black using a soft-edged brush, the shadow will only show up where it overlaps the table.

8 We could continue to wrap this watch over multiple surfaces, as Dalí did in his original. But it's this very fact of apparently not knowing when to stop that contributed to his rejection by other surrealist artists. We'll paint in an appropriate background, darken the table top and, using great restraint, stop right there.

MORE INFO

● The Liquify filter is a great way to move large chunks of a layer around. But you do need a very large brush in order to avoid leaving pieces behind – often, the brush size is much bigger than we'd expect. If you make a mistake while working within this filter, you can always Undo the previous step; and, as in the rest of Photoshop, using `ctrl` `alt` `Z` `⌘` `⌥` `Z` will undo backwards through multiple steps.

● As well as distorting watches, Dalí loved to play around with distortions of the human form. Using the Liquify filter, nothing could be easier: we can twist, extend, mutate and distort limbs as much as we like. The trick, as always, is knowing when to stop – it's all to easy to end up with a cartoon-like result when working with this tool.

● Dalí's melting watch has become so iconic that there's now even a real working wristwatch made in the gloopy design. How's that for life imitating art! Check www.artwatches.com for details.

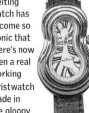

SHORTCUTS

 MAC WIN BOTH

Francis Bacon

The painter Francis Bacon (1909–1992) was a noted English figurative artist, known for his striking, often nightmarish imagery.

Bacon frequently painted triptychs – three part works reminiscent of medieval altar screens – which portrayed a figure from three different views. His paintings of human figures often had grotesquely distorted heads and limbs: this is, incidentally, a feature that's easy to replicate in Photoshop using the Liquify filter, which we'll use here to a limited extent.

Bacon's most famous painting is probably the so-called Screaming Pope, or – to give it its full title – *Study after Velázquez's Portrait of Pope Innocent X* (1953). While we're not going to attempt a slavish copy of Bacon's work, we'll look at how to replicate some of the techniques he used, taking the original Velázquez portrait as our starting point.

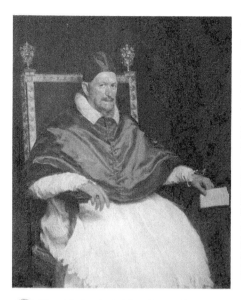

1 The original portrait of Pope Innocent X was painted in 1650 by Diego Velásquez, and so is thankfully out of copyright. This means that although Bacon had to create his masterpiece from scratch, we can use the original and build upon it.

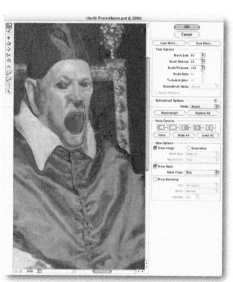

2 A startling feature of Bacon's painting is the open, screaming mouth. While we could copy an open mouth from another painting, we can just as easily open the one he has using the Liquify filter. With a small brush, push out from the mouth to create the illusion of a gaping hole. We can also use this filter to coarsen and exaggerate his features somewhat.

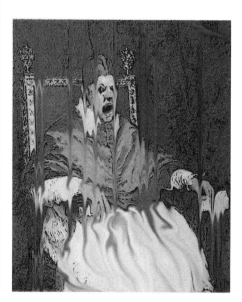

5 We can make use of those streaks to create folds and wrinkles in that large expanse of white robe. Again using the Smudge tool, tweak out each streak over the robe and bend it into the shape of a fold in the fabric. Smudge up from the bottom as well: any color that's slightly different to the body of the robe can be used to create shadows and highlights.

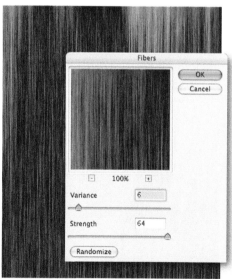

6 To create the strong vertical texture – Bacon himself described it as 'a head painted as if folded in on itself like the folds of a curtain' – we can use the Fibers filter. Fill a new layer with black, and set the background color to black and the foreground to dull yellow. A small Variance setting creates widely spaced streaks; a high Strength setting creates streaks that reach all the way down to the bottom.

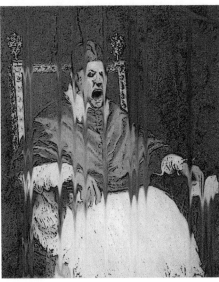

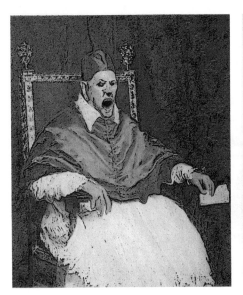

3 To give the painting a harder edge, we can use a combination of the Dry Brush and Poster Edges filters. Using the Filter Gallery, it's easy to combine the two effects to make a starker image, Here, I've also painted in some teeth and darkened the interior of the mouth.

4 We'll reproduce the streaks in the original painting in two ways. First, using the Smudge tool set to around 80%, start at the top of the image and hold *Shift* as you drag vertically downwards, making strong streaks in the image. Vary the opacity of the tool to create a more realistic impression.

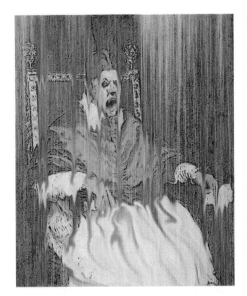

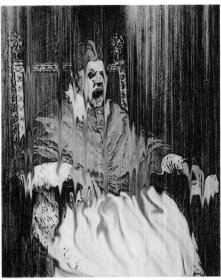

7 So that we can see through the streaks to the painting beneath, change the mode of the Fibers layer from Normal to Screen. In this mode all the black disappears, leaving us with just the pale yellow. Experiment with other modes as well: Hard Light and Overlay, for example, produce dramatic results.

8 To increase the power of the image, add an Adjustment Layer to increase the contrast: both Curves and Brightness/Contrast will do the job well, so use whichever one you're happier with. Here, I've also added a Hue/Saturation adjustment, selecting the reds in the image and taking the magenta and yellow out to create a robe color more suited to Bacon's original.

MORE INFO

● This tutorial involves several steps that work directly on the image – the Liquify and Smudge procedures in particular. To avoid hard-to-rectify mistakes later, it's always worth duplicating the layer before performing either of these tasks, so you can always revert to an earlier version if you need to.

● Painting the interior of the mouth in step 3 is not a difficult process, although the idea of painting teeth may seem daunting at first.

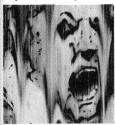

The trick is to use a small, soft-edged brush at an opacity of around 40%. Where painting with solid white will always look artificial, at a low opacity you have the opportunity to build up the teeth in stages: because we can see through the brushstrokes, they appear to blend into the rest of the painting to a far higher degree than if we'd just painted them solid to start with. The same applies to the dark interior of the mouth.

SHORTCUTS

 MAC WIN BOTH

175

Roy Lichtenstein

The artist Roy Lichtenstein (1923-1997) was one of the foremost proponents of Pop Art in the 1960s.

The pop art movement, which included Andy Warhol and Jasper Johns, began in the 1950s as a way of making art come more in line with popular mass culture. The movement took many forms, but Roy Lichtenstein is best known for his adaptations of the art style found in comic books of the period.

The Lichtenstein style is best known for its stark, graphic images, strong outlines, and cartoon lettering. The dot screen which overlays much of the colored areas refers back to the dots used to print comic books: as they were printed on low quality paper, a coarse dot had to be used to avoid the ink bleeding into the paper, and this dot was clearly visible to the reader.

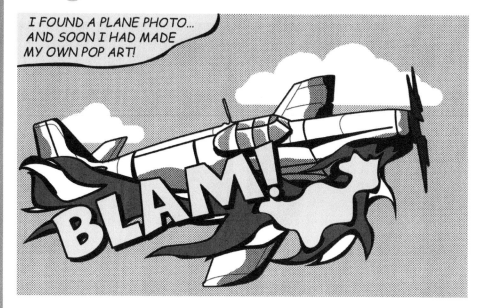

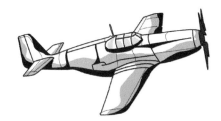

3 Hold ⌘ *ctrl* and click on the plane layer's thumbnail to load its selection once more, then make a new layer below the outlines and fill this with white to match the plane. Make another new layer, with the plane region still selected: paint shading colors in green, with blue for the windows, and red for the propeller.

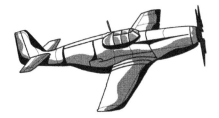

4 Click the eye icon next to the Texture layer in the Layers palette, and drag it above this new shading layer. Change its mode to Multiply, using the pop-up menu at the top of the Layers palette; then press ⌘ ⌥ *G* *ctrl* *alt* *G* to make a clipping mask with the layer beneath, so it only shows up where the two overlap.

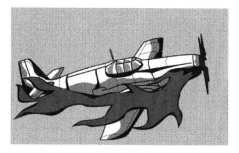

7 To complete this flame, draw another path just inside the black area. Don't try for an exact fit: the variable thickness of line is part of the style. Then turn this into a selection, and fill it with red.

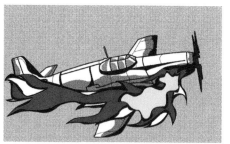

8 Repeat this process on new layers to make the yellow flame, and the white smoke beneath it. Don't try for a realistic effect, but keep the flames stylized in keeping with the original.

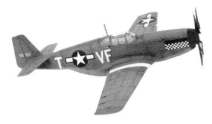

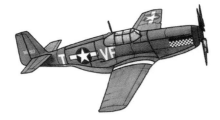

1 Almost any image can be used as the basis for a Lichtenstein painting, as we'll draw over it in outline in the next step. Here, we've chosen a plane, as this is the object used in his most famous painting, the iconic *Whaaam!*

2 Make a new, empty layer. Load up the pixels in the plane layer by holding ⌘ ctrl as you click on its thumbnail in the Layers palette, then use Edit > Stroke to make a black outline, 5 pixels wide, on the new layer. Use the Pen tool to draw in the contour and edge lines within the plane; then, with all the Pen paths visible – but not selected – switch to the Brush tool. Choose a hard-edged brush 5 pixels in diameter, and press *Enter* to stroke the pen paths with black.

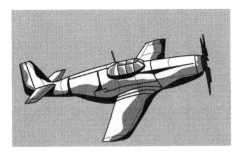

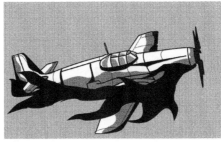

5 To make the sky, fill the background layer with a pale blue. Duplicate the Texture layer and move it to the bottom of the layer pile. Set its mode to Multiply, and lower the opacity to around 50%. You'll be able to see through it to the blue background beneath.

6 On another new layer, at the top of the layer stack, paint in the red fire. This is most easily done by drawing the outline with the Pen tool: press *Enter* to turn this path into a selection. Set the foreground color to black, and press ⌥ ← alt ← to fill the selection with the chosen color.

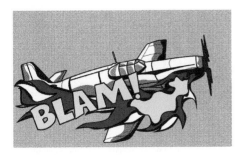

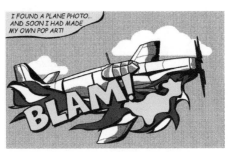

9 The text here has been made using the font Comics Cartoon. The exclamation mark has been drawn in, as the equivalent in this font is far too weak. Filled with yellow, it's given a black stroke.

10 The shadow on the BLAM lettering is made by duplicating the layer, filling it with black and moving it behind the original text. The clouds and caption are easily added on new layers.

MORE INFO

● Although I've provided the dot screen texture (steps 4 and 5) for this tutorial, it's easy to make your own. First, create a layer filled with solid gray. Then use Filters > Pixelate > Color Halftone, and set all the angles to 45°. This way, they'll line up and so look like a single color. When you apply the filter, the size of the dot will depend on how dark the gray base is. The darker the gray, the larger and closer together the dots will be. Experiment with different gray levels to get the effect you want.

● The font used for the caption here is Comics Sans MS, which comes as standard on most computers. The only drawback with this font is that it doesn't come with an italic version; here, the whole text block has been sheared horizontally to simulate italic text.

● When drawing the pen paths for the outlines in step 2, it can be hard to see where you've drawn before you stroke the paths. Try reducing the opacity of the Plane layer, so you can see the drawn paths more clearly.

SHORTCUTS

Andy Warhol

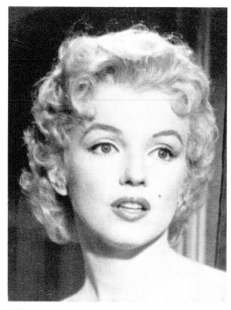

The word 'iconic' is used frequently in the world of contemporary art, often claiming an inflated status for the subject. But the work of Andy Warhol (1928–1987) can truly be said to fall into this category. In particular, two of his pop art screen prints are now so well known that they form part of everyday popular culture: his Campbell's Soup Can and his image of Marilyn Monroe.

I'm not able to show the original Marilyn image for copyright reasons, but we can use this production still from one of her movies for which the copyright has expired.

Of course, this is a technique that can be applied to any image, and is perhaps the most copied modern art style of all. You'll find tutorials for creating this style on many websites; but it would make this book incomplete if we were to miss it out.

1 The original photograph needs to be cropped to just the size of Marilyn's head, and enlarged to fit the space. It's essential that it's in black and white; if you're working with your own photograph, desaturate it using `ctrl` `Shift` `U` `⌘` `Shift` `U` first.

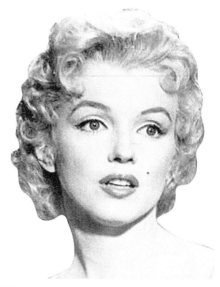

2 The cutout should be smooth around the head, but not trying to follow every hair: Warhol cut out his version with a scalpel, and that's the effect we're aiming for. Use Unsharp Mask to sharpen the image, which has become fuzzy once enlarged.

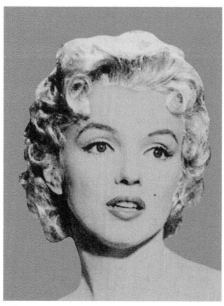

5 Lock the transparency of the color layer by pressing `/` (see More Info). Choose a strong yellow and, using a hard-edged brush, paint over the hair area. Because the transparency has been locked, there's no danger of painting over the edge of the image, which has already been filled with the skin color.

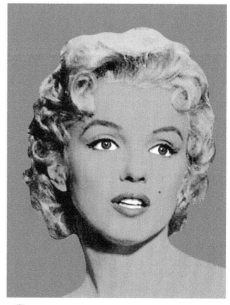

6 Switch to white and paint in the eyes and the teeth. It doesn't matter if you go slightly over the edge on the teeth, since we'll be painting the lips in afterwards. If you make a mistake, it's easy to resample the skin color and paint it out again.

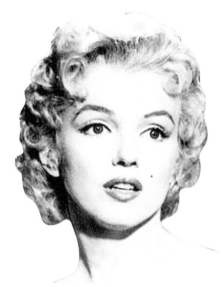

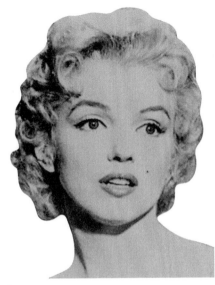

3 The sharpened version of the image added detail and texture, but we need a starker version for the effect to work. Duplicate the Marilyn layer, and change the mode of the new layer from Normal to Hard Light. This produces a stronger, stylized result.

4 Make a new layer, and set its mode to Multiply so we can see through it. Hold *ctrl* ⌘ and click on the Marilyn layer's thumbnail in the Layers palette to load it as a selection, then fill with a flesh color on this new layer.

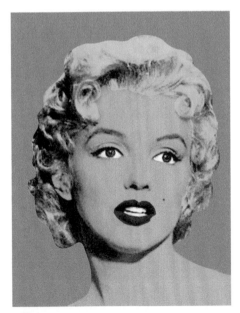

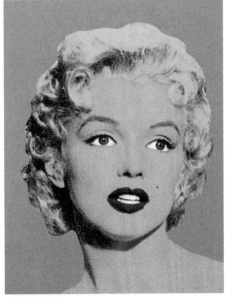

7 I don't know if Marilyn Monroe wore this shade of eye shadow, but it was clearly popular enough in the 1960s for Warhol to want to use it here. When painting this and the teeth, go slightly over the edges rather than being too precise: we want to recreate the feeling of a slightly misaligned screen print.

8 Even though all the colors are in the right place, the finished result needs more. With no texture, the background in particular simply looks flat and lifeless. The answer is a scan of a piece of rough paper, placed on top and with its layer mode changed to Hard Light so we can see through it.

ON THE CD

✔ image

✔ 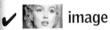 texture

Aa font

MORE INFO

● In step 3 we could have used Brightness and Contrast or even Curves to add contrast to this image. But duplicating it with a Hard Light layer in this way gives us an instant result, which we can control by lowering the opacity of the duplicated layer.

● Choosing the right colors can be a little hit and miss. To help you, the file on the CD includes a layer called Colors, which holds swatches of color sampled from the Warhol original:

back   face   lips

eyes   hair

Make this layer visible if you need it, and sample colors from here by holding the *alt* *ctrl* key as you paint with the Brush tool.

● To lock the transparency in step 5, either press *∕* or choose the Lock Transparency icon at the top of the Layers palette:

This will prevent anything painted on the layer from spilling out beyond the already filled area.

SHORTCUTS

 MAC WIN BOTH

179

Bridget Riley

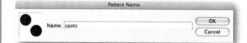

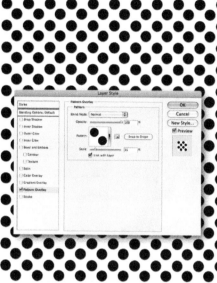

Bridget Riley was born in 1931 in England, and became the leading proponent of op art, as typified by her 1964 painting *Metamorphosis*, above.

The movement's name is short for optical art, and is chiefly concerned with the fallibility of the human eye – the way in which we can be fooled by what we look at. As the author John Lancaster put it, 'Optical Art is a method of painting concerning the interaction between illusion and picture plane, between understanding and seeing.'

Unlike the sort of optical illusions you'll see in puzzle books, op art tends to employ strong geometric forms and seeks to confuse and disturb.

Bridget Riley initially worked almost exclusively in black and white, producing variations on her work using squares and circles. Later on, she experimented with adding color to her paintings.

1 To recreate this painting we first need a regular array of dots. Draw a circular ellipse, and fill with black; then hold `alt` `Shift` `⌥` `Shift` as you drag it diagonally to make a copy at 45° to the original. Select both with the Rectangular Marquee tool, and choose Edit > Define Pattern.

2 Now that we have those dots as a pattern, we can fill our entire canvas with them. Make a new layer, filled with white; then choose Pattern Overlay from the Layer Styles menu in the Layers palette. Here, we can choose the size of our pattern.

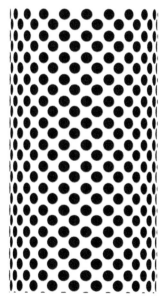

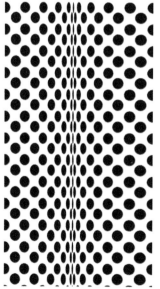

5 The Spherize filter tends to be a little over-enthusiastic, and distorts the dots in the middle by making them much wider. Scale this layer horizontally so that the dots in the middle are truly circular: that way they'll join up to the original array of dots when we reveal this layer again.

6 Split this layer in half down the middle by selecting one half with the Marquee tool, and cut that half to a new layer (`ctrl` `Shift` `J` `⌘` `Shift` `J`). Move both halves over to one side, rearranging them so that the narrow dots which were at the edges of the cylinder now appear in the middle.

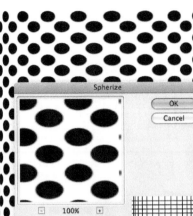

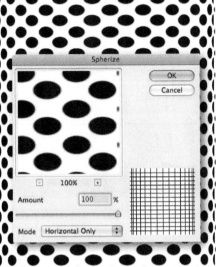

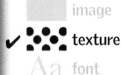
3 In order to work with the pattern and distort it, we need to turn that Layer Styles layer into a regular, editable layer. The best way to do this is to make a Merged Copy by pressing `ctrl` `alt` `Shift` `E` `⌘` `⌥` `Shift` `E`.

4 Now duplicate this new layer and hide the original – we'll need to use it again later. To create the effect of the dots rolling around a cylinder we'll use the Spherize filter; but rather than wrapping around a sphere, choose Horizontal Only as the mode, to create a cylindrical effect.

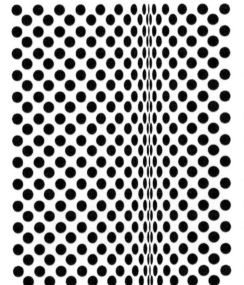

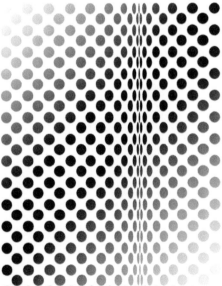

7 When we view the original layer, we'll need to rearrange the two halves of the spherized version so that they line up with the original dots. Generally, this is just a matter of dragging the component parts left and right until they align correctly.

8 The last step is to make the two opposite corners fade away. Make another new layer, and choose the Gradient tool. Set its mode to Foreground to Transparent (using the pop-up menu on the Options bar), and set the foreground color to white. Drag diagonally from each corner to create the fading effect.

MORE INFO

● In step 2, we could have just chosen Edit > Fill and selected Pattern as the fill type, and this would have flooded the layer with our chosen pattern. The advantage of using the Layer Style approach is that it allows us to scale the pattern as we fill our layer with it: often, we don't know how large we want a repeating pattern until we see it in place. The only drawback is that we need to make a visual copy of the layer in order to apply filter effects to it afterwards.

● Bridget Riley produced a very similar image to this using squares instead of dots. Try reproducing the effect shown here with a checkerboard pattern instead, to make your own unique Riley artwork.

● The final step, fading the corners away to white, is unusual in an op art work: generally, the artist aims for a purely geometric, flat texture. But the effect here is a good one, adding interest to the painting, and is worth keeping in our version of the image.

● The only tricky part here is making the spherized halves align with the original grid. Remember, these can be squeezed horizontally until they fit the space.

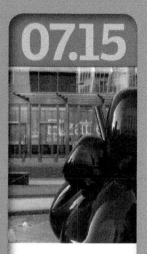

Jeff Koons

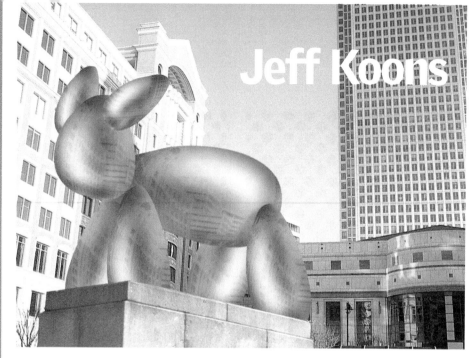

The contemporary artist Jeff Koons (born 1955) is best known for two styles of work: his oversized reproductions of everyday kitsch objects, and his highly pornographic models of his wife, the former porn star and one-time Italian politician Cicciolina. Needless to say, it's the first style we'll be attempting to emulate here.

Among the objects Koons reproduces are giant ballon sculptures, cast in shiny, gaudily colored metal. Often taller than a man, these sculptures are at once appealing and baffling: how can anything in such obvious bad taste be so entertaining to look at?

Building a Koons balloon animal is not a tricky task, and it's one of the few examples in this book for which there's no accompanying image on the CD. Everything here can be made from scratch with no photographic sources, directly in Photoshop.

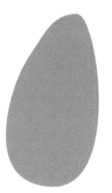

1 Begin by drawing a balloon shape (left) on a new layer. Fill with a midtone gray.

2 Use the Burn tool, set to Highlights, to add some shading around the bottom and right side of the balloon (right); then switch to the Dodge tool to add a highlight down the left-hand side. Remember, you can hold the ⎇ *alt* key with either tool to temporarily use the other one.

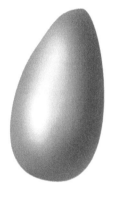

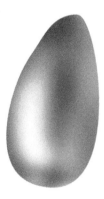

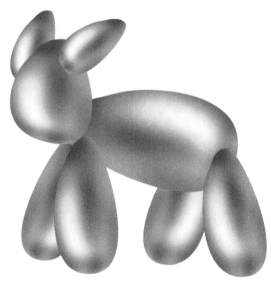

4 A little more Dodge and Burn helps to even out the texture. Because we added the Curves effect as an Adjustment Layer, we're seeing through it as we add extra shading, so the tools will produce unexpected results: paradoxically, darkening the image can actually make it lighter.

5 Duplicate the single balloon several times to build the animal. Here, we've distorted and rotated the separate balloon elements to make the legs, body, head and ears.

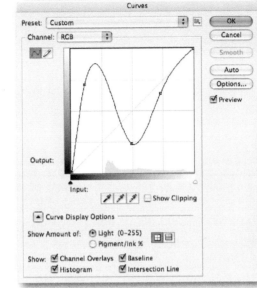

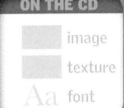

3 At the end of the previous step, our balloon looked like it was made of plastic, rather than metal. Here's how to add shininess to the surface.

Make a new Curves Adjustment Layer (chosen from the pop-up menu at the bottom of the Layers palette). Click and drag in the curve at the mid point, and drag it downwards; then click either side of this mid point and drag upwards, to make an N-shaped curve as seen

in this dialog. The result of this operation is to make the surface appear shiny. It works by virtue of the fact that metal reflects light in unpredictable ways, adding its own highlights and shadows.

It can take a while to get the curve to work well, but experiment with the technique and you should find it possible to create spectacular effects in a relatively short time.

MORE INFO

● The result we get in step 3 depends on a combination of the shading and the Curves adjustment: the shape shown here is only an example. You may need to vary it to achieve a similar effect on your own shaded artwork, depending on the exact amount of shading.

● To place the model in an outdoor setting, as in the main image, it was necessary to add some reflections. This was done by taking a section of the background and applying the Spherize filter to it: this piece then uses one of the balloons as a clipping layer, so it only shows up where the two overlap. The opacity of this layer was then reduced to 10%. Further copies of this Spherized background were copied above each balloon in turn, and distorted to fit.

● Because the Curves and Hue/Saturation were added as Adjustment Layers, they would normally affect the background as well. To make the main image, each of the balloons was loaded as a selection by holding ⌘ *Shift* ctrl *Shift* and clicking on their thumbnails; then the selection was inversed, and the mask for each Adjustment Layer filled with black to hide their effect in that area.

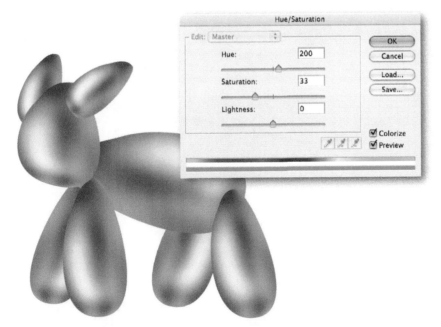

6 With the body complete, it's time to add some color. Make another Adjustment Layer, this time using Hue/Saturation, above the Curves layer. Check the

Colorize box, and drag the Hue and Saturation sliders until you get the metallic color that looks best for your model. You can always change it later!

SHORTCUTS

183

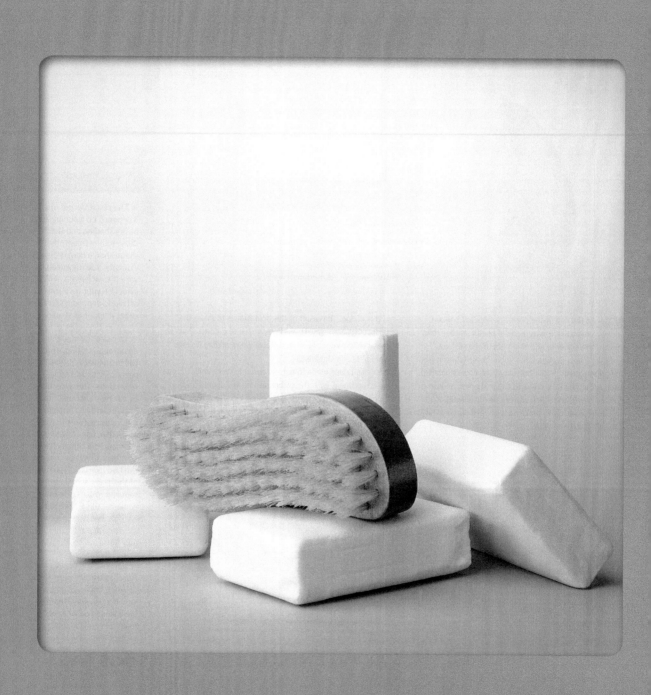

Packaging

In 1885 William and James Lever bought a small soap factory in Warrington, in the north of England. They were so proud of the soap they made there that, rather than sell it loose in grocer's shops – as had previously been the way all goods were sold – they decided to give it a name, Sunlight Soap, and to package the bars in their own wrappers.

Sunlight Soap was among the first pre-packaged goods. The Lever brothers were innovative marketeers; so much so that in 1930 Lever Brothers became Unilever, the first modern multinational company.

Over the years packaging design has become more and more standardized, enabling consumers to recognize what type of product they're looking at from the packaging alone. We can distinguish at a glance between cans of beans and cans of cat food, between soap powder and cereal boxes, without having to search the container for the appropriate wording.

In this chapter we'll look at what makes products identifiable by their containers, and see how to reproduce the most typical examples of each product category.

packaging

1. The act, process, industry, art, or style of packing.

2. Material used for making packages.

3. The manner in which something, such as a proposal or product, or someone, such as a candidate or author, is presented to the public.

American Heritage Dictionary

Pharmacy cartons

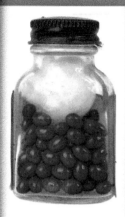

Once upon a time, we'd all have gone off to the local drugstore to ask our friendly pharmacist what would be the best remedy for croup, or rickets, or gout. And he or she would spill a few capsules from an unmarked bottle, which would either cure us or kill us.

Today the experience is rather different: when we search the shelves for an appropriate remedy we're overwhelmed with choice, with a dozen different marketed brands each claming to be better than the next, despite the fact that they appear to contain exactly the same ingredients.

There are several tricks that many drug manufacturers commonly use to make their products appear cleaner, faster, more efficient and more clinical. We'll look at how to simulate their packaging here.

1 Start with the background. Fill the background layer with mid gray, then use the Dodge tool, set to Highlights, to make several diagonal stripes across it. This is the first step in making the background look as if it's covered in metallic foil.

3 Let's add a human element to our image. This woman looks like she's in need of some serious painkillers. Use Filter > Sketch > Stamp to produce this black and white version of the image. Raise the Smoothness value enough to produce clean outlines, but not so much that the features are lost.

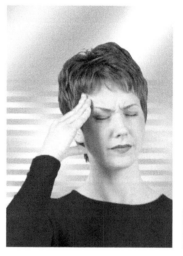

5 To give the lettering a bit of a lift and a slightly three-dimensional feel, add a bevel using Layer Styles. Rather than the standard variety, choose Outer Bevel from the pop-up list at the top of the dialog. This mode applies the bevel effect to the background, making the text appear raised.

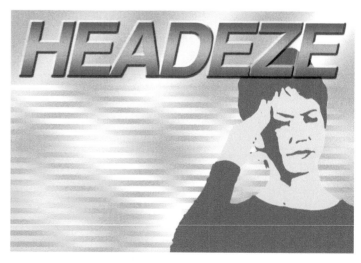
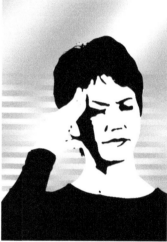

2 Make a series of rectangular selections within this background: the easiest way to do this is to use QuickMask mode (see More Info panel for details). Once the selection has been made, turn it into a new layer using `ctrl` `J` `⌘` `J` then flip it horizontally to make this simple striped effect.

MORE INFO

● To make the striped texture in step 2, you first need to create an array of horizontal stripes. The easiest way is to use **Q** to enter QuickMask mode, and make a rectangular selection. Fill this so it stands out from the background. Then hold `alt` `⌥` as you use `Shift` `↓` to make a copy 10 pixels below; then release `alt` `⌥` and nudge down a couple more times. Repeat this process until you have an array of horizontal bars; when you leave QuickMask by pressing **Q** once more, you'll have a striped selection. Use `ctrl` `J` `⌘` `J` to turn this selection into a new layer.

4 Use Hue/ Saturation to colorize the woman, giving her a blue tint – see More Info for details. For the lettering, I've used good old Helvetica. Choosing the Bold Oblique weight makes the drug name appear faster, as oblique styles always do. The orange–yellow–orange fill is a standard gradient, added as a Gradient Fill in the Layer Styles palette.

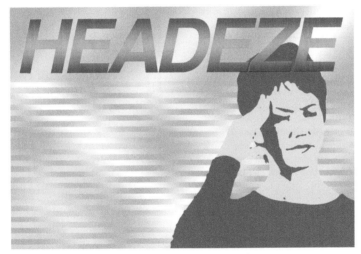

● To color the woman in step 4, open the Hue/ Saturation dialog and check the Colorize button. Raise the Lightness value to brighten the black, then drag the Hue and Saturation sliders to get a subtle blue. We now need to add the color overlay. Duplicate the woman layer, choose a pale blue and press `alt` `Shift` `Backspace` `⌥` `Shift` `Backspace` to fill with the chosen color (the `Shift` key prevents the color from leaking out of the edge of the layer), then change the mode of this layer from Normal to Multiply so we can see through it.

6 The rest of the text is set in the same font, again using the oblique style to give the sense of rapid action. Set in red, a white stroke is added using Layer Styles in order to make the text stand out from the background. I've also added a clock here, since this is something drug companies like to do: it doesn't say anything specific, but it implies quick results.

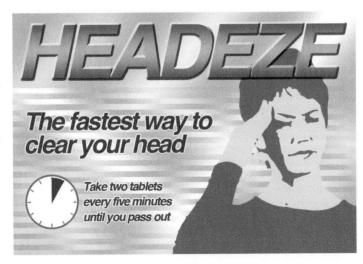

SHORTCUTS

 MAC WIN BOTH

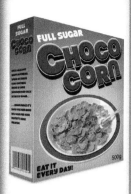

There are several occasions in this book where we look at how to draw flat artwork for packaging. Although it's interesting to see how different products are marketed, it's not until we see our designs appearing on an actual box that we really come to appreciate them.

Rather than explain each time the technique is used in the book, we'll go through it once here and then refer to these pages elsewhere.

Of course, you don't need to go quite as far as this: adding the reflection is appropriate for some boxes, such as this medicine carton, but would probably not suit a cereal box, for instance.

As is always the case, the final judgment is always up to you. See how the various options are constructed, then take your pick as to which you include.

1 This is the box we created on the previous tutorial. To make it fit a three-dimensional form, we first need to merge all the visible layers together so we can work on them as one. The best way to do this is to make a Merged Copy (see More Info). Then enter Free Transform mode (*ctrl* T ⌘ T) and distort the box using perspective distortion to make it appear to be receding away from us – see the More Info panel for details.

3 The side we created in step 2 can now be distorted using the same technique we used for the face, but in the other direction. We need to darken this side to give the sense of a light direction: it makes the object look more three-dimensional. Finally, select a thin border about 2 pixels wide on the side nearest the face, and brighten it up. This gives the impression of cardboard rolling around an edge, and is far more effective than a simple butt joint.

5 With the reflections of the face and side complete, we need to lower their opacity to make them more convincing. Select them both, and choose New Group from Layers from the pop-up menu on the Layers palette: lower the opacity of this group to around 50%, to start with. Placing the elements into a group means we can reduce the opacity of the entire group, and add a layer mask to it if we wish.

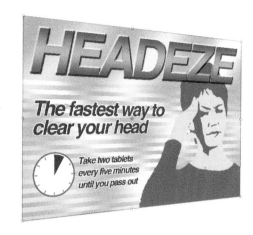

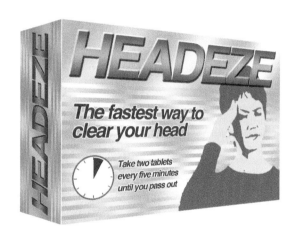

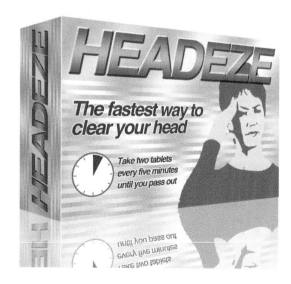

2 The side of the box is our first building project. The elements are already there – the metallic background, the title, the stripes; all we need to do is rearrange them slightly (and hide the figure of the woman) to make a suitable image for the side.

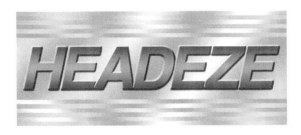

4 To make the reflection, duplicate the face and side layers, and flip them vertically. We can now use the Shear component of Free Transform to stretch them downwards: hold `ctrl` `Shift` `⌘` `Shift` as you grab a center handle on one of the sides, and drag it downwards. The `ctrl` `⌘` key moves just that side; the `Shift` key constrains the movement to purely vertical. Repeat the process with the side. Here., I've separated the original and the reflection to show the two more clearly: you won't be working with this gap.

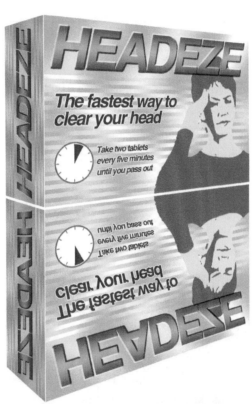

6 To complete the effect, I've created a simple black background with a blue gradation (made with the Gradient tool) to give the suggestion of a backdrop behind the surface. The reflection works well against black: I've also added a layer mask to the reflection group, and used the Gradient tool to fade the reflection away gradually. The pill adds an additional dimension to the image; it's duplicated to make the reflection.

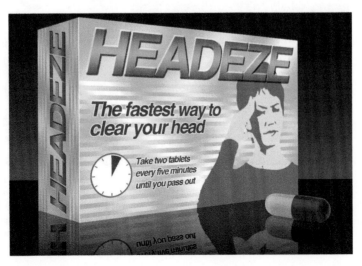

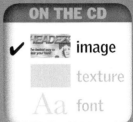
MORE INFO

● We need to make a Merged Copy in step 1 so we can work on all the layers as one. Don't flatten your image: instead, when all the layers you want to show are visible, click on the topmost layer in the stack and press `ctrl` `alt` `Shift` `E` `⌘` `⌥` `Shift` `E`. This will place a Merged Copy at the top of the pile.

● We use Perspective Distortion in step 1 to place the box at an angle. We can do this by choosing Edit > Transform > Perspective; or, we can simply use the Perspective mode within the standard Free Transform mode. Press `ctrl` `T` `⌘` `T` to enter this mode, then hold `ctrl` `alt` `Shift` `⌘` `⌥` `Shift` as you drag one of the corner handles up or down. This will move the facing handle in the opposite direction, producing a smooth perspective transformation. If you then want to change the apparent viewing height of the box, just hold `ctrl` `Shift` `⌘` `Shift` as you drag one of the side handles up or down.

● In step 5, we place the reflected elements into a group before lowering their transparency. By doing this, we're able to add the transparent capsule in step 7 quickly and easily.

SHORTCUTS

`MAC` `WIN` `BOTH`

Cereal boxes

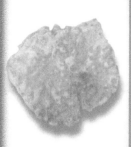

Cereal boxes do much more than hold breakfast cereal. For one thing, as one wag had it, they're generally more nutritious than their contents.

Whatever your views on the amount of sugar we're feeding to our children, we can't escape the fact that cereal makes up the daily breakfast for a huge number of households. And, while we're munching, we study the back of the box because there's often nothing else readable to hand.

Cereal boxes have evolved a graphic style all of their own. They go for bright, welcoming colors, and the lettering tends towards a bevel effect with a strong stroke and a drop shadow.

We'll put all the typical elements together in our version of the breakfast staple.

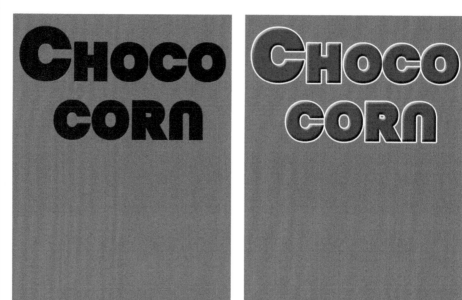

1 Begin with the name of the cereal. To make the contents appear filling the manufacturers often opt for a chunky, sometimes slightly wacky font; this is called Strenuous. We'll set it on a strong, dark orange background.

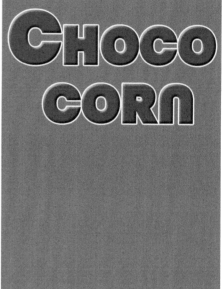

2 Use Layer Styles to add the effects. Here a simple bevel adds highlights and shading to the lettering, giving it an instant three-dimensional look. The type is often left black; I've changed it here to red, and used Layer Styles to add a white stroke.

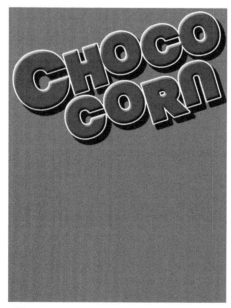

5 A good solution to the text problem is to tighten up individual characters so their strokes run into each other (see More Info panel). We can also nudge some letters up and down: highlight each one, and use `ctrl` `alt` `Shift` `⌘` `⌥` `Shift` with the up and down cursor keys to move them.

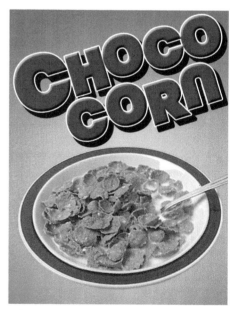

6 The cereal bowl itself is essential – we have to show what the stuff looks like, after all. To give it a healthy glow, make a new layer behind it, and use the Gradient tool set to Foreground to Transparent, with yellow as the foreground color, to make this warm, sunny background.

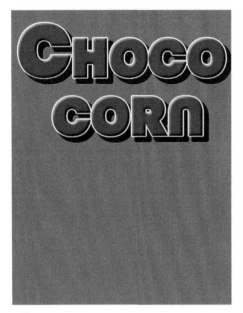

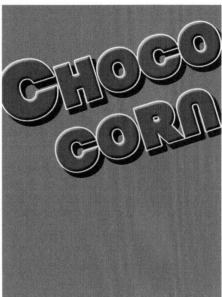

3 The solid black shadow is a common cereal title technique. This can be added using Layer Styles as well. The system is designed for soft shadows, but if you change the Spread value to 100% you can change the Size value to make it match the stroke size.

4 Rotating the text gives it a more dynamic, more playful feeling. After all, this is supposed to be a fun food, not something that your mother would nag you to eat. But we don't want it butting out over the edge – and we don't really want to reduce the text size either.

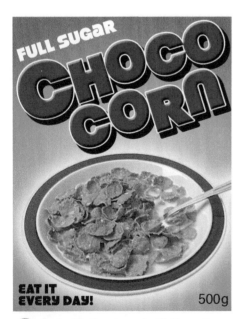

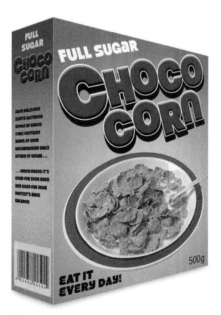

7 The bowl itself needs an extra lift; I've used Layer Styles to add an Outer Glow to it, changing the color of the glow from the default yellow to pure white. Add more text to fill up the spaces: it's these additional elements that really make the cereal box start to look more convincing.

8 The background from the box front, as well as the title, have been repurposed here to make the box side. Both the front and the side have been distorted to turn the flat artwork into a 3D image: see the previous pages for more details on this technique.

MORE INFO

● We've used red lettering on a yellow-orange background – warm colors that suggest an appetizing, warming breakfast. Many cereal varieties vary the colors to make them more distinctive: Kelloggs Cornflakes goes for a distinctive white background, Rice Krispies is generally pale blue, and so on. The only cereals that use green or brown backgrounds tend to be of the muesli variety, which make overt claims of health – appealing to adults, perhaps, but off-putting to most kids.

● In step 5 we've tightened up the letter spacing, or 'tracking' as it's known. We can do this for the text as a whole, using the Character palette; here, though, we want more overall control. Place the cursor between each pair of letters, and use *alt* Shift ⌥ Shift and the left and right cursor keys to nudge the following character left and right. Adjusting the tracking by eye means we can apply different values to each pair of letters.

● In step 6 we can use the Gradient tool to add the glow behind the bowl. The tool should, of course, be set to create circular gradients, chosen from the icon in the tool's Options bar.

SHORTCUTS

MAC   WIN   BOTH

Wine labels

The buying of wine is an art that's shrouded in mystique – from the moment a young man wants to impress his date, to the billionaire who spends thousands on a single bottle.

We're savvy enough consumers to know that we shouldn't rely on packaging alone, but when we're buying unknown wines we have little to go on but the label. Whether we go for the traditional, the ultra modern, the cut price or the gold embossed, we're affected by the label to a degree larger than most of us would care to admit.

We're going to put together a traditional red wine label, of the kind you'll see in every liquor store. The quality of the bottle's contents is entirely in the mouth of the imbiber.

1 No need to give you the font for this one: Old English, or a variation on it ships with just about every computer ever sold. Use the parchment background (see page 110), and set the first letters of each word in red to make them stand out.

2 To create the offset 'shadow', duplicate the lettering, then make a layer mask for the copied version. Load the text as a selection by holding *ctrl* ⌘ and clicking on its thumbnail in the Layers palette; then nudge the selection a little to the left and up, and fill with black on the mask to hide all but the remaining edge.

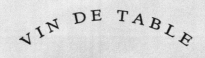

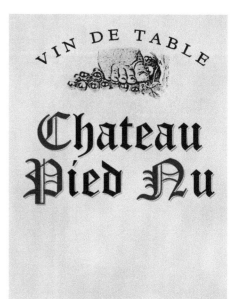

5 The text is spaced out by tracking – see More Info for details on this. To give the text a shallower curve, press the Warp Text button once more and reduce the Bend value. Because this type remains live, we can change the Bend value at any time.

6 Every traditional bottle needs a graphic; it's often a view of the chateau where the wine is made (or, sometimes, a more picturesque one nearby). I've opted for a naked foot crushing a bunch of grapes, to match the name of the wine.

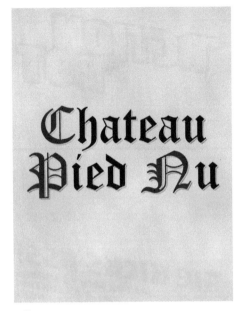

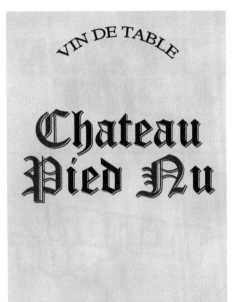

3 Here's the 'shadowed' text shown with the original text visible again (I'd hidden it in the previous step to show the effect more clearly). Here, the shadow has been filled with a gold-like color, and the Dodge tool dragged across it a couple of times to give the effect of a slight shine.

4 The text above is plain old Times Roman – any traditional serif font will do here. Use Warp Text (the button appears on the Options bar when the Type tool is active) to add an arc to straight text. Here, a Bend value of 50% has been used to give the text a slight curve – leave the Horizontal and Vertical settings alone.

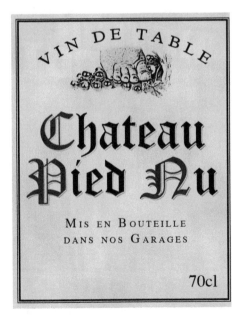

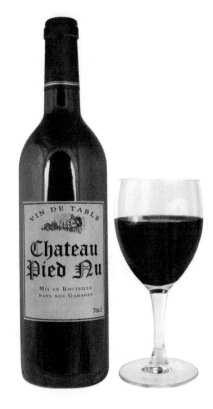

7 The border is made by making a rectangular selection on a new layer, and using Edit > Stroke to apply a 2 point black stroke; then, on a slightly smaller selection, a 4 point stroke is added. Don't forget the extra text elements for greater realism.

MORE INFO

● To recolor the initial letters in step 1, select them wih the Type tool and choose a red from the Swatches palette. Alternatively, make a new layer using the type layer as a Clipping Mask (see page 233); paint in here on red to apply the color.

● In step 5, we add tracking to the lettering – spacing it all out – by selecting the type and holding *alt* *Shift* ⌥ *Shift* while pressing the left and right cursor keys to add or remove additional space. But there's a problem here: if all the text is selected, the type will become unbalanced. That's because Photoshop will add extra space after the 'e' of 'Table', and with this much space the text would look like it's lurching to one side. The solution is to select from before the 'V' of 'Vin' to just before the 'e' of 'Table': that way, the space after the 'e' isn't extended along with the rest of the lettering.

● The bunch of grapes with the naked foot image is a pair of photographs that have been desaturated and treated with the Poster Edges filter to achieve this graphic effect. If you have the time and inclination, you can produce more convincing engraving effects – see page 50 for details on the technique.

SHORTCUTS

 MAC   WIN   BOTH

Action figure box

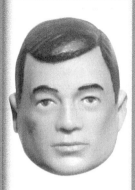

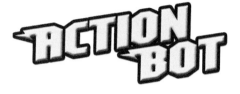

Action Man, G.I. Joe... however we came to know him, the first doll for boys (although we'd never admit him as such) sparked the imagination of a generation.

Manufacturers have been marketing action figures at boys and girls ever since. It's grown into a multi-million dollar industry; no kids' movie is complete without its range of spin-off figures in every moviegoer's pocket.

Making these colorful, overpriced lumps of articulated plastic sell requires the manufacturer to make them as appealing as possible in their boxes. There's been a long tradition of boxes with cutout holes that follow the shape of the lettering or other design element; they offer a tantalising glimpse of the goodies within, without showing absolutely everything. Of course, you have to buy the box to find out what else is inside.

1 THe font we've used here is Superheterodyne, in which the capitals and lower case forms are identical except for the lightning flashes on the capitals. Rotating the text adds interest and action; the black stroke and bevel are added using Layer Styles.

2 The main text is duplicated, and then edited to make the rest of the wording: that way, we can be sure they're both at the same angle. Inverting the colors ties the two text elements together, without the bottom text detracting from the title.

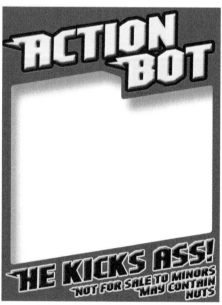

5 Now that we have a selection for the hole, inverse that selection using `ctrl Shift I` `⌘ Shift I` and fill the outer portion with the color of your choice, on a new layer. Adding a Drop Shadow using Layer Styles gives the box its depth; use a large shadow to accentuate the sense of depth.

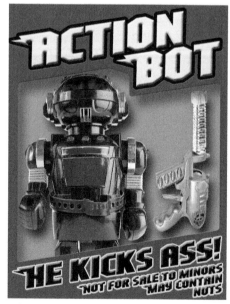

6 Fill the background with a cardboard color. To avoid copyright issues, I've filled this box with a robot and its gun. These also have a drop shadow attached to their layers, using Layer Styles once again; but because they're right up against the backing board, we need closer, tighter shadows.

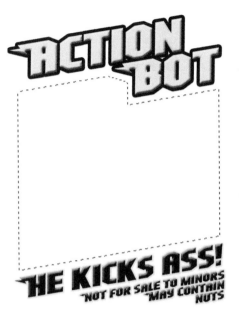

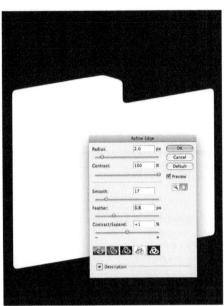

 We can make a selection inside the text area with the Lasso tool: hold *alt* ⌥ as you draw to make the tool trace straight lines between click points. We can draw this shape as a straightforward polygon, and smooth it in the next step.

 Open the Refine Edge dialog, and set the Contrast value to 100%. When we now raise the Feather setting, we end up rounding off those corners: if it weren't for the high contrast, we'd be making them fuzzy. The simplest way to create rounded corners!

MORE INFO

● In step 8, we need to give a slight thickness to the cardboard, to accentuate the fact that the robot is in a container behind it. To do this, first load up the card layer we created in step 5 as a selection by holding *ctrl* ⌘ and clicking on its thumbnail in the Layers palette. Now inverse the selection using *ctrl Shift I* ⌘ *Shift I*, make a new layer, and fill with a very pale brown. Don't deselect: instead, make sure one of the selection tools is active (but not the Move tool) and nudge the selection a couple of pixels down and to the right, using the cursor keys; then delete the selection, You'll be left with a thin border that makes a convincing impression of thickness.

● If we wanted to view this box from an angle, it wouldn't be as simple as rotating and skewing it, as we did with the cereal box earlier in this chapter: we'd need a photograph of the robot from a different angle as well. Assuming we don't have a limitless supply of robot photographs, the only viable solution is to find a photo from a suitable angle, and then distort and build the angled box around that. It's the only way to guarantee a perfect match.

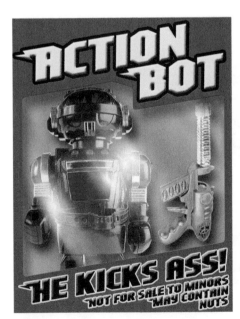

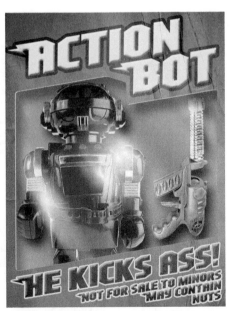

 We need to add some cellophane to this box. Make a new layer, and fill with 50% gray; then paint diagonal stripes on it with the Dodge tool. Apply Filter > Artistic > Plastic Wrap to make a shiny effect, and set the mode of the layer to Hard Light so we can see through it. See More Info on page 197.

 A piece of crumpled card is added as a texture to make the box look old and tatty. Because the texture would cover the whole canvas, we need to add a layer mask to hide the window portion; load up the selection of the card made in step 5, then inverse it and delete on the crumple layer mask.

Container perspective

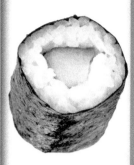

Drawing box artwork is one thing; making it fit around a three dimensional object is another skill entirely. In this tutorial we'll skip over the details of how the box art is created, and concentrate on the process of fitting it around the sushi.

A common mistake that many Photoshop artists make when constructing boxes is to build the box first, and then find suitable objects to go inside it. It's one approach, but it's bound to cause problems: finding a photograph of the chosen object from exactly the right angle will be almost impossible, and distorting it may not produce good results.

The trick is to find your object first, and then build the box around it to match the perspective of the object photography. That way you can be sure the box will fit, since you're constructing it for this express purpose.

1 The box artwork is made in two sections – one for the top, and one for the front side. The font is called Zorque, and the effects are added using Layer Styles. This is a popular contemporary Japanese style of rendering text, which can look rather brash and toylike to Western eyes.

3 Draw the other side of the box with either the Lasso or, better, the Pen tool. This can take a while to get exactly right; adjust the shape until the perspective works. Fill this with a darker version of the green color.

5 With the two sides in the right place, all you have to do now is to move the top left corner (still in Free Transform) until the perspective of the box looks right. This is largely a matter of judging it by eye: you'll know when it works.

7 Shadows added to the interior later halp the sushi look like it's in there. Giving the interior of the lid some thickness adds realism, and makes it look much more like a three-dimensional object: see More Info for a simple way to do this.

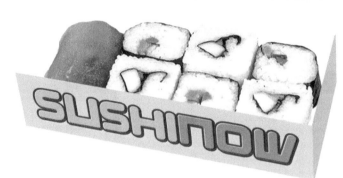

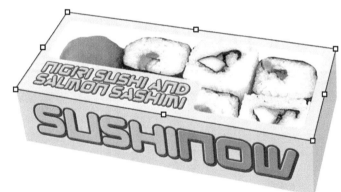

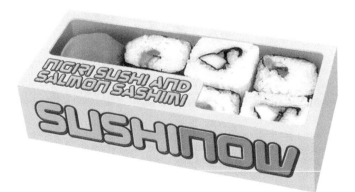

2 Make a single layer from the front side of the box, and use Free Transform to distort it to match the angle of view of the sushi. It can help to view the layer at 50% opacity, so you can see the sushi through it. Darken this layer slightly, as it's partly in shadow.

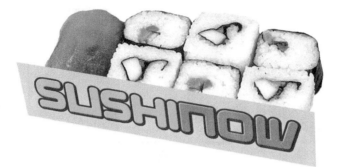

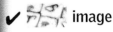
4 To make the lid fit, enter Free Transform mode and skew it, using the center handles, until the bottom and right edges line up with the two visible sides of the box. Don't leave Free Transform yet!

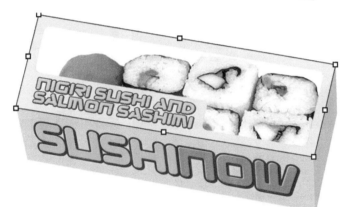

MORE INFO

● To make the interior edge of the lid in step 7, select the hole with the Magic Wand tool. Fill this selection with mid gray on a new layer. Nudge the selection down and to the right a couple of pixels; you should be moving the selection area, not the contents. Delete the selection, and you'll be left with just the edge. Darken or lighten it as appropriate using Dodge and Burn.

● To make the cellophane effect in step 8, begin with a layer filled with mid gray:

6 The inside of the box is a new layer behind all the others. Fill with a mid gray, then make a selection of one side that goes up to the inside corner of this box. Darken this area, to give the box a more convincing interior.

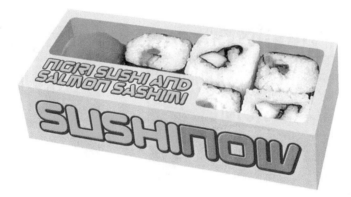

Then use the Dodge tool to add some streaky highlights:

Then use the Plastic Wrap filter to make it shiny:

8 The cellophane is made using the Plastic Wrap filter – see More Info. Finally, on a new layer draw white lines with the Brush tool (set to a small, hard brush) over the three edges facing us; reduce the opacity of this layer to 30% to make more rounded edges.

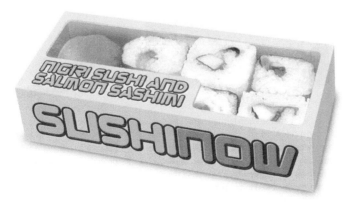

Finally change the mode of this layer to Hard Light, and it will look like a plastic sheet. Raise or lower the brightness (and contrast) as required.

SHORTCUTS

 MAC   WIN   BOTH

Soup cans

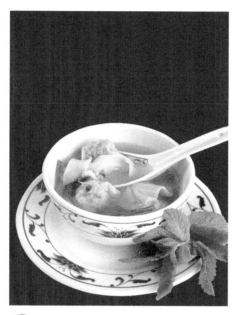

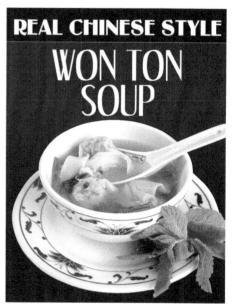

However much work a food stylist, home economist and still life photographer might put in, it's hard to make soup look appetizing. This might be the packaging the words 'serving suggestion' were invented for: add a sprig of parsley, a couple of handfuls of herbs and you've got something far more appealing. We'll try to make our won ton soup look as tasty as possible by means of tasteful packaging.

But creating the label is only half the battle: we then have to wrap it around a can. The technique we'll use involves both Smart Objects and the Image Warp distortion, so is only possible for users with Photoshop CS2 or higher. It's a powerful technology, well worth the upgrade price on its own, as we'll see: once we've wrapped the label, we can still edit it.

1 The photograph of our won ton soup is about as appealing as we can make it – certainly, the colorful leaves help distract the eye from the beige soup itself. The rich purple background aims to speak of quality and sophistication.

2 We've used two Ray Larabie fonts, Dream Orphans and Guanine, for the wording. A slight graduation from dark to light helps the bowl look as if it's sitting on a surface; the darker band at the top makes the text stand out more clearly.

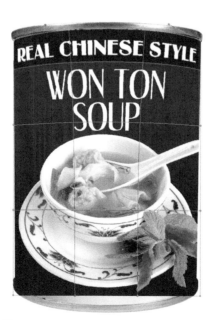

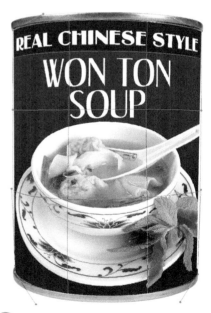

5 Click the Image Warp button on the Options bar, to get the Warp grid. Drag the top two handles up, to make the top of the label fit the can; drag them outwards as well, towards the edges. This will help give the impression of the label wrapping around the can, as the sides are now viewed in perspective.

6 Drag the bottom handles to make the bottom of the label fit the can, then drag the four cross points within the grid outwards as well. This is a tricky procedure, as grid points will move when you drag those nearby; it's hard to control this grid, and there's really no option but to persevere until you get it right.

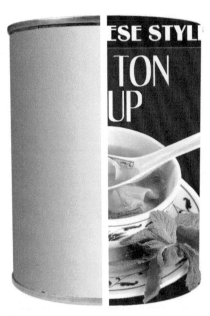

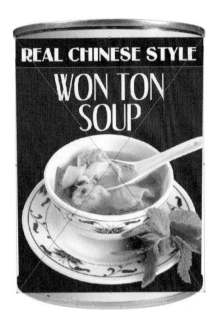

3 Our photograph of a soup can has a blank but shaded label (left). Select all the label elements, and convert them to a Smart Object (see More Info for details); then make a clipping mask with the can layer, so the Smart Object only shows up where the two overlap.

4 We need to distort the label to fit, so use `ctrl` `T` `⌘` `T` to enter Free Transform. Scale the artwork so the top left and right corners of our label match the corners of the label as seen on the photograph of the can.

MORE INFO

● In step 3, we have multiple layers making up our label: two for the text, the bowl, the background, and so on. Select them all, and choose Convert to Smart Object from the pop-up menu in the Layers palette. This will make them appear to be a single layer. We can now use Free Transform and even Image Warp on this layer as a whole, allowing us to distort all the layers together.

● Smart Objects allow us to edit their contents as well. Double-click the Smart Object icon in the Layers palette and it will open in a new window, with all the layers intact. We can change, hide or delete any of these layers, or even add new ones; it's just like working on a regular Photoshop document. But when we save or close the window, the distortions we applied will be reapplied instantly. That's how we manage to change the soup label in step 8.

● One further bonus of Smart Objects is that when we enter Free Transform for a second time, all the Image Warp handles are where we left them – we don't need to start again. So if we find later that the label doesn't fit perfectly, we can easily adjust the settings.

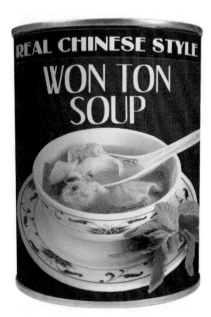

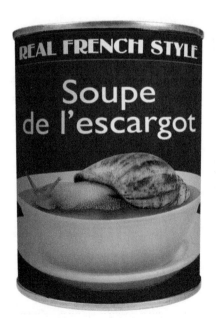

7 When we change the mode of the Smart Object label from Normal to Multiply, we can see through it to the shaded label beneath. The shading from that label is seen on our version on top, producing a convincing impression of light and shade.

8 It may have taken a while to get the mesh to fit the shape of the can perfectly, but it's well worth the effort – and not just for this illustration. The real power of Smart Objects lies in their editability: it's an easy matter to replace our won ton label with another one entirely – see More Info for details.

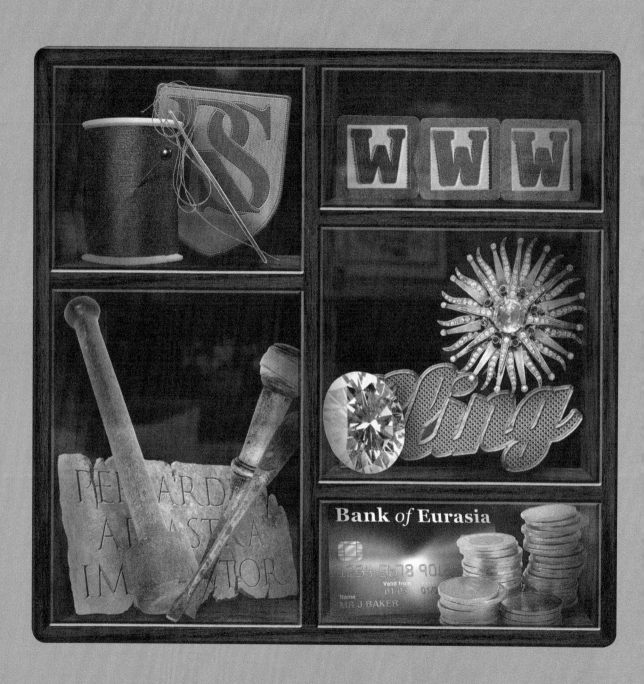

Any other business

So far in this book we've looked at how to choose and use typefaces well and wisely. We've explored the basic rules of design and composition, from perspective to the Rule of Thirds.

We've seen how to create a variety of posters, how to make graffiti, and how to design book covers for anything from historical non-fiction to trashy 1950s pulp stories. We've seen how to create medieval manuscripts, picture postcards, cereal boxes and soup cans. We've even discovered the secrets of some of the greatest painters of this or any other age.

There are some designed objects that don't fit within any of the categories we've covered so far. Stained glass windows, for example, or credit cards, or carved stone. This chapter is for the miscellaneous.

miscellany

1. A mass or mixture of various things; a medley; esp., a collection of compositions on various subjects.
    'Tis but a bundle or miscellany of sin; sins original, and sins actual.
    – Hewyt.

2. Miscellany madam, a woman who dealt in various fineries; a milliner. [Obs.]

Webster's Revised Dictionary

Credit cards

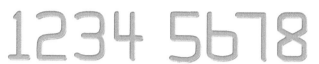

The idea of the credit card was first put forward in the novel *Looking Backward*, written by Edward Bellamy as long ago as 1887. It tells the story of a young American who falls into a sleep induced by hypnosis, and wakes up in the year 2000, by which time the United States has become a socialist Utopia.

Well, at least he got the credit card part right. Bellamy mentions them, by name, no less than eleven times in the book, as the lead character frequently uses them to buy goods.

Although they have little to do with socialist Utopian states, credit cards have steadily replaced both cash and checks since their introduction in the 1950s. Key elements apply to all cards: the embossed name and numbers, making the card machine readable, are an essential part of the system.

1 I've been unable to find a font that accurately reproduces that found on credit cards – and so I've drawn my own characters. They're colored gray with a slight touch of blue. Apply an Inner Bevel using the Layer Style dialog, with a small size – just 2 pixels should be enough, as these characters are going to be very small.

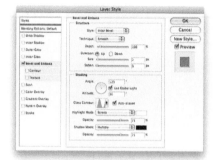

3 The hologram is a tricky element. First, we'll draw a round-cornered rectangle and place a picture of a bird on it. Merge the two layers and desaturate, then darken the rectangle corners to make some variation in tone. Open the Curves dialog, and draw a step curve like this one: the result will be a solarized view, which looks convincingly like a real hologram.

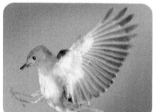

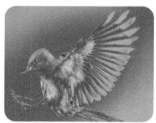

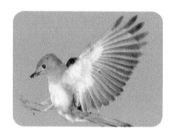

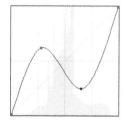

5 Credit cards use a bewildering variety of background images – some photographic, some pure design. I've drawn this abstract pattern using the Brush and the Dodge tool to add highlights, but you can use any image you like. The fictional bank name here has a very small bevel added, using Layer Styles, to add some life to it.

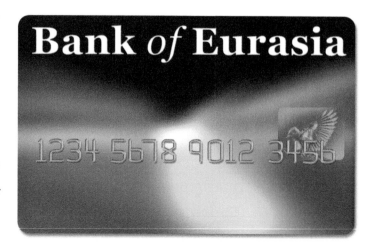

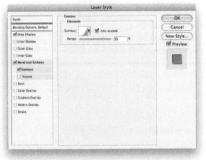

2 To add some metallic shine to this, we can use the Contour section just below the Bevel and Emboss section. Choose an upwards curve from the Contour pop-up, as shown here – or experiment with some of the other curves to see the result. You can even draw your own.

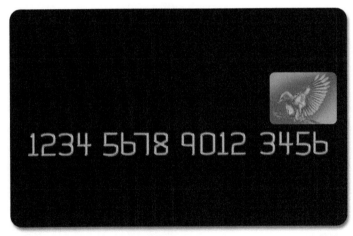

4 We can draw our credit card using the Round Corner Rectangle mode of the Shapes tool. The Shapes tool can be set to Fill Pixel mode (see More Info); drag on a new layer to fill with the foreground color. If the corner radius is not right, Undo and then change it on the Options bar.

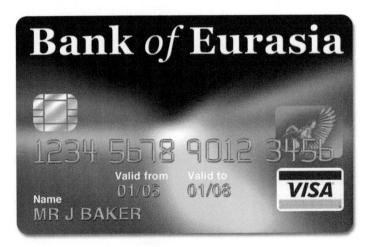

6 The computer chip below the word 'Bank' has to be drawn, copying the real thing. Draw it in gray, then use the Dodge and Burn tools to add diagonal stripes to make it look metallic. The card holder's name and the dates have the same layer style applied to them as the numbers; the other wording is set in straightforward Helvetica.

MORE INFO

● Although the credit card numbers have not been made into a font, I've drawn the full set here – copy them in the order you want to make a convincing set of figures. But remember, it's always four groups of four figures for standard cards.

● The Shapes tool, used for the hologram backing in step 3 and for the card itself in step 4, has three modes: it can create Shapes layers, draw Pen paths or paint pixels directly. The modes are chosen using the three icons on the Options bar:

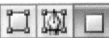

In this instance it's easiest to use the Pixel Fill mode, the last of the three buttons, to create our card.

● The position of the elements on a card varies from card to card. But it's common practice to place the numbers so they overlap the hologram – an additional fraud protection.

● A drop shadow has been added to the numbers when placed on the card, to make them stand out from the surface. This should be a very small shadow that's barely noticeable: we don't want the numbers to look as though they're floating.

SHORTCUTS

Carving in stone

1 First, take your lump of stone. I've provided one on the CD, but there are many sources of stone and marble on the internet: look for free textures for 3D modelers. You'll find an excellent selection at www.mayang.com/textures.

3 Change the color of the text to around 50% gray, and change the mode of the layer to Hard Light. It will more or less disappear, depending on whether you hit exactly 50% gray: this doesn't matter. It's just there as a basis for the embossing.

5 Let's make some cracks in this stone to go with the lettering. Make a new layer, above the type; then select both and press ctrl ⌥ G ⌘ alt G to use the stone layer as a Clipping Mask. Select areas of the new layer with the Lasso, and fill with mid gray.

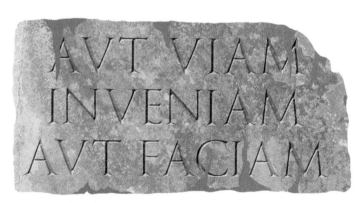

7 We need to chip away at the outer stone, to tie in with the large cracks we've made. Make a layer mask for the stone layer, and erase V-shaped notches at the ends of the cracks. We'll need to hide the lettering where it intersects with these cracks as well – see More Info for how to do this.

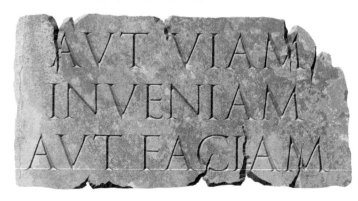

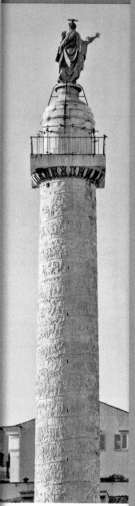

The Trajan Column, in Rome, completed in 113AD, commemorates the emperor Trajan's victory in the Dacian wars. It tells the story of his conquests in pictorial form on a continuous spiral that winds all the way around the column.

We won't attempt anything quite as ambitious. But we do have a good method of carving text onto stone without having to raise a chisel.

2 The text is set in Optimus Princeps, a wonderfully evocative font that accurately reproduces the Roman style of carved typography. Don't be tempted to use Times Roman instead, it just won't look right!

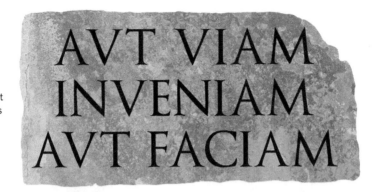

4 Choose Bevel and Emboss in the Layer Styles dialog. We only need to make a couple of changes from the default settings here: set the Technique to Chisel Hard, and the direction to Down. Increase the Size setting to create an appropriate carved appearance.

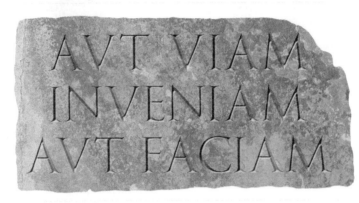

6 Change the mode of this layer to Hard Light as well, and copy the Layer Styles from the text layer onto it – hold alt ⏎ and drag the style in the Layers palette. The carved effect will now show through on this layer as well.

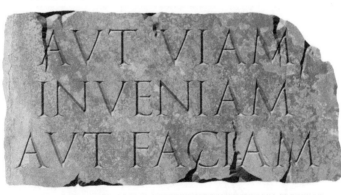

8 One of the best features about creating this effect with live text, rather than text that has been rasterized to become a regular pixel layer, is that we can change the wording or the font at any point – and the effect will remain in place.

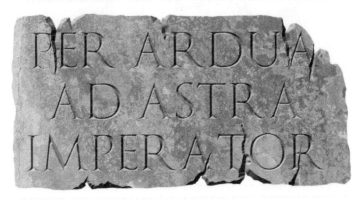

MORE INFO

● In step 4 we choose Chisel Hard as the style for the Inner Bevel. There are three modes here: Smooth, which is the standard bevel method, and the two Chisel modes – Hard and Soft. Rather curiously, Chisel Soft produces a harder-edged effect, with clear striations in the bevel edges: this effect would work well on wood, but is too rough for polished marble.

● In step 7, we need to hide the text where it intersects with the cracks. This is a straightforward procedure: first, load up the pixel area taken up by the cracks by holding ctrl ⌘ and clicking on the layer's thumbnail in the Layers palette. Then switch to the Type layer, and, with the selection still active, choose Layer > Add Layer Mask > Hide Selection. This will make a new layer mask, with the selected area already painted out.

● When we change the text in step 8, we retain the Layer Style that produces the incised effect – and, of course, we keep the layer mask added in step 7 as well. All that changes is the wording: the rest of the effect is exactly as we intended it to be.

SHORTCUTS

MAC　WIN　BOTH

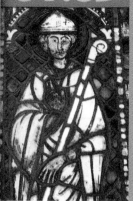

Stained glass windows

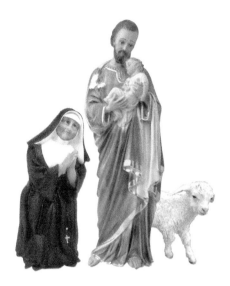

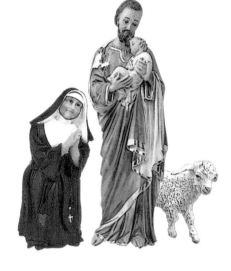

1 The first step is to locate and combine your picture elements. We've used figures from the Hemera Photo-Objects collection: a saint, a nun, both images of figurines, and a photograph of a real sheep.

2 To make them seem more painted, each of these figures has had the Poster Edges filter applied to it (found in Filter > Artistic). Since black is a rather dull color for glass, I've also brightened the nun's robes, adding color using the Curves dialog: simply achieved by raising the curve on both the red and the blue channels.

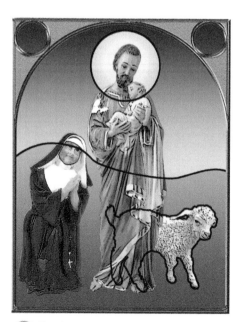

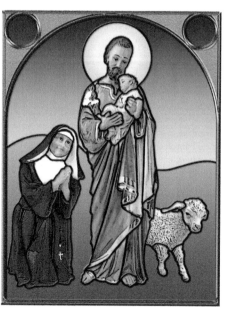

5 To make the leading, first create a new layer above the figures. Hold ⌘ ctrl as you click on the thumbnail for the Sheep layer, and use Edit > Stroke to add a 6pt black stroke to the new leading layer. Repeat this process for the hills and the halo layer. Don't worry about the outlines cutting through the saint!

6 Now hold ⌘ ctrl as you click on the saint layer's thumbnail. Press *Backspace* to delete the area from the leading; add a stroke in the same way as before. Layer Effects adds an inner bevel and slight shadow to the leading. Use a hard-edged brush with a 6 pixel size to paint in additional leading within the figures.

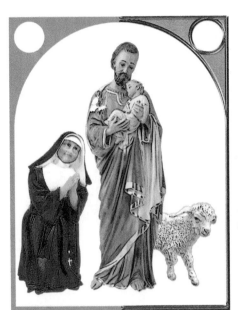

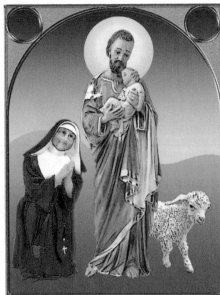

③ Stained glass works best within a suitably shaped frame. The basic outline (left) was drawn on a new layer, using a combination of the Rectangular and Elliptical Marquee tools to draw the shapes. Then, Layer Styles are used (right) to add embossing, as well as a sandstone texture using the Texturizer filter.

④ The hills, sky and halo are drawn on separate layers. After drawing the shape for the hill, fill it with pale green: then choose a darker green and use the Gradient tool, dragged from bottom to top, to add a deeper hue. The same process is used for the sky; the center of the halo is lightened with the Dodge tool.

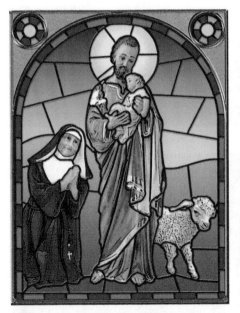

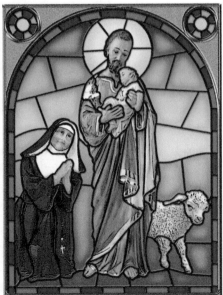

⑦ Add further leading to the background to break it up into manageable panes. The border is first drawn on the leading layer, then alternate panes are selected with the Magic Wand tool, and filled with red and blue on a new layer behind the leading.

⑧ Finally, let's add some glow. On the leading layer, use the Magic Wand to select the interior of the large panes of glass. Flatten the hills and sky into a single layer, then use ⌘ J ctrl J to make a new layer from the selection. In Layer Effects, add an inner glow, adjusting the size and choke until the effect looks right.

MORE INFO

● In steps 5 and 6 we're loading selection areas from several layers, but only working on the one layer – the leading. Using the ⌘ ctrl key to load a layer's pixels as a selection, while working on a different layer, is a useful ability that we'll use many times in this book.

● To draw the straight lines in step 7. first click the brush at one end of the line; then hold *Shift* as you click the other end, and a straight line will be drawn between the two click points.

● Making the curved band of glass in step 7 is easier than it looks. On the frame layer (made in step 3), select the interior of the arch with the Magic Wand. Then, on the leading layer, press *Backspace* to delete the existing leading; add a stroke as before. Then use Select > Modify > Contract to reduce the size of the selection by around 24 pixels, and add another stroke. All the interior lines are drawn one at a time.

● By default, the inner glow added in step 8 will be at the edge of the selected panes of glass. Change the mode to Center rather than Edge to make an interior glow.

SHORTCUTS

MAC   WIN   BOTH

Quick and dirty neon

1 The lettering I've used here is Junegull, made by Ray Larabie. It has the curved corners that are ideal for turning into neon, and will save us some time. Alternatively, you could use the approach described on page 20 for turning any font into one that's suitable for the neon process.

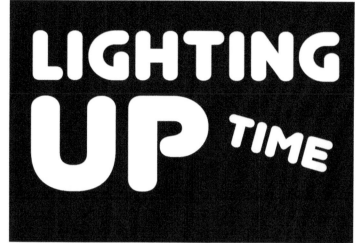

Neon lettering is made of glass tubes that have been heated up and bent into shape. It's not possible to create hard corners using this technique, as the example above shows: to make the letter R, the neon has had to be bent backwards in front of itself.

Creating accurate neon lettering is a long and fairly tortuous business. I deal with it in some depth in my book *How to Cheat in Photoshop*, so I won't repeat the same procedure here. Instead, let's look at a quick and simple way to make neon lettering using Layer Styles. The advantage of this method is that it's easy to create, and once the Layer Style has been defined it can be applied to any other object. The disadvantage is that it isn't an exact reproduction of neon – but it's a speedy alternative.

3 While we"re not going to attempt to make the creases as the tube doubles back on itself, we can insert breaks where each section of tube is masked to join the next. Make a layer mask for the neon layer, and use a hard-edged brush to paint out small gaps in each letter. Try to paint out the gaps in appropriate places.

5 Make another new layer, and fill with black; then hold *alt* ⌥ as you drag the Layer Style from the neon layer onto this new one, and the style will be copied across. There are some places where the reduced neon effect really doesn't work, such as inside the 'M' of 'Time'; delete these with the Eraser tool.

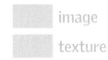
2 Load up all the words as a selection (see More Info for details), then make a new layer and apply an 8pt stroke to it (left). Using Layer Styles, add a bevel and emboss (center); then add an Outer Glow to make the neon shine. The neon style is included in the file Art&Design.asl on the CD.

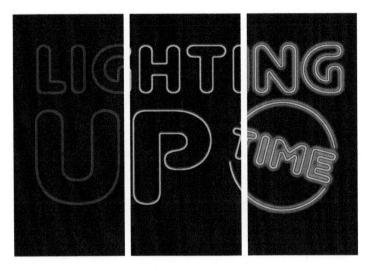

MORE INFO

● In step 2, we need to add multiple layers as a single selection. To do this, first hold *ctrl* ⌘ and click on the thumbnail of the first layer in the Layers palette, to load up its pixels as a selection. Then hold *ctrl* *Shift* ⌘ *Shift* and click on each additional layer's thumbnail in turn: when you do so, the pixels on that layer will be added to the selection.

4 Let's add a second row of neon inside the first. Hold *ctrl* ⌘ and click on the neon's thumbnail to load the selection, then use *ctrl* *alt* *R* ⌘ ⌥ *R* to open the Refine Edge dialog. Use the Contract slider to make the selection a lot smaller, and raise the Contrast slider to hide any fuzziness in the edges. Then hit *Enter* to apply the effect.

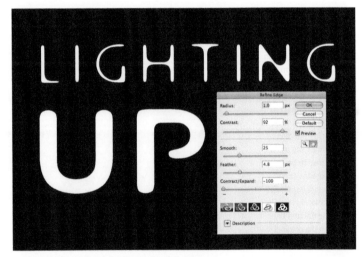

● When we paint gaps in the letters in the layer mask in step 3, we're likely to be left with hard ends. A good solution is first to make the gaps slightly larger than you want them to end up. Then switch the foreground and background colors so that we're painting in white, which will paint back in on the layer mask. Choose a small, hard brush that's the same size as the neon tubing, and carefully paint back the end of each piece of tubing. The result will be neatly rounded ends that look far more convincing.

6 We could add color to the neon by changing the color of each layer, and modifying the colors in Layer Styles to match. But here's a much quicker way: make a selection around the word 'UP', and make a new Hue/Saturation adjustment layer using the pop-up menu at the bottom of the Layers palette. When you drag the Hue slider, the adjustment will be confined to the area you selected.

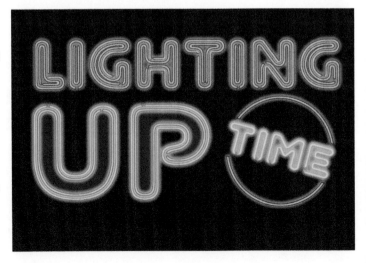

● In step 6, I've revealed the original lettering behind the neon effect – reduced in opacity, so it's only just visible. This gives the impression of the wooden backing to which the neon tubing is attached, and which allows it to be read clearly in daytime.

Writing under water

Since the dawn of time people have been fascinated by fire and water. The invention of the aqualung has helped divers to discover the wonders of the deep.

Closer to home, the British artist David Hockney made an early name for himself with *A Bigger Splash*, the first painting to depict the pattern of sunlight reflected on a swimming pool as a graphic illustration. The painting is also unusual in that the subject, a diver, has disappeared beneath the surface.

We'll use the texture already present in our swimming pool to place text on the bottom of the pool.

1 We can see the distorted tiles through the surface of the water, and it's this rippling distortion that we want to emulate. The pattern of sunlight on the surface follows the 'contours' of the water, outlining the various rippling hills and valleys that make up the surface.

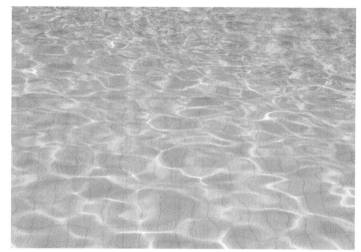

3 Use Layer > Rasterize > Type to turn the text into a regular pixel layer, then use Free Transform to distort it so it's seen in perspective. This effect is achieved by holding *ctrl* ⌘ as you drag each corner handle: the modifier key allows each corner to be moved independently. It can take a while before the effect looks right, so be experimental and try to match the original perspective of the pool.

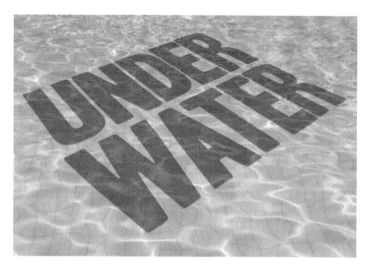

5 Now for the clever bit. Hide the gray version of the water, and choose Filter > Distort > Displace. You'll be presented with this dialog: choose a horizontal and vertical scale of 20 to begin with. When you click OK you'll be presented with a standard Open dialog: navigate to the .psd file you saved in the last step, and click on that.

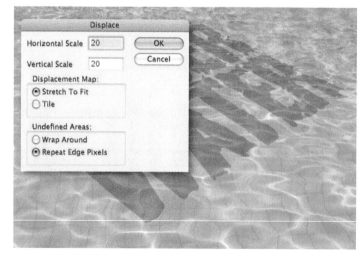

Displace	
Horizontal Scale 20	OK
Vertical Scale 20	Cancel

Displacement Map:
- ● Stretch To Fit
- ○ Tile

Undefined Areas:
- ○ Wrap Around
- ● Repeat Edge Pixels

2 Because we're going to distort the text, we need to choose something bold and straightforward. This is Headline One, a plain sans serif that will be perfect for our needs.

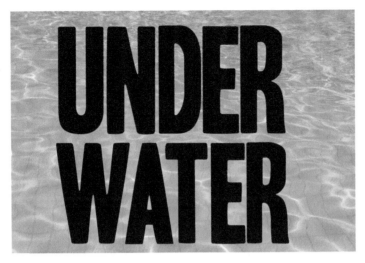

MORE INFO

● In step 4, we blur the water before saving it as our displacement map. That's because the original gray version of the water is too intricate, and will produce a very fiddly outline on the text. Here's the text distorted by itself:

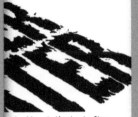

And here's the text after adding some blur to the displacement map:

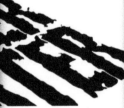

4 Duplicate the water layer, and desaturate it using `ctrl` `Shift` `U` `⌘` `Shift` `U`. Drag the copy to the top of the layer stack. Now, we need to blur the gray version and increase the contrast slightly: use Filter > Blur > Gaussian Blur to add around a 2 pixel blur (see More Info for the reason why). With the layer at the top of the stack, save the document as a .psd file on your hard drive.

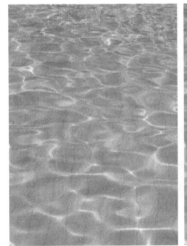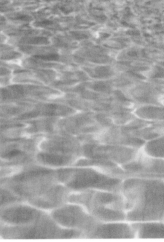

The second version gives us the distortion we want – following the major contours of the water, without replicating each little ripple.

● When you save the .psd file in step 4, it's only the uppermost visible layer of the saved file that's read by the Displace filter – so you can carry on working on the rest of the image beneath it.

6 The Displace filter distorts the image according to the 'displacement map' we saved in step 4: the brighter the image, the more it's distorted. Here, I've moved an unblurred copy of the gray water and made a clipping mask with the distorted text, setting its mode to Hard Light so that the bright ripples stand out on top.

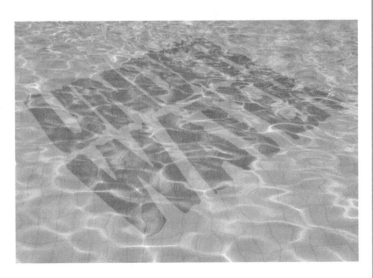

Fabric badges

Every school child who has ever worn a uniform has had one of these badges emblazoned on their chest. They're worn by retired colonels, and security guards alike: the badge of belonging.

Creating these badges in Photoshop is, like any other task, a question of replicating the material and style of the original. The fabric part is easy – it's just a scan of a coat.

The only tricky part here is the stitching, which requires us to create a Photoshop brush specially to do the task. But even though this might take us a few minutes, it's very much easier than having to draw individual cotton strands all the way around the object – and we can save the brush and use it again.

1 This piece of fabric is a photograph of the inside of a coat. I've desaturated it and sharpened it slightly to make an all-purpose gray fabric background. The odd shadows and creases will simply add to the texture.

2 There are several ways to draw the shield shape: you could use the Pen tool and draw it from scratch, or use a combination of rectangular and elliptical Marquee tools. Or you could use the shape on the CD. Color it using Hue/Saturation.

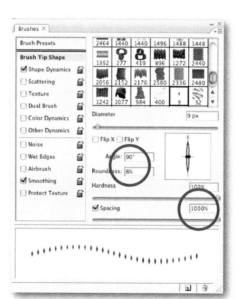

5 Time for our new brush. Select a small brush – this one's 9 pixels in size – and open the Brushes dialog. In the Brush Tip Shape section, set the Roundness to just 8% for a very thin brush, and the angle to 90°. Drag the Spacing slider to its maximum value of 1000%, so we get big gaps between each stroke.

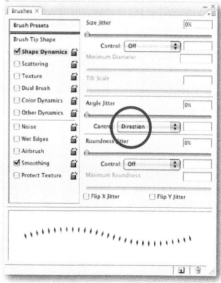

6 Switch to the Shape Dynamics section of the Brushes palette, and look at the section marked Angle Jitter. We'll leave this value at 0 – the 'jitter' is the amount of random variation – but set the Control pop-up here to Direction. This makes the brush follow the direction of painting.

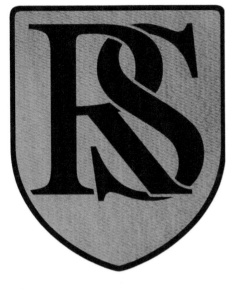

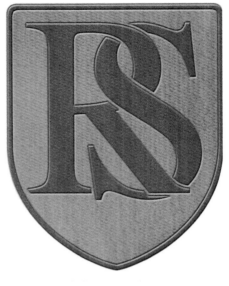

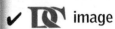
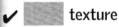
3 We created this monogram on page 18, so we can reuse it here. The outer band was created by modifying the outline of the shield shape (see More Info for details); this band is then merged down into the monogram layer to make a single layer.

4 Hold *ctrl* ⌘ and click on the monogram layer's thumbnail to load it as a selection, then switch to the fabric shield layer and use *ctrl J* ⌘ *J* to make a new layer from it. In the Bevel/Emboss section of Layer Styles, select Pillow Emboss as the style and recolor.

MORE INFO

● In step 3 we need to make a border around the edge of the shield. Do this by first holding *ctrl* ⌘ and clicking on the shield layer's thumbnail in the Layers palette to load it as a selection, then use Select > Modify > Contract to reduce this selection by 16 pixels. We now have a shape 16 pixels smaller than the shield. Inverse the selection using *ctrl Shift I* ⌘ *Shift I*, so everything outside this reduced shape is selected; then, with the shield layer selected, choose *ctrl J* ⌘ *J* to make a new layer from the selection. The result will be the border around the edge.

● In step 7, we'll get a double edge around the outer border when creating a Work Path. We don't want stitching at the very outside of our badge, so select that outer path by holding *alt* ⌥ and clicking on it with the Direct Selection tool (*A*) and then delete it.

● In step 8 I've painted the stitching in white so it stands out. The color you use depends entirely on the colors in your badge; you can always change the stitching color later, or reduce its transparency if you think it stands out too much from the background.

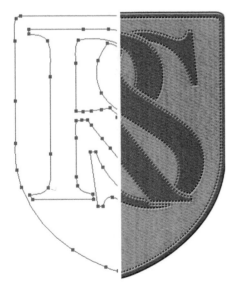

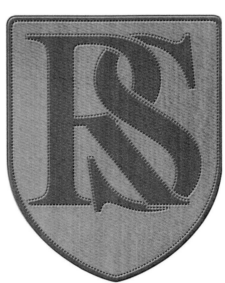

7 We can make the Brush tool follow a Pen path automatically – but first we need a Pen path. Load the outlines as described in step 4, then choose Make Work Path from the pop-up menu in the Paths palette. With the path visible and the Brush tool selected, make a new layer and press *Enter*.

8 The *Enter* key makes the Brush tool paint along the line of the current path. Switch to the Pen tool, and press *Enter* again to hide the path: you'll have just the stitching on a new layer. Add a small bevel and a tiny drop shadow using Layer Styles to give the stitching some three-dimensionality, and the badge is complete.

Button badges

If you have a cause, get a badge. It's the literal equivalent of wearing your heart on your sleeve: badges proclaim your political, social, musical or anarchic views to anyone who passes you in the street.

While the more conservative may scoff at badge-wearing youths, it's directly paralleled by the dazzling array of medals and ribbons worn by senior soldiers and boy scouts.

As I write this, a friend peering over my shoulder tells me that he used to have a job designing badges. They always tried to avoid the circular designs, apparently, as they were so difficult to press correctly: the machines that punched the paper and fixed it onto the badges were notoriously inaccurate, it seems. Still, we can make it work in Photoshop...

1 Start with a circular selection. On a new layer, fill this with the color of your choice. It doesn't matter too much what it is – we can always change it later if we need to.

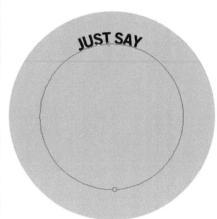

2 With the Shapes tool set to Path mode, draw a circle rather smaller than the size of the badge. Switch to the Type tool and when you click on the path, the tool will type onto the path, following its shape. The text used here is OldSansBlack.

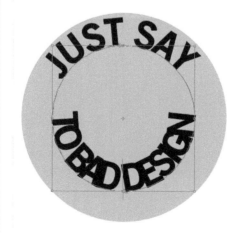

5 The text was upside down at the end of the last step because we dragged it around the circle, so it kept the same orientation it had originally. We need to flip it the other side of the line, so hold *ctrl* ⌘ once again to grab the I-beam, and drag it to the other side of the path.

6 We now need to shift the text down so its top, rather than the bottom, aligns with the path. Select all the text with the Type tool, and use *alt* Shift ↓ ⏷ Shift ↓ to shift the text baseline down a couple of times, until it sits with the tops just touching the line.

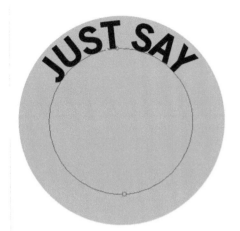

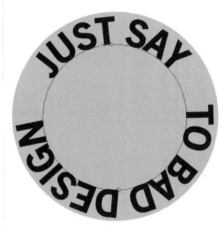

3 Make sure the text is centered, and enlarge it to the size you want. If you hold *ctrl* ⌘ you'll get an I-beam which you can drag where you want it; it will snap to the top center marker, so you know the text is centered on the badge.

4 To make the other half of the text, first duplicate the layer. Click in the text with the Type tool, then Select All and retype the new words. Grab the I-beam again with the *ctrl* ⌘ key, and drag the type to the bottom half. You'll notice it's upside down.

MORE INFO

● The Shapes tool, used in step 2, has three different modes: it can create a new Shapes layer, make a Pen path or draw filled pixels:

We want the middle of these three: we can only set text along a standard path.

● Paths with text on them behave rather differently to other Photoshop objects. When we distort the path using Free Transform, only the path itself will be distorted, and not the text attached to it: the text will reflow along the new path. So in step 8 here, I reduced the size of the text circles slightly to make them fit better within the badge. The text itself didn't get smaller, but it tightened up slightly as it reset itself to fit on a smaller radius.

● Once the basic badge has been made, complete with bevel shading and drop shadow, it can be reused to make any number of badges: simply copy it and recolor as necessary. If you want to use a design on the badge that wraps around the edges, as opposed to simple text, then make a clipping mask with the badge layer and the design will only show up where it overlaps the badge beneath.

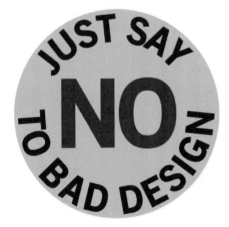

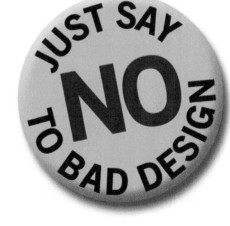

7 With the upper and lower text now centered around the perimeter of the badge, we can add our interior text – a giant NO set in red, in the same font. You'll see badges like this all over the place: from a distance you can tell they're protesting, but you can't always tell what about.

8 To make the badge itself look three-dimensional, switch to its layer and add an Inner Bevel using Layer Styles. Add the maximum amount of Softness for a really smooth edge; the drop shadow makes it sit just above the surface of the paper. Rotating the design also helps it to look more like a real object.

Leather work

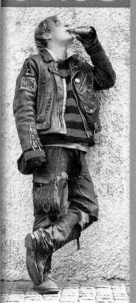

The leather jacket has long been a symbol of rebellion. From Marlon Brando in *On the Waterfront*, through The Fonz in *Happy Days*, right up to Harrison Ford in *Indiana Jones*, the jacket has signified an outsider, a maverick, someone beyond the bounds of respectable society.

No jacket is complete without a slogan emblazoned on the back. It might be painted on, or – if the wearer pays a little more – it will be made out of pieces of dyed and shaped leather, sewn onto the top of the jacket.

We'll look at how to create both methods, since the effect is largely the same (until the jacket starts to get worn, of course).

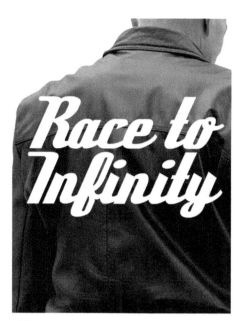

1 The text here is set in the Ray Larabie font Deftone Stylus, which perfectly captures the 1950s automotive feel. It's a highly stylized script, which would be equally at home spelling out the name of a car in gleaming chrome.

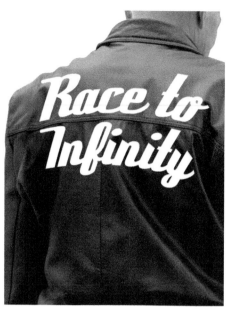

2 We can use the Warp Text dialog (click the button on the Options bar when the Type tool is active) to bend the text into shape. Adding a little horizontal distortion within the dialog gives it a feeling of some perspective.

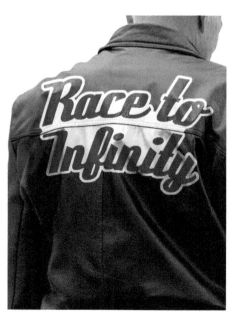

5 Make a layer from the expanded region, and brighten it using the Curves dialog, raising the curve center. You'll need to use Hue/Saturation to take some of the color out of it as well. If we were merely painting on the jacket, we'd stop here; we'll continue for a stitched look.

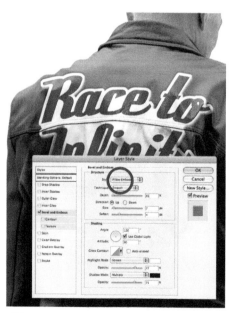

6 To give the new layer some depth, use the Bevel/Emboss settings in the Layer Styles dialog. From the Style pop-up menu choose Pillow Emboss. This has an effect both inside and outside the layer, giving the impression of stitching between the two. You may need to soften the effect if it's too harsh.

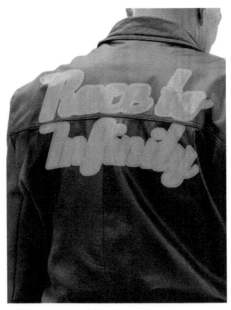

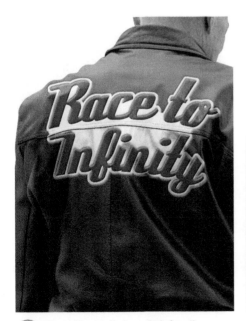

3 Hold `ctrl` `⌘` and click on the text layer's thumbnail to load it as a selection, then go to the jacket layer and use `ctrl J` `⌘ J` to make a new layer. Use Hue/Saturation to brighten and colorize the text; adding some Unsharp Mask gives it definition.

4 To make the backing, we need to make a larger selection. Load up the type selection as in the previous step, and use Select > Modify > Expand to make it 8 pixels larger. As we can see here, there are holes; use the Lasso tool to loop around these to include them.

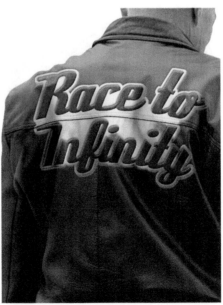

7 We need to copy the Layer Style from the previous layer onto the main (red) text layer. To do this, hold `alt` `⌥` as you click on the style in the Layers palette, and drag it to the red text layer: the style will be copied between the two. Reduce the radius and softness as needed for a tighter effect.

8 Although we made the lettering out of the jacket texture, some additional shading helps it to look as if it's wrapping around the jacket. Load up the selection of the white text layer, and make a new Hard Light layer (see More Info) above it. Use the Burn tool to darken it, following the lines of the creases.

MORE INFO

● In step 8 we need to make a Hard Light layer to hold the shadow. We could simply make a new layer, using the text outline as a clipping mask, and paint on this in black; but the Hard Light layer gives us more control over the shading, and stores the selection so we can continue to work on it later. Hold `ctrl` `⌘` and click on the white text layer's thumbnail to load the selection, then make a new layer using `ctrl Shift N` `⌘ Shift N`. In the dialog which pops up, specify that the layer mode should be Hard Light, and that the layer should be filled with Hard Light Neutral color:

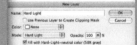

When the layer's created, inverse the selection using `ctrl Shift I` `⌘ Shift I` and delete to remove everything outside the selection. You won't see anything, because the layer is filled with 50% gray, and that's invisible in Hard Light mode. But when we add shading using Dodge and Burn, anything that's brighter or darker will show up: the layer makes the perfect base for shading work.

SHORTCUTS

 MAC   WIN   BOTH

Enamel pin badges

In Great Britain, enamel shield badges are worn by school students to indicate that they have rank and authority over their fellow students. These things have been around, virtually unchanged, for over a hundred years; they're instantly recognizable, and are frequently parodied.

We can create the enamel effect easily, adding our own lettering. We'll stick with the traditional 'prefect' badge, although you may wish to substitute this for a more ironic or playful word.

The key to making this work is softening the edges, which we round over using the Refine Edge dialog. This is found in Photoshop CS2 and higher, so if you have an earlier version of the application you won't have this feature.

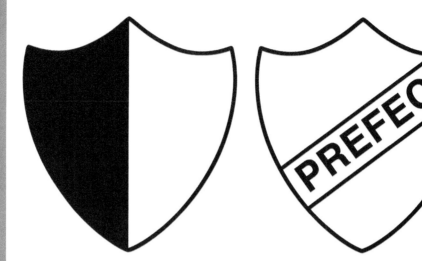

1 Begin by drawing half a shield, with the Pen tool. This is the only tricky part. Fill it with black, then flip it to make a full shield (half shown, left). Use Edit > Stroke to make the outline, on a new layer; choose around an 8 point stroke to begin with.

2 The disgonal lines are easily added on a new layer, using the Shapes tool set to Pixel mode (so they paint directly onto the layer). The text here is plain old Helvetica: we want a simple, boring, readable font for this job.

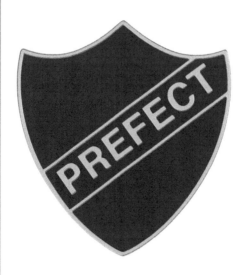

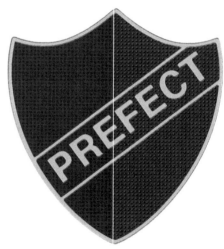

5 Select the original badge area, and make a new layer filled with your choice of color. Red is traditional for these badges, although other primary colors such as blue and green are also used occasionally. Darker colors will help the gold to stand out, so choose dark rather than bright red.

6 Create an array of dots by drawing one and duplicating it (left). I've made an array on the CD for you. Use the shield layer as a Clipping Mask using *ctrl* *alt* *G* ⌘ ⌥ *G* so the dots only show up where they overlap the red layer beneath; add some bevel and emboss (right) to give them texture.

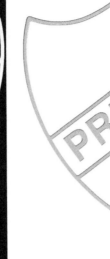

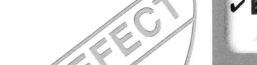

3 Load up all the layers as a selection (see More Info) and use *ctrl* *alt* *R* *⌘* *⌥* *R* to open the Refine Edge dialog. Drag the Smooth slider to round off the edges, creating subtle curves at the corners of the lettering and at the joins.

4 Make a new layer from the selection, and use Layer Styles to make a gold effect (see page 236 for how to do this). Use a very small bevel, just one or two pixels in size: the lettering should look almost flat on the badge surface.

MORE INFO

● In step 3, we need to load up all three layers we've created – the shield outline, the diagonal lines and the text – as a single selection. To do this, hold *ctrl* *⌘* and click on the thumbnail of one of the layers; this will load it as a selection. Then hold *ctrl* *Shift* *⌘* *Shift* and click on the thumbnails for the other two layers, to add them to the selection.

● When we open the Refine Edge dialog, there are several ways in which we can view the selection. For our purposes, we want the last choice, on the right:

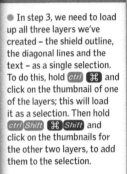

This will show the selection in white on a black background, which makes it easy for us to see exactly what we're going to get.

● To create the Hard Light layer in step 8, load up the selection by *ctrl* *⌘* clicking on the shield thumbnail, then choose New Layer. Specify Hard Light as the mode, and fill with Hard Light Neutral color (this is an option in the New Layer dialog). After it's created, inverse the selection and delete the area outside it. Now, when you use the Dodge and Burn tools on it, only the highlights and shadows will be visible.

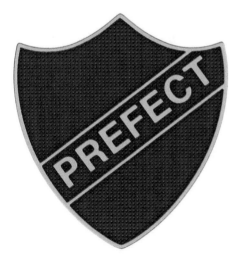

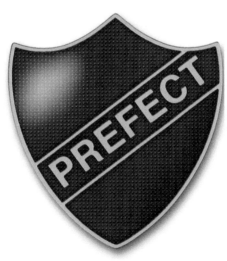

7 To add some realism, use Layer Styles to add a Drop Shadow to the gold layer. Set the Distance to zero, so the impression is equal all round the gold. The shadow will spill over the edge, so use *ctrl* *alt* *G* *⌘* *⌥* *G* here as well to make this layer join the Clipping Mask set.

8 Add a shadow to the red fill layer for a little extra realism. Make a new Hard Light layer the same shape as the shield, and use the Dodge and Burn tools on here to paint in a little extra shading and a highlight on the top left – see More Info if you need help here.

SHORTCUTS

 MAC   WIN   BOTH

Bling bling

The term 'bling bling' first appeared in the 1990s, coined by a New Orleans group of rap artists called, appropriately enough, the Cash Money Millionaires.

Although it started as a street style, bling bling quickly spread beyond the hip-hop culture in which it began and entered the mainstream, where jewelry manufacturers suddenly found themselves able to sell items that attained previously undreamed-of levels of vulgarity, with price tags to match.

It's a style that's instantly recognizable, and one that's relatively simple to create – we just need to define a Layer Style for the gold outer, and a diamond pattern for the inner lettering.

1 Two kinds of fonts tend to be used for bling bling jewelry – chunky sans serifs and slab serifs, and stylized italics. We'll take the latter route: this is Deftone Stylus, by Ray Larabie.

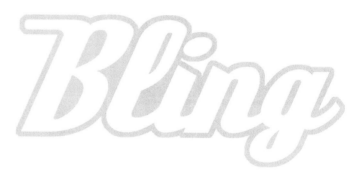

3 To make the gold outer work properly, we need to remove the text region from this layer. Load up the text area again, then press *Backspace* to delete it from the yellow layer. With a hard brush, paint in any stray holes in the B and L.

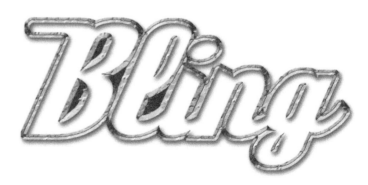

5 To give the gold a more realistic appearance, try adding some texture using the Texture pane beneath Bevel and Emboss. Keep the depth to a fairly small amount or it will swamp the image: I've used about 18% here.

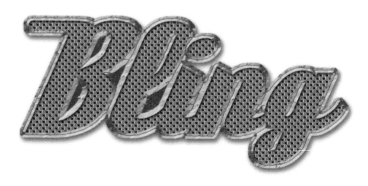

7 When we put the diamond text together with the gold outer edge, we start to get a feel of the bling jewelry effect. To make the diamond text look as if it's recessed, use Layer Styles to add an Inner Shadow to the layer.

2 Load up the font's area by holding `ctrl` ⌘ and clicking its thumbnail in the Layers palette. Then use Select > Modify > Expand to make it 16 pixels larger. On a new layer, behind the text layer, fill this selection with yellow.

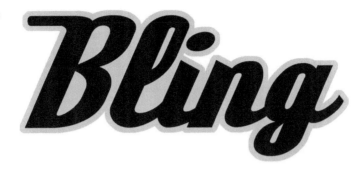

4 The gold effect is added using Layer Styles. Check the Bevel and Emboss tab, applying an Inner Bevel using the Chisel Hard method; in the Shading pane, add a Gloss Contour. See page 236 for more on creating shiny effects with Layer Styles.

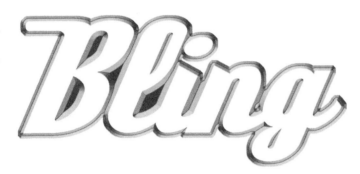

6 This diamond pattern is made from a photograph of a real diamond – see More Info for details. It's applied to the text layer as a pattern using Layer Styles, so we can reduce its scale to 25%, producing this densely packed look.

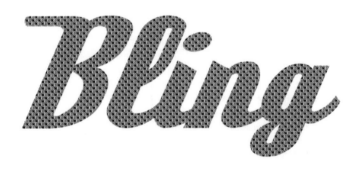

8 Adding a black background always helps to make jewelry look better. Here, I've added three sparkles: these are created with the sparkle-shaped brush (it's one of the default brushes). I've also added a distorted diamond to the 'i'.

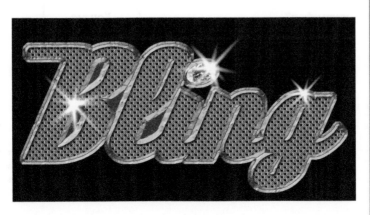

MORE INFO

● The diamond pattern in step 6 is defined as follows. First, take a picture of a real diamond: reduce it and make three copies, placed at corners of a square. Make a square selection with the Marquee tool that touches the centers of each diamond:

With the background layer hidden so that the diamonds have a transparent background, choose Edit > Define Pattern, and give the new pattern a name.

● When the diamond pattern is applied using Layer Styles, we can change its scale. It will look sharp at 100%, 50% and 25%, and a little soft at intermediate sizes; use these sizes if you can, for a better result.

● The sparkle brush used in step 8 is a default Photoshop brush:

17	23	36	44	60	14
26	33	42		Star 55 pixels	

Use it at a large size, on a new layer. In case you have trouble locating it, I've included a sparkle in the Photoshop file that you can use instead.

www.wrong

A few years ago I was looking for a boat to take me from the south of England to northern Spain. After a short search I found exactly the right crossing – except Google had dropped me into the middle of a frame-based site, with the main frames missing. There was no indication of which company was offering this service, and the URL was a meaningless string of numbers so there was no way to guess.

Good design on the web isn't just a matter of aesthetics, it can crucially affect your business.

On these pages I've pointed out some of the major irritations that I see daily on the internet. This is by no means an exhaustive list of errors: it's a minefield out there, and you have to tread carefully.

www.who?
'Use your browser's Back button to return' – how many times have you seen that instruction on a website? The problem is that most users don't come in through the front door. They'll start with a Google search and end up somewhere in the middle. Make it easy for them to get to your home page – always give them a dedicated button.

www.wacky
It's a common enough situation. Your logo has always been in black and white, because it's cheaper to print that way. But hey, this is the internet, color comes free – so let's do a glistening chrome version! On second thoughts, let's not. Especially if it's unreadable.

www.waving the flag
It doesn't really matter how patriotic you are: waving flags, like any other off-the-shelf animated GIF elements, simply look distracting and awful. Leave the flag-wearing to the politicians.

www.word wrapping
If users have to enlarge type so they can read it, make sure that any type on the page won't then be too big to read to avoid this sort of mishap. Make the text big enough in the first place.

www.wrong font
Once you've chosen a font for your text, stick with it. It always looks clumsy when an edited piece of text ends up with one or two words in a different font from the rest.

www.when?
Placing a News slot on your front page is a great way to show that your site is current, up to date and moving with the times. Unless you fail to update it, of course, in which case all it will do is show that your site is out of date, poorly maintained and unloved.

www.waiting for visitors
It's easy to place a visitor counter on your site. But if you don't expect many visitors then all it will do is show how unpopular your site is: wait till you have some traffic before boasting about how much you have.

www.where?
At some point, a user may have to read your website's URL over the phone to a friend. What are the chances of this one being written down correctly? If you don't want to lose users, give them an address they can understand.

http://174.257.33.5592/?qu

Firefox Help   Firefox Support   Plug-in FAQ

End of seaso

Widget
UNIVERSAL & GIZMO

Departments

GROMMETS
SUB GROMMETS
WIDGETS
BUDGETS
GADGETS
GIZMOS
WAZZATS
WIDGWATS
GIZMOIDS
CLEARANCE

CREATE

NEWS... NEWS... NE

January 14, 2003

Hi, and welcome to our website!

We've been working day and nig around the world. And now we'v you're looking here, and if you c updating our site and scouring th regularly and see what we've con is not only the most entertaining become your favorite - so don't c Click the link at the bottom of th

You are visitor no.
0000031

Done

www.welcome
You know when you go on vacation, and you go out for an evening meal to a tourist area? Outside the seedier restaurants you'll find waiters beckoning you inside. It's off-putting and counter-productive.

www.whatever

If you have important information, don't place it in a flashing sign at the top of your site. Most web users are so used to flashing banner ads that they'll ignore them, even if this one turns out not to be an ad from another site. Don't make them confuse your info with junk.

www.waiting...

If your site is so long, or so graphic intensive that it doesn't load in a couple of seconds, then you're going to lose viewers. Unless there's an exceptionally good reason for filling your site with graphics, then keep them to a minimum.

www.wow, that's a long page

Web pages have links for a reason. It's so you can break up your site into manageable chunks. A scrollbar this size tells your viewers that they've got an awful lot of page to wade through.

www.what?

There's a tendency among arty, designer sites to replace obvious links with teasers. If the site is created in Flash, these will often be floating so you have to chase them around the screen. Don't treat your users like this – let them find what they're looking for.

www.whoops!

Cascading Style Sheets, pop-up windows, Flash navigation – all very well, as long as it behaves itself. But users shouldn't have to scroll just to see a window that the site has opened. If you can't fit it in the main window, miss it out and do something simpler.

www.watermarks

Web authoring programs allow us to create custom backgrounds behind our pages. Often, you'll see watermark effects, where the company logo is repeated a hundred times in the background. Because you can never push your logo too hard, right? Wrong. It's awful.

www.wordy wordy

The internet is not a book. It's not even a magazine. Reading text on screen is harder than reading it on paper, and when something more interesting is just a click away you need to work harder to keep your readers' attention. Keep text chunks short, pithy, and narrow enough to take in at a glance. The art is all in the cutting.

www.width matters

Visitors to your site should never, ever, have to scroll horizontally to see the whole site. If it won't fit on a standard monitor, then redesign it so it does: the monitor width is your only physical constraint.

SALE now on CLICK HERE

INSPIRE

EXPECT

Widget

About the comp
Key members of
Client list
Our mission
Why we are diff
Getting to know
Example of the
Typical workflo

... NEWS... NEWS... NEWS... NEW

Widget

ie very best grommets, widgets and gizmos from
el free to browse! You'll find just about anything
nost likely it doesn't exist. We're constantly
more fantabulous goodies, so be sure to check back
e sure you'll agree that Universal Widget & Gizmo
on the whole internet, but one that will quickly
ersal Widget & Gizmo your home page today.
y to make this page your home page, and you'll

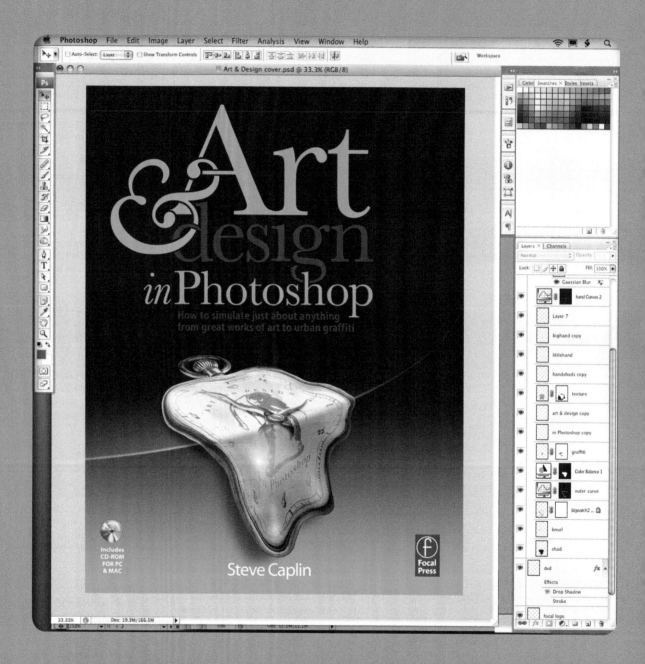

Photoshop
reference

This book assumes you know your way around Photoshop to a fair degree. There are countless books out there whose sole purpose is to show you how to use the application, and this isn't one of them.

But knowing how to use Photoshop can mean different things to different people. You might spend your whole life retouching photographs, without ever looking at special effect filters. Or you might understand the workings of each filter inside out, but have never experimented with layer masks and never dabbled with QuickMask.

This chapter is here to bring everyone up to speed. It's by no means an exhaustive Photoshop instruction manual, but should provide a handy reference that will help you to understand the key concepts.

Photoshop

From Adobe Photoshop, a well-known and widely-used graphics editor.

Verb

to photoshop *(third-person singular simple present photoshops, present participle photoshopping, simple past and past participle photoshopped (transitive)*: to digitally edit or alter a picture or photograph.

Usage notes: Photoshop is a registered trademark of Adobe Systems, and they object to its usage as a common verb.

Wiktionary.org

Selection tools

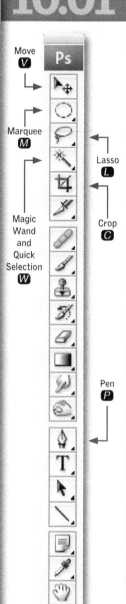

Move
V

Marquee
M

Magic
Wand
and
Quick
Selection
W

Lasso
L

Crop
C

Pen
P

Quick
Mask
Q

MOVE TOOL Select and move layers

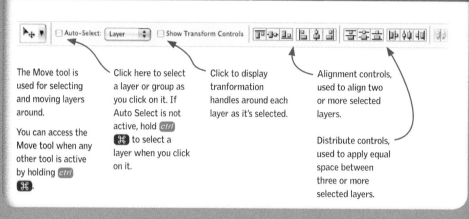

The Move tool is used for selecting and moving layers around.

You can access the Move tool when any other tool is active by holding *ctrl* *⌘*.

Click here to select a layer or group as you click on it. If Auto Select is not active, hold *ctrl* *⌘* to select a layer when you click on it.

Click to display tranformation handles around each layer as it's selected.

Alignment controls, used to align two or more selected layers.

Distribute controls, used to apply equal space between three or more selected layers.

MARQUEE TOOL Make rectangular and elliptical selections

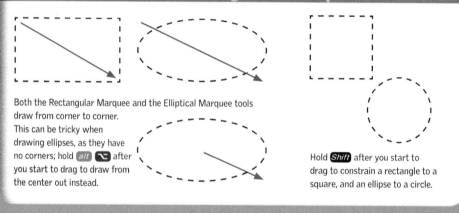

Both the Rectangular Marquee and the Elliptical Marquee tools draw from corner to corner. This can be tricky when drawing ellipses, as they have no corners; hold *alt* *⌥* after you start to drag to draw from the center out instead.

Hold *Shift* after you start to drag to constrain a rectangle to a square, and an ellipse to a circle.

SELECTION TOOL TRICKS Adding and subtracting

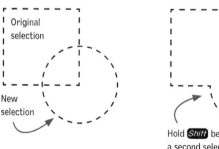

Original selection

New selection

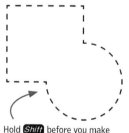

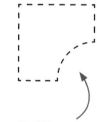

Hold *Shift* before you make a second selection to add the new one to the old.

Hold *alt* *⌥* before you make a second selection to subtract the new one from the old.

Hold the Spacebar while you're drawing a selection to move it around. When you release the Spacebar, you can continue to drag the selection.

Hold *alt* *Shift* *⌥* *Shift* before you make a second selection to produce an intersection of the new selection with the old.

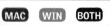

MAGIC WAND + QUICK SELECTION TOOLS Automatic range selection

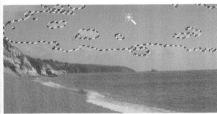

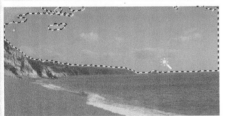

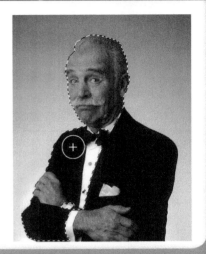

The Magic Wand selects ranges of similar colors, such as this sky (left). To add to the selection, hold *Shift* and click in a different area (right).

The Tolerance setting on the Options bar determines the color variation that the tool will include in its search. A figure of 32 is a good starting point.

Press *Shift* *W* to switch between the Magic Wand and the Quick Selection tool (right). This is used for isolating people or objects from a background, and selects all the tones over which the tool is dragged. Use *Shift* and *alt* *⌥* to modify the selections.

LASSO Basic selection

The basic tool for tracing a selection. But it's hard to control for accurate selections; best used while holding *alt* *⌥*, which allows you to trace straight lines between click points.

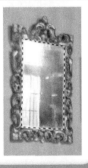

CROP Crop + rotate

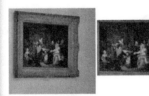

The Crop tool allows us to both crop and rotate images. When the Perspective button is checked on the Options bar, we can remove distortion from images.

PEN Smooth selection

A sophisticated tool for drawing smooth paths, which can then be stored within images and turned into selections later. The professional's choice of selection tool.

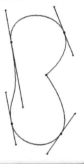

QUICK MASK Selection by painting

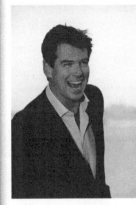

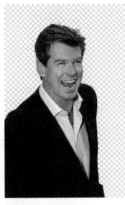

The default method is for 'masked' (unselected) regions to be highlighted in red. Many Photoshop users prefer to switch this around, so selected areas are shown: double click the QuickMask icon to change the settings. Paint black to select, white to deselect.

Change the highlight color if there's a lot of red in your image

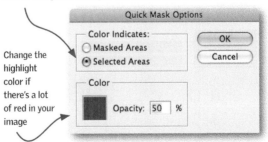

QuickMask is one of the best ways of making selections in Photoshop. Press *Q* to enter QuickMask mode, and use any of the painting tools to fill in your selection. When you've finished, press Q again to leave QuickMask to work with your selection.

You can used a soft-edged brush in QuickMask to get a feathered selection – or use Gaussian Blur on a QuickMask selection to soften the edges numerically, if you prefer. All the standard painting tools and filters can be used within a QuickMask selection.

227

Painting tools 1

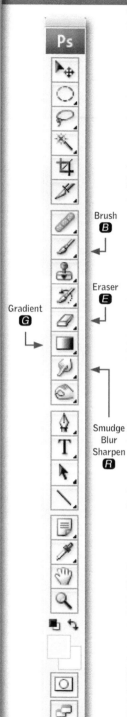

Brush
B

Eraser
E

Gradient
G

Smudge
Blur
Sharpen
R

BRUSH TOOL The basic painting tool

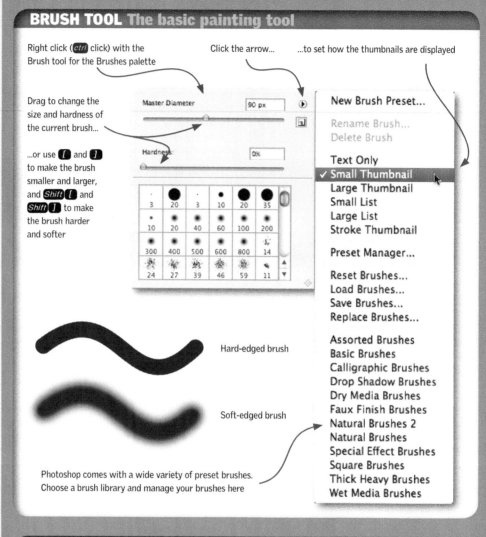

Right click (*ctrl* click) with the Brush tool for the Brushes palette

Click the arrow...

...to set how the thumbnails are displayed

Drag to change the size and hardness of the current brush...

...or use **[** and **]** to make the brush smaller and larger, and *Shift* **[** and *Shift* **]** to make the brush harder and softer

Master Diameter   90 px

Hardness: 0%

3	20	3	10	20	35
10	20	40	60	100	200
300	400	500	600	800	14
24	27	39	46	59	11

New Brush Preset...

Rename Brush...
Delete Brush

Text Only
✓ Small Thumbnail
Large Thumbnail
Small List
Large List
Stroke Thumbnail

Preset Manager...

Reset Brushes...
Load Brushes...
Save Brushes...
Replace Brushes...

Assorted Brushes
Basic Brushes
Calligraphic Brushes
Drop Shadow Brushes
Dry Media Brushes
Faux Finish Brushes
Natural Brushes 2
Natural Brushes
Special Effect Brushes
Square Brushes
Thick Heavy Brushes
Wet Media Brushes

Hard-edged brush

Soft-edged brush

Photoshop comes with a wide variety of preset brushes. Choose a brush library and manage your brushes here

GRADIENT TOOL Creates smooth color transitions

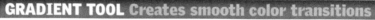
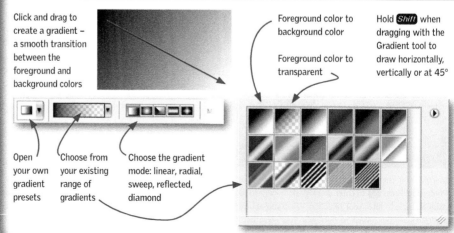

Click and drag to create a gradient – a smooth transition between the foreground and background colors

Foreground color to background color

Foreground color to transparent

Hold *Shift* when dragging with the Gradient tool to draw horizontally, vertically or at 45°

Open your own gradient presets

Choose from your existing range of gradients

Choose the gradient mode: linear, radial, sweep, reflected, diamond

ERASER TOOL Removes portions of a layer selectively

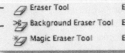

Eraser: deletes layer where you brush

Background Eraser: deletes colors similar to the color you first click on, as you brush

Magic Eraser: deletes colors similar to the one you first click on, throughout the image

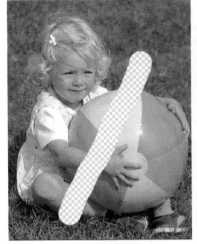 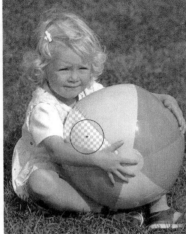 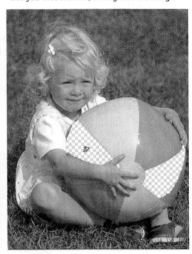

Background Eraser options: Sample continuously   Sample once   Erase background color   Do not erase foreground color

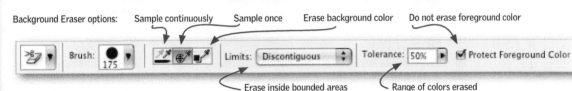

Erase inside bounded areas   Range of colors erased

SMUDGE, BLUR, SHARPEN TOOLS Smear and refocus pixels

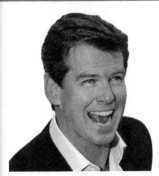 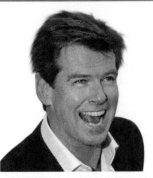

The Smudge tool is used to smear pixels. Use with the Spatter brush style, or with a small soft brush, to recreate the effect of windswept hair.

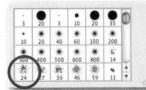

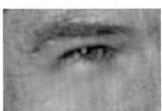

The Blur tool is used to soften harsh edges, such as around the eyes in this greatly enlarged view.

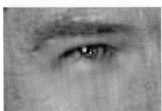

The Sharpen tool is used to add contrast, such as the sparkle that has been painted back into this eye.

Choose from the fly-out tool icon, or press Shift R to change between these three tools.

Painting tools 2

DODGE AND BURN Darken and brighten the image

The Dodge and Burn tools are used to add light and shade to an image. Burn darkens, and Dodge lightens.

Each tool can affect the Highlights, Midtones and Shadows (see examples here); Right click or `ctrl` click to select which.

Switch between these tools by holding `alt` `⌥` when either tool is active.

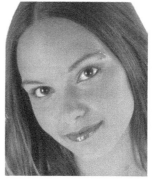

The original image.

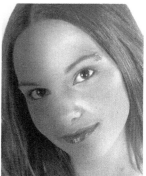

Set to Highlights, Burn (on the left) adds grayish shadow, while Dodge (right) brightens and enhances color.

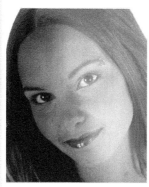

Set to Midtones, Burn (left) produces rich shading, while Dodge (right) merely adds brightness.

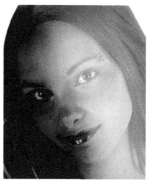

Set to Shadows, Burn (left) greatly increases saturation, while Dodge (right) gives a washed out look.

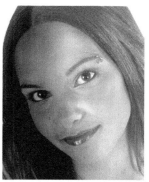

Here, a combination of Burn set to Midtones and Dodge set to Highlights produces the best result.

Healing **J**

Clone **S**

History Brush **Y**

Dodge and Burn **O**

HISTORY BRUSH Revert to an earlier state of the image

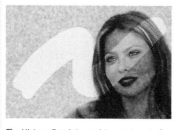

The History Brush is used to paint part of an image back to an earlier state, set by the History Palette. Here, we're able to revert a swoosh through this image, despite several operations having taken place.

The History Brush works well in conjunction with the Background Eraser (see previous page) to revert areas inadvertently erased.

History brush pinned at this position

Current state of the document

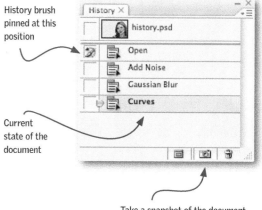

Take a snapshot of the document in its current state

CLONE TOOL Copy a portion of an image from one location to another

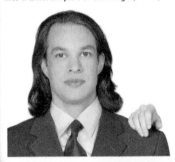
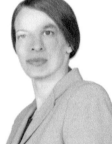

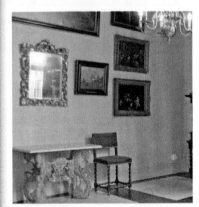
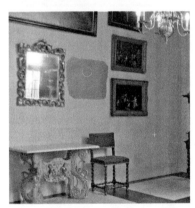

Hold *alt* ⟍ and click to set the clone source (above), then paint a copy into a different part of the image (below).

As of Photoshop CS3 the Clone tool has its own dialog, permitting a much wider range of effects:

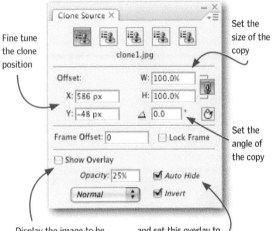

Fine tune the clone position

Set the size of the copy

Set the angle of the copy

Display the image to be cloned as a translucent overlay...

...and set this overlay to hide automatically when you start to clone

HEALING TOOL Seamless removal of unwanted elements in an image

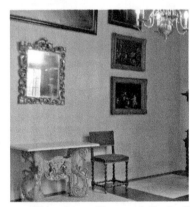

Hold *alt* ⟍ and click to set the source point such as the blank portion of wall, bottom right.

Paint with the Healing Brush. Don't worry that the result is much darker than the original...

...as when you let go of the mouse button it will blend in perfectly.

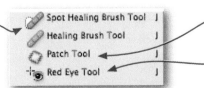

Spot Healing Brush works in the same way, but no need to set a source point – results are not as good.

Patch Tool is similar to the Healing Brush, but used for large areas: trace the area as if using the Lasso, then drag selected region to clone source point.

Red Eye tool used for painting out redeye caused by flash photography.

Working with layers

THE LAYERS PALETTE How to control your layers

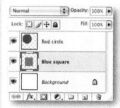

Layers are like sheets of glass upon which the image is painted. We can drag and change the layer order to set which layer is on top.

We can lower the opacity of a layer, so we can see through to the layer below.

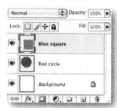

Click to select layer mode (see below)

Click and drag to change layer opacity

Click for pop-up menu showing more layer options

Lock layer transparency and position

Layers can be combined into groups for ease of organization

Click eye to hide and show layer

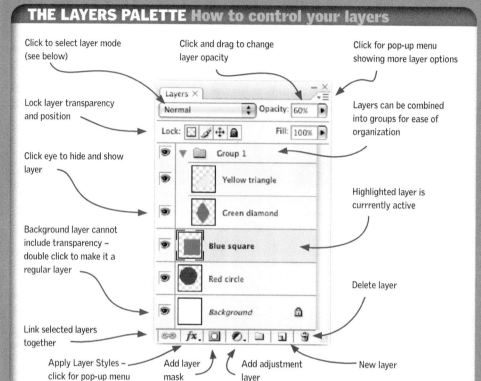

Highlighted layer is currrently active

Background layer cannot include transparency – double click to make it a regular layer

Link selected layers together

Delete layer

Apply Layer Styles – click for pop-up menu

Add layer mask

Add adjustment layer

New layer

LAYER MODES Change the way layers interact

Layer modes determine the way in which we see through a layer to the layers beneath. There are a lot of these, and the most common ones are shown here. You can cycle through all the layer modes by pressing `ctrl Shift =` `⌘ Shift =`.

One of the most useful layer modes is Hard Light, shown bottom right. Because this hides the midtones, allowing the light and shade to show, we can use it to create initially invisible layers on which to paint shading.

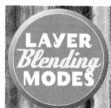

Normal mode. There are two layers in this document: the plaque and the wall behind it.

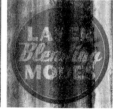

In Multiply mode, the plaque layer darkens up the wall, making everything darker.

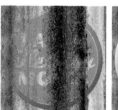

In Darken mode, the plaque is visible only where it's already darker than the wall behind.

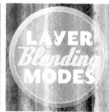

Screen mode: the plaque brightens the wall. This mode is the opposite of Multiply.

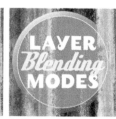

Lighten mode: the plaque is visible only where it's brighter than the wall.

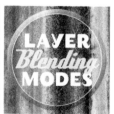

Hard Light mode: midtone gray disappears, leaving just the highlight and shadow visible.

LAYER MASKS Allow us to hide and show parts of a layer

Although there are three separate eraser tools in Photoshop, erasing is an irrevocable step: once part of a layer has been erased, it's gone forever.

Using a layer mask is a better option: it's created by clicking the icon at the bottom of the Layers palette (see left).

Painting in black on the layer mask hides the layer, and painting in white reveals it again. We can paint in gray, by lowering the opacity of our brush, for partial transparency.

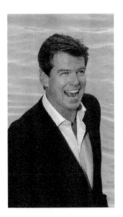
This is our original layer.

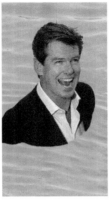
When we paint in black on the layer mask, we hide the layer.

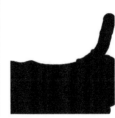
This is the layer mask itself, showing the area we've painted out.

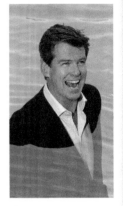
If we paint with gray instead of black, we can partially hide the layer.

ADJUSTMENT LAYERS Apply Curves, Levels and so on in an editable manner

Adjustment Layers let us apply contrast, color and other adjustments to layers that are editable, and can even be turned off entirely. They work like looking through sheets of colored glass at the layers beneath.

The advantage of Adjustment Layers is that we can apply changes that we can later adapt easily; we're also able to copy adjustments between layers.

Adjustment Layers are selected from the pop-up menu at the bottom of the Layers palette.

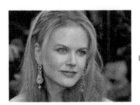

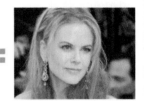

All Adjustment Layers come with a Mask, so we can paint out areas where we don't want the adjustment applied

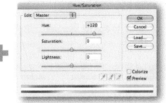

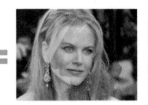

CLIPPING MASKS Constrain the visibility of layers to the layer beneath

Clipping masks are layers that constrict the visibility of the layer above. Here, the Red circle layer uses the Blue square layer as a clipping mask, so it's only visible where the two layers overlap. Multiple layers can be stacked up this way, using the bottom one as a clipping mask.

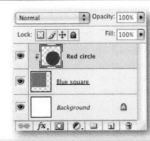

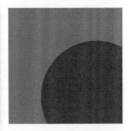

To make a clipping mask, select the uppermost layer and choose Layer > Create Clipping Mask. There are two alternative methods: use the shortcut ctrl alt G ⌘ ⌥ G, or hold alt ⌥ and click between the two layers in the Layers palette. Note: if you have an old version of Photoshop this is called 'grouping'.

233

Layer styles: basics

VIEWING AND CREATING LAYER STYLES

Layer Styles add special effects to all the pixels in a layer. Unlike applying filters or painting directly onto a layer, Layer Styles can be turned on and off at any time, added to, modified or copied to other layers.

In this example we'll use the simple circle with a hole in it, above, to which we'll apply a variety of styles and effects.

Switch to a layer style by clicking on it in the side panel so it's highlighted

Click the Eye icon to show or hide all effects

Click the Eye icons to show or hide individual effects

Create new layer styles from the pop-up menu at the bottom of the Layers palette

Click to collapse palette view so effects are not expanded

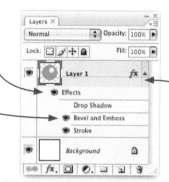

BEVEL AND EMBOSS Add depth and shading

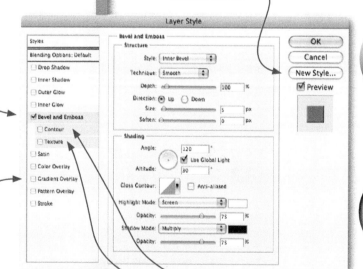

Basic Inner Bevel applied to object

Click here to save style to disk for later use

Turn individual styles on and off by clicking their check boxes

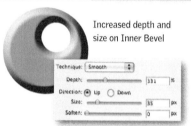

Increased depth and size on Inner Bevel

Changing Technique from Smooth to Chisel Hard creates a carved look

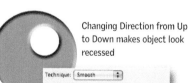

Changing Direction from Up to Down makes object look recessed

Checking the Texture category under Bevel and Emboss allows us to add the impression of raised textures

Checking the Contour category under Bevel and Emboss allows us to modify the shape of the beveled edge itself

SHORTCUTS

MAC **WIN** **BOTH**

DROP SHADOWS Make a layer look as if its above the surface

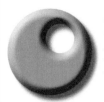

Drop Shadows make objects appear to be floating above the surface

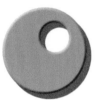

Set the Size value to zero for a hard-edged shadow

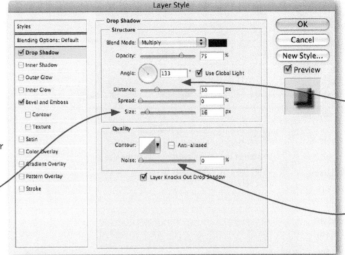

You can drag directly on the image to change the Distance and Angle values

Add noise for a more realistic photographic shadow effect

MORE LAYER STYLES Stroke, satin, glows and more

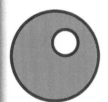

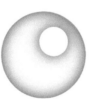

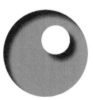

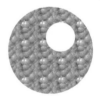

Stroke: a border around the edge, which can be set to inside, outside or centered on the object

Satin: adds a shiny appearance, but matt rather than metallic

Inner Glow: A glow that can be set to radiate from the center or come in from the edges

Inner Shadow: creates a cutout appearance, especially good for text

Gradient Overlay: applies any of the current gradients to a layer

Pattern Overlay: places any loaded patterns over the layer, which can then be scaled

USING LAYER STYLES Maintaining editability throughout the process

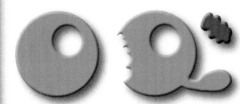

STYLES AND TEXT
Fully Editable

Layer Styles apply to the layer as a whole, not just to the pixels already present. After we apply the effects to this layer (left), we can extend, delete or paint on the layer and the styles will still apply to the entire layer (right).

When we apply layer styles to text, we don't need to rasterize the text first (turn it into editable pixels). This means that the style can be applied to text that we can edit later: we can change the wording, font and color as we wish.

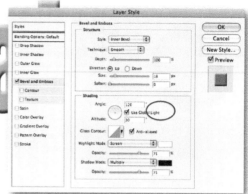

The Secret
of
the Orrery

Layer styles: metal

METAL: CREATING THE BEVEL

We use metallic styles a few times in this book, and they're created using Layer Styles. There are many variations, and you can easily spend an evening toying with the settings to produce the effect you want. Here, we'll go through the basics of setting up a metallic style, showing how it's created step by step so that you can see how to modify it.

There are several filters that create metallic effects, from Photoshop's own Chrome filter to a number of third party solutions. But they all depend on regular pixel layers to have their effect. The advantage of using Layer Styles is that we can apply the effect to live text, and then edit the text as we wish.

This style is included on the CD so you can load it directly without having to build it, if you wish to do so.

① Begin by choosing Bevel and Emboss from the Layer Styles button at the bottom of the Layers palette. Adjust the size of the bevel with the slider to suit the size of your artwork.

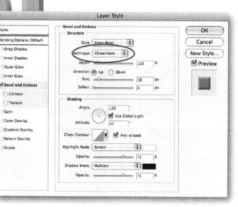

② Change the Technique pop-up from Smooth to Chisel Hard. This produces a hard-edged bevel, which will look much more like a metal finish.

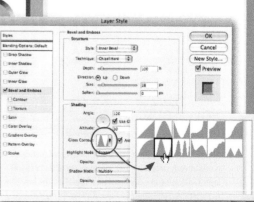

③ We can begin to bring a metallic feel to the text by changing the Gloss Contour setting. Try out the available shapes to see how they look: click on the thumbnails to change them.

METAL: ADDING THE DETAIL

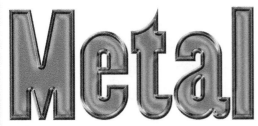

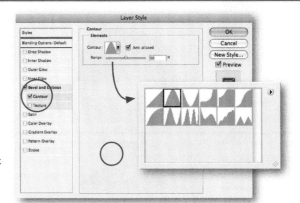

④ Click on the Contour checkbox to turn it on and switch to that pane. This applies a shape to the bevel itself. You don't have to use this step if you don't want a shaped bevel.

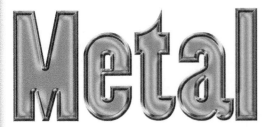

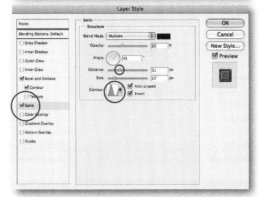

⑤ Click on the Satin checkbox to turn it on, and switch to its pane. By changing the distance, size and contour we can change the apparent reflections this creates.

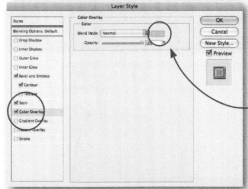

Click here to open the color dialog to pick a different color

⑥ Finally, add a Color Overlay. Choose a grayish blue color for steel and silver (more gray than blue), and a strong orange for a gold effect.

METAL: VARIATIONS

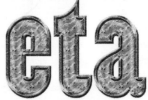

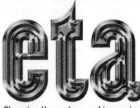

Changing color overlay to orange produces a gold effect

Increasing the bevel width removes the flat area from the face

Adding texture produces a mottled surface

Changing the contour and increasing the bevel width adds interest

Adjusting images

CURVES Allow us to control contrast and color together

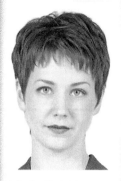

Adjusting the brightness and color of an image is the key not only to producing crisp images in Photoshop, but also to make elements of a montage fit together.

There are several ways to do this in Photoshop, and we'll look at the most popular here – beginning with Curves, which gives us the highest amount of control over the image.

Choose whether to adjust the whole image or a single channel

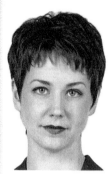

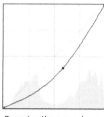

Dragging the curve down darkens the midtones (see original, above left)

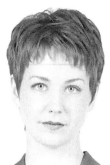

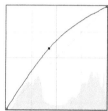

Dragging up on the curve brightens the midtones

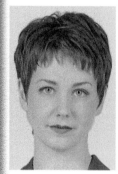

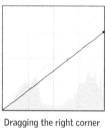

Dragging the right corner down lowers the total brightness of the image

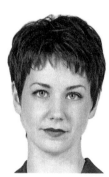

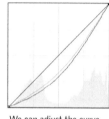

We can adjust the curve for each channel: here, we reduce the blue and green

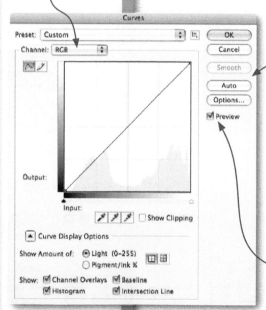

Try an automatic adjustment first

With this image we first drag the center of the curve down to darken the skin tones...

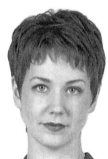

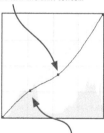

...then raise the lower portion to lighten the shadows in the hair

Turn the Preview box on and off to compare the before and after images, while you still have the dialog open

ADJUSTMENT LAYERS

All the adjustments shown here can also be applied as editable Adjustment Layers – see page 233 for details.

BRIGHTNESS/CONTRAST Simple and straightforward correction

The Brightness/Contrast dialog has just two sliders, and is easier to use than Curves. It works well when you simply want to beef up a dull looking image, but offers a lower degree of control.

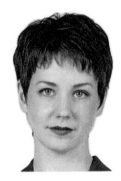

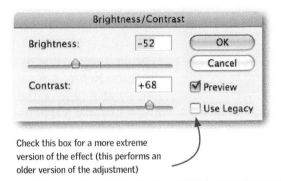

Check this box for a more extreme version of the effect (this performs an older version of the adjustment)

HUE/SATURATION The best adjustment for making major color changes

You can change colors selectively using the pop-up menu

Drag to change the hue – but watch out, it can make big changes

You may need to reduce the saturation when changing colors

Hold *alt* ⌥ and press Cancel to revert the dialog

Check the Colorize button to color the entire image uniformly

LEVELS The photographer's choice for image adjustment

Levels performs a largely similar job to the Curves adjustment, except that while we can drag the midpoint we can't add extra points to the graph. Levels features a histogram showing the ratio of light to dark in the image, which photographers find particularly useful.

Choose which color channel to work on

Drag sliders to set the darkest, lightest and mid point values

Drag triangles to set the overall brightness and black density

Use Auto Levels for a quick fix, which can then be adjusted by dragging the sliders

Histogram shows the balance of light and shade

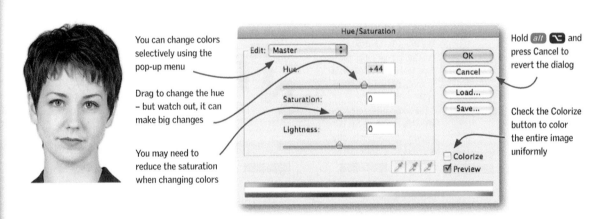

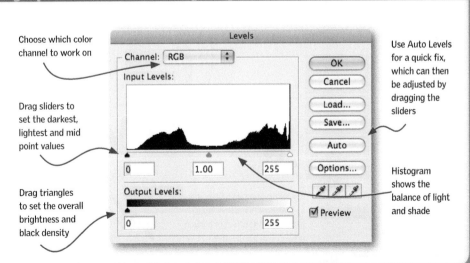

239

Ps

Type
tool
T

If you click in your artwork with the Type tool, you'll type on a single line until you press the Return key, at which point you'll type on the next line – just like a typewriter.

If you click and drag the Type tool, you'll create a text box. When you type in here, the text will wrap itself automatically when you get to the end of a line.

Drag to change height and width

Drag to change height

Drag to change width

WARPING TYPE Distorts type in an editable manner

The Warp Text button, on the Options bar when the Type tool is active, allows us to apply custom distortions to live text.

The text remains editable after the distortion has been applied, and we can modify or remove the distortion at any time.

Choose a distortion from the pop-up list

Drag to set the amount of the current distortion

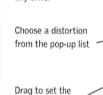

WARPING

Warp Text

Style: Arc

⦿ Horizontal ◯ Vertical

Bend: +50 %

Horizontal Distortion: 0 %

Vertical Distortion: 0 %

OK
Cancel

WARPING

WARPING

The Horizontal Distortion (above) and Vertical Distortion (right) sliders add the effect of horizon and vertical perspective

THE TYPE OPTIONS BAR Controls many aspects of the current text block

Switch between horizontal and vertical type

Choose your font. You can also click in here and type the first few letters of the font you want, such as T for Times

Type the size, or choose from the pop-up list. With type selected, press *ctrl* *Shift* > ⌘ *Shift* > and *ctrl* *Shift* < ⌘ *Shift* < to make text larger and smaller

Align left, center, or right

Open Warp Text dialog (see facing page)

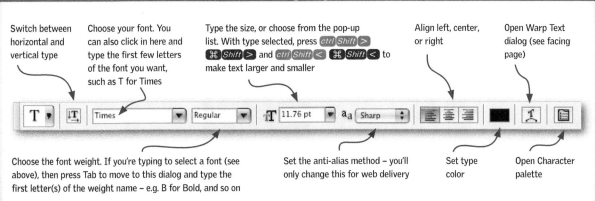

Choose the font weight. If you're typing to select a font (see above), then press Tab to move to this dialog and type the first letter(s) of the weight name – e.g. B for Bold, and so on

Set the anti-alias method – you'll only change this for web delivery

Set type color

Open Character palette

CHARACTER AND PARAGRAPH PALETTES Fine-tuning controls

Kerning control: the amount two characters overlap each other's space. Type a value, or click and drag the pop-up slider

Modify characters' height and width: mainly useful to restore text that has been distorted using Free Transform

Raise and lower selected characters. You can also use *alt* *Shift* ↓ ⌥ *Shift* ↓ and *alt* *Shift* ↑ ⌥ *Shift* ↑ to increase and decrease the values

Choose hyphenation method

Leading control: the space between lines of type. Set Auto for an optically pleasing setting, or choose a custom figure. With type selected, you can also press *alt* ↓ ⌥ ↓ and *alt* ↑ ⌥ ↑ to increase and decrease the leading for the selected paragraph

Tracking control: sets the space between characters over a whole word or text block. You can also press *alt* → ⌥ → and *alt* ← ⌥ ← to increase and decrease the spacing

Set text in Bold, Italic; All Caps, Small Caps, Superscript and Subscript; Underline and Strikethrough

Align text left, center, right; justify (normal), justify with last line centered, justify with last line aligned right; justify with last line expanded to fit width

Indent left margin

Indent first line of each paragraph

Insert space between paragraphs, before selected paragraph

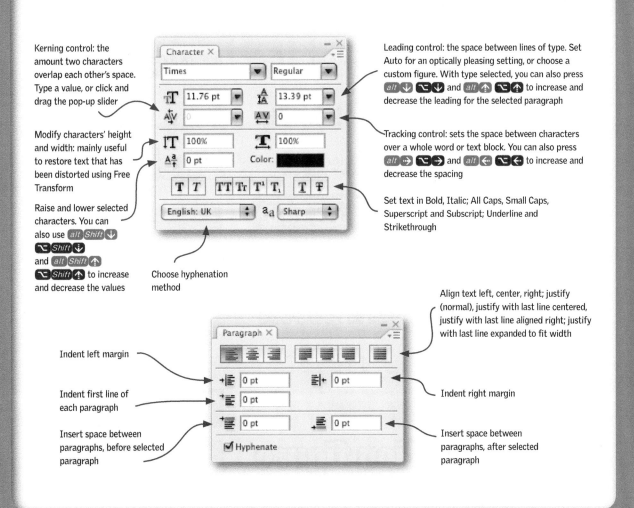

Indent right margin

Insert space between paragraphs, after selected paragraph

What's on the CD

Photoshop files

Double click their icons on the CD, or use the Open dialog in Photoshop and navigate to them.

Font files

Windows Vista: select the font file, then right click and choose Install.

Windows: place the fonts in the folder C:\ Windows\Fonts.

Mac: Double click the files and press the Install Font button.

Layer styles

Open the Layer Styles palette in Photoshop. From the pop-up menu in the top right, choose Load Styles... and navigate to the file **A&D styles.asl** in the folder Layer Styles on the CD. The styles will now appear in your Styles palette, after all your existing styles. Once loaded, you do not have to have the CD inserted in order to continue using the styles.

Custom brushes

Open the Brushes palette in Photoshop. Choose Load Brushes... from the pop-up menu at the top, and open the file **A&D brushes.abr** in the folder Brushes on the CD.

PHOTOSHOP FILES

You'll find Photoshop files to accompany all the tutorials in this book. These contain the starting images, as well as any additional textures and picture elements you may need. They're in the folder named Photoshop Files.

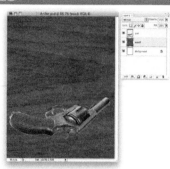

BRUSHES

Only one custom brush is used in this book – on page 212, in the tutorial on fabric badges. The stitching brush is in the folder marked Brushes on the CD.

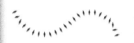

LAYER STYLES

Several of the tutorials require the use of Layer Styles. You can build these yourself, of course, and instructions are given in the text. But for some of the more complex styles, it can be tricky to get it exactly right; so I've included these on the CD, in the folder named Layer Styles. These are the styles that are included:

Steampunk

Steampunk infill

1950s thriller

Science fiction

Swinging 60s

Western poster

Pulp fiction

Thriller

Action figure

Cereal box

Pharmacy

Sushi

Bling bling

Bling diamond

Credit card

Enamel badge

Neon tube

Stone carving

FONTS

These are all the fonts used in the tutorials in this book. You'll find them in the folder named Fonts on the CD.

In one or two instances I have been unable to contact font authors. If you are the designer of one of these fonts, apologies for my failure to contact you first. If you would like your font removed from the CD please let me know through Focal Press.

My grateful thanks to all the font authors who have selflessly created these fonts and allowed us to use them freely:

Christophe Feray
www.wcfonts.com

Manfred Klein
http://manfred-klein.ina-mar.com

Ray Larabie
www.larabiefonts.com
www.typodermicfonts.com

Andrew Leman
www.cthulhulives.org

Paul Lloyd
http://www.moorstation.org/typoasis/
designers/lloyd/index.htm
LJP101267@hotmail.com

Graham Meade
www.moorstation.org/typoasis/designers/
gemnew

Pat Snyder
www.patsnyderartist.com

Dieter Steffmann
www.steffmann.de
*Please note: Dieter Steffmann's fonts are licensed for personal use only, and may not be used for commercial purposes

Julius B. Thyssen
http://jthz.com

Walter Velez
http://www.geocities.com/wvelezart

Ben Weiner
www.readingtype.org

A Yummy Apology .... Graham Meade
ACKNOWLEDGEMENT ..... Ben Weiner
Aquiline Two .... Manfred Klein
Baveuse .... Ray Larabie
Blackletter HPLHS .... Andrew Leman
Bullpen .... Ray Larabie
Cairo .... Author unknown
Cantebriggia .... Paul Lloyd
Chopin Script .... Dieter Steffmann*
COMICS CARTOON .... Pat Snyder
Credit Valley .... Ray Larabie
Deftone Stylus .... Ray Larabie
Dream Orphans .... Ray Larabie
Echelon .... Ray Larabie
Euphorigenic .... Ray Larabie
Fette Egyptienne .... Dieter Steffmann*
Foo .... Ray Larabie
Geosans Light .... Manfred Klein
GREENFUZ .... Ray Larabie
Guanine .... Ray Larabie
HEADLINE ONE HPLHS .... Andrew Leman
Honey Script .... Dieter Steffmann*
JUNEGULL .... Ray Larabie
Kenyan Coffee .... Ray Larabie
Kyrilla Sans Serif .... Manfred Klein
Marketing Script .... Dieter Steffmann*
Victoriana .... Paul Lloyd
OldSansBlack .... Manfred Klein
OPTIMUS PRINCEPS .... Manfred Klein
PLASTISCHE PLAKAT ANTIQUA .... Dieter Steffmann*
Saddlebag .... Dieter Steffmann*
Salernomi-J .... Julius B.Thyssen
Slab Serif HPLHS .... Andrew Leman
SUPERHETERODYNE .... Ray Larabie
STRENUOUS .... Ray Larabie
Timeless .... Manfred Klein
TrueCrimes .... Walter Velez
Velvenda Cooler .... Ray Larabie
Vipnagorgialla .... Ray Larabie
WC Wunderbach Mix ..... Christophe Feray
ZORQUE .... Ray Larabie

Index

About the author

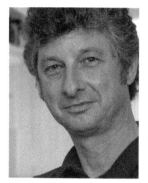

Steve Caplin is a freelance digital artist and author working in London, England. His satirical photomontage work is regularly commissioned by newspapers and magazines both in the United Kingdom and around the world, including *The Guardian, The Independent, The Sunday Telegraph, The Sunday Times Magazine, Radio Times, Readers Digest, Men's Health* and *l'Internazionale*.

Steve has worked for advertising agencies including Saatchi & Saatchi, Bartle Bogle Hegarty and Lowe Howard Spink, and his work has won two Campaign Poster Awards and a D&AD Pencil award. He has lectured widely in England, Norway, France and Holland, and has taught digital design at the University of Westminster and the London College of Printing.

Steve is the author of nine books: *How to Cheat in Photoshop* (four editions), *How to Cheat in Photoshop Elements 6* (co-authored), *Icon Design, Max Pixel's Adventures in Adobe Photoshop Elements*, and *The Complete Guide to Digital Illustration* (co-authored). He has also co-authored three mainstream books: *Dad Stuff* (published in the United States as *Be the Coolest Dad on the Block*), *More Dad Stuff* and *Stuff the Turkey*.

A regular conributor to *MacUser* magazine since 1990, Steve is also a beta tester for Adobe software and has a pathological interest in gadgets.

When he's not sitting at his desk Steve plays the piano well, the accordion moderately and the guitar badly, and enjoys making improbable constructions out of wood.

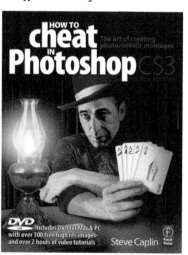